Shooting Stars

The Brief and Glorious History of Blackburn Olympic F.C. 1878-1889

Graham Phythian

A *SoccerData* Publication from Tony Brown

Published in Great Britain by Tony Brown,
4 Adrian Close, Beeston, Nottingham NG9 6FL.
Telephone 0115 973 6086. E-mail soccer@innotts.co.uk
First published 2007

© Graham Phythian 2007

All rights reserved. No part of this publication may be reproduced, stored in a retrieval system, or transmitted in any form, or by any means, electronic, mechanical, photocopying, recording or otherwise without the prior permission in writing of the Copyright holders, nor be otherwise circulated in any form or binding or cover other than in which it is published and without a similar condition including this condition being imposed on the subsequent publisher.

Cover design is by Bob Budd.

Printed and bound by 4edge Ltd, Hockley. www.4edge.co.uk

ISBN 978-1899468-83-6

CONTENTS

Preface		5
1.	A Blueprint For Victory	7
2.	Balance Of Power	12
3.	Hole-i'th'-Wall	15
4.	Baptism Of Fire	20
5.	The Shape Of Things To Come	26
6.	Mr. Hunter Changes Teams	33
7.	Cup Fighters	36
8.	To The Seaside For The Semi	43
9.	Little Tin Idol	48
10.	The Road To Trent Bridge	53
11.	Showdown With The Rovers	63
12.	The Jack Southworth Affair - And Other Tribulations	69
13.	Things Fall Apart	73
14.	Shadows Of The Past	77
Appendix I:	Complete Results	82
Appendix II:	Sketches Of The Players	103
Appendix III:	*The Times* April 2nd 1883	117
Appendix IV:	"Our Football Teams"	118
Appendix V:	East Lancashire Charity Cup	119
Appendix VI:	International Players	120
Bibliography		121
Acknowledgements		123
Index		125

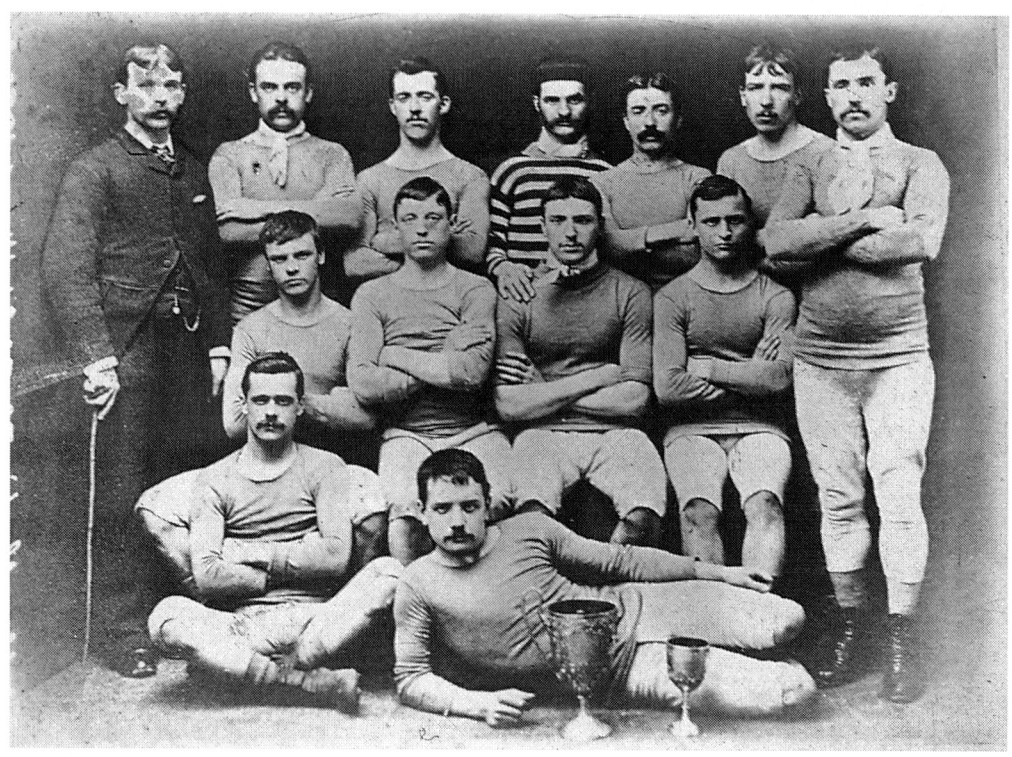

The Olympic team, from around May 1882. The trophies are the Blackburn Association Trophy (won 1879 and 1880) and the Livesey United Trophy (won 1878).

    The players are believed to be: back, from the left, W Bramham, A Warburton, W Astley, T Hacking, A Astley, J Yates, T Gibson; centre, J Beverley, J Hunter, T Dewhurst, J Ward; front, an unknown player and A Matthews.

    The date is deduced from the fact that the East Lancs Charity Cup is not in evidence, so it is before August 1882. Alf Astley is still in Olympic colours and neither Wilson nor Costley are present.

    The unknown player on the front row may be either R Wensley (Costley's predecessor on the left wing) or W "Tich" Parker, first reserve for the Cup final XI.

PREFACE

Why another book about Blackburn Olympic?

As a select band of readers is aware, my first effort on the subject was a novel: *Olympic FC: The Forgotten Giant-Killers*, a limited edition published at my own expense some ten years ago. I believe it was well received by the couple of hundred people who took the time to read it. Looking back now I'm only too aware of the book's faults and omissions. My first reason for revamping the tale is a corrective return journey. And 2008, of course, is the 125th anniversary of the team's Cup Final battle with the Old Etonians.

Moreover, since publication of the first book, I have received communications from interested parties, which have helped to shed light on some aspects of the club's history. Pride of place goes to letters from descendants of two of the Cup Final team: Warburton and Costley. With fresh leads like those, it would have taken someone with a stronger will than mine to turn away to another project.

When I gave the 1998 book its subtitle – *The Forgotten Giant-Killers* – it was simply to give it an eye-catching "hook". The idea was to appeal to football buffs' yen for obscure information: the "WOW factor", if you will. What I didn't realise at the time was just how close to oblivion Blackburn Olympic were in danger of slipping. For instance: the *News of the World Football Annual*, that usually reliable treasure house of data, for a long time asserted that the first FA Cup-winning team with an all-English XI was West Bromwich Albion in 1888. It took a letter from the author to rectify matters. And Blackburnians are, quite rightly, quick to celebrate anniversaries of the Rovers' triumphs. Yet in 1908, 1933 and 1983 there's not a trace of a mention in the local newspapers of Olympic's 1883 victory – one which, with hindsight, was of immeasurable importance to the history of the game.

So central is Olympic's achievement in the development of football in those days that I found it impossible to omit constant references to the landmarks beyond the team's immediate story. The frame of reference includes – as it must – the early years of the Rovers, and the prolonged, involved (and occasionally sinister) power struggle between the town's soccer rivals. But there is far more to it than this. The origins of the offside rule, the switch to the two-handed throw-in, Lord Kinnaird's unbeatable FA Cup Final appearance record, the beginnings of the 2-3-5 playing system, the world's first ever floodlit match, the arrival of professionalism and the Football League, the tale of the Sheffield Zulus – all of these and more make an appearance in these pages. I foresee many a pub bet being won with the help of this book!

When this fighting, mould-breaking Blackburn Olympic side takes up its rightful place in the soccer Hall of Fame alongside the likes of Stanley Matthews, Dixie Dean or the Corinthians, then I'll feel that my labours have been worthwhile.

G. P. P.

*If a chap had no conscience, but plenty o' cheek
He can net a month's profit i' less than a week;
If he's young, strong an' plucky, an' gwos a good speed
It's twenty to nothin' that mon will succeed;
If his mate at his elbow should happen to fall
He can sprint off his body – let t'weak go to t'wall!
... Goo in for a win, sell yo'r soul for a place,
Oather do or be done, it's a neck and neck race.*

William Billington (Blackburn dialect poet): "*Goo in for a Win*"

1: A BLUEPRINT FOR VICTORY

> Blackburn Olympic v. St John's – on the ground of the former, at Oozebooth, on Saturday afternoon last, the Olympic played their first match under their new name ... After change of ends the visitors were sorely pressed, their citadel being repeatedly assailed by the Olympians.
> *Blackburn Times* (Feb 16th 1878)

> Goal taking seemed to be the order of the day.
> *Blackburn Standard* (Nov. 9th 1878), after Blackburn Law 0, Olympic 7

Imagine a Saturday afternoon in late 1877 in Blackburn. The racket of the cotton mills, foundries and engineering works is silent. In its place, the hubbub of the teeming crowds of Northgate and the Blakey Moor Market, the rumble and the clatter of horse-drawn trams along Preston New Road, and the murmur of the citizens taking the air in Corporation Park. On several of the open spaces down among the factory chimneys of the grimy town, and on its windswept edges of green moors and farmland, some flurries of activity, accompanied by the odd shout or cheer, are visible. On looking closer, we see that a number of football games are in progress.

These are proper matches, organised between church, pub, or work-based teams. But there is much that would surprise a touchline observer from modern times. There are no goal nets or pitch markings, and a tape instead of a crossbar is a common sight. The terrains are often makeshift: rough and muddy, rarely level, and even – in one famous instance – with some boards and turf covering a pit in the middle of the pitch. Players' kit is usually rolled-up trousers, old shirts of a variety of colours, and workaday boots with blocks of wood hammered into the soles for grip. Play can be rough and reckless, and tackles are full-blooded and often violent.

The rules have yet to reach their later fine-tuned sophistication. The penalty kick does not exist, as all free kicks, from whatever position on the field, are indirect. The throw-in is still slung one-handed from the touchline. The touchline itself can be an uncertain fixture, sometimes dependent on the vagaries of the line of spectators along the edge of the playing area. Since there is neither penalty area nor halfway line, the goalkeeper may handle the ball anywhere on the pitch.

The names of the teams we would encounter reveal their points of origin within the town: St Mark's (later to evolve into Witton FC), Park Road, Queen's Own, James Street, Furthergate, Christ Church. And a colourful constellation: Silver Star, Red Star, White Star, Blue Star, and the one with greater staying power than the rest, Black Star. The home pitch of this last mentioned is Mill Hill, by the railway line from Preston. Black Star's major claim to fame will be a tough little half back known as Tommy Gibson, an ironmonger's dresser by trade.

Back then the Association aristocrats of the town were already the Rovers, formed in 1875 by old boys of the Grammar School. In their early years the out of town opposition would include Darwen, Partick from Glasgow, the Manchester Wanderers, and the Sheffield Association.

The next year – 1878 – the Blackburn Football Association was formed. Mill-owner Councillor Boothman was elected Chairman, and a trophy was offered to the winners of a knockout tournament along the lines of the FA Cup. Rovers, their eyes set on loftier horizons, declined to take part.

Perhaps getting wind of the forthcoming Association and its trophy, some of the smaller clubs underwent a beefing-up process. And when Black Star and James Street joined forces, as a result of a meeting in a coffee house in Randal Street in February 1878, some rare footballing talent started to play under the same flag.

The very choice of name of this new club – Blackburn Olympic – seemed to give notice of its members' intentions. It was James Edmondson, the treasurer and first captain, who hit upon the euphonious title. It was as if their aim from the very beginning was to become front-runners, and to take their ambitions beyond the borough.

Or as the *Standard* was to say – albeit with the wisdom of hindsight and in the afterglow of the Cup Final – five years later:

> "It was a happy thought of theirs to select that name, for its very meaning must have endowed them with zeal and cleverness."
> (April 7th 1883)

There was a certain topicality to the choice of name too. In the news at the time was the uncovering by German archaeologists of the site at Olympia, where the Greeks had held their Games in antiquity. The dig had begun in 1875, and the discoveries were soon to fire the imagination of sports fans across the Western world.

The Olympic's first ever game was on February 9th 1878, a 2-0 win against St John's, played at Oozebooth. The venue, more correctly known as Higher Oozebooth, was also the first home of the Blackburn Cricket Club, on some open farmland a couple of hundred yards from what would be Olympic's permanent home at Hole-i'th'-Wall. Centre forward Walter Askew scored the club's first ever goal. Joe Beverley, who had taken the field just to make up the numbers, was a revelation: in goal for the first half, he then replaced Askew as leader of the attack, and scored the second. In the report in the *Blackburn Standard*, special mention was made of the skills of ex-James Street forward Johnny Duckworth (later to play for the Rovers), Askew, J. Foulds, and, almost inevitably, Tommy Gibson. Other players who caught the eye in that first abbreviated season were:

> Andrew Mackereth, renowned for constructive wing play and the odd lethal crack at goal;

> Alfred Astley, print worker and newsagent by trade, with a shop on Church Street, a solid midfielder, who could combine well with Tommy Gibson. (Alfred's younger brother, William, would play in the 1883 Cup Final);

> Robert Westwell, another free-scoring forward in the first year or so of the club's existence.

Then there was the mercurial, outrageously talented Joe Beverley. "Bev" was born in Buttery Street, Blackburn in November 1857. An ex-pupil of St John's Church School, and a member of the Black Star club before joining Blackburn Olympic, he was on his way to a Cup-winner's medal (with Rovers) and four England caps. As regards all-round talent, despite his youth and small, slight stature he would have few equals on the football field. A prolific goalscorer, a bewildering dribbler, an unerring tackler when in defence, and the one-armed throw-in expert (it was said that with Beverley, a throw-in was as good as a free kick), in many ways he would become the legs and lungs of the team. The *Football Annual* of 1882 would describe him as a "good all-round player; can play back, half-back, or forward; is fast and has plenty of judgment." The Rovers, of course, tried to win him over. By the time of the great FA Cup runs in the early to mid-1880's, he would become a symbolic bone of contention between the two clubs.

There is an-oft-repeated story surrounding the half back pair Gibson and Alfred Astley. The former, showing typical single-mindedness, in the early years of his career refused to wear any other colour than his "lucky" amber and black hooped shirt. This was despite the fact that Olympic's accepted colour in those days was magenta. Eventually Astley gave in to the irresistible force of his team-mate's will and started to wear amber and black hoops too, so as to balance out the colour scheme. This caused "much jovial comment". By 1880, with entry in the FA Cup demanding a more uniform approach, the team colours would be the familiar light blue.

Later that month of February 1878 the new team travelled across town to take on Furthergate. Again the win was 2-0, Duckworth and Beverley the scorers. The victorious side were praised for their "capital cross-play", which sounds like appreciation of their long ball passing skills. It's quite possible that in the crowd that day was a twelve-year-old by the name of James Ward, a Furthergate School pupil who would later play for Little Harwood, and then graduate via Blackburn Olympic to an England cap whilst still aged nineteen.

The first published team line-up of the Olympic was for the Feb. 23rd victory over the 17th Lancers:

Goal: L. Cook;
Backs: T. Gibson, G. Little;
Half-back: J. Edmondson (capt.)
Forwards: J. Foulds, J. Duckworth, J. Bradshaw, J. Beverley, R. Westwell, W. Askew, A. Mackereth

The score was another 2-0 win, and the reporter enthused:

" ... by a combined effort Olympic scored a simply beautiful goal."
Blackburn Standard (Mar. 2nd 1878)

The blueprint for success was already in evidence. Not for this new team the bullish individual charges at goal that typified many of the élite sides of the day; combination play was the way of the future. With their seven forwards on that occasion, the Olympic's attacking interplay must have been worth seeing.

The first trophy was soon gathered in. Livesey United, whose home base was the Cherry Tree Cricket Ground out on the Preston Old Road, organised a knock-out competition. Seven local clubs (much the same participants as in the following year's Blackburn Association Trophy) took part.

All games were played at Cherry Tree, and it was there that Olympic met their opponents St Mark's in the final tie in April. The team was the same as the one given above, except that Bradshaw dropped back to partner Edmondson, and J. Cook replaced J. Foulds in the forward line. St Mark's won the toss and chose to play the first half with the strong wind at their backs. The Olympic defence, although continually under pressure, managed to keep a clean sheet until half-time. L. Cook in goal was in especially fine form.

One minute after change of ends Beverley showed that Olympic could boast individual as well as collective skills. He dribbled the ball upfield into a scoring position, whence he struck a powerful shot, "the ball flying under the tape amidst loud cheers". (*Blackburn Standard* Apr. 20th 1878). With fifteen minutes left "Bev" gave a repeat performance, the Olympic thus winning the Livesey United Cup by 2-0. It was to be another five years or more (and another three trophies on the sideboard) before they would be defeated in the final of any competition.

The following season, 1878-9, was to see the new club flexing its muscles, finding its realistic level. It soon became clear that, locally at least, they had few equals. There were early victories over Livesey United (1-0), and a 7-0 drubbing of Blackburn Law. A trip to Haslingden, and a 2-1 victory over a team of doughty pit workers – "a very amiable and interesting game" – further increased optimism.

Out of the fifteen recorded games played that winter, they suffered just the one defeat: a 0-1 reverse against Enfield, in the gathering gloom of a late November afternoon up at Clayton-le-Moors. Reports state that Olympic had the better of the play. By February they had reached the final of the inaugural Blackburn Association trophy. There had been a couple of hiccups on the way: it had taken two replays to dispose of St Mark's. The first game in the final, against the Queen's Own side that contained a smattering of Rovers players, had resulted in a 1-1 draw. One week before the replay there was an even sterner test: the team's first ever match with the Rovers, on Alexandra Meadows.

The *Blackburn Times* describes that historic meeting:

> "This long-talked-of match was played on the ground of the Rovers, last Saturday, in the presence of about 1,000 spectators. A strong breeze from the west was the only drawback to one of the fastest and finest games ever played in Blackburn. The splendid all round play of the Olympic was much admired, every player acting in concert, and though a much lighter team than their opponents they won very cleverly by three goals to one. The Rovers played with one or two Second XI men, and appeared to be especially deficient in the quality of speed; in addition to this, Duckworth, one of their right forwards, was not in his usual fine form. Messrs. Bradshaw and Astley, Olympic forwards, contributed in a great measure to the success of their team, which now takes rank as one of the best, if not the best, in town.
>
> "Teams:
> "Olympic: L. Cook; J. Edmondson, J. Holden; A. Astley, T. Gibson: J. Bradshaw, A. Mackereth, J. Beverley, W. Askew, R. Westwell, W. Hanson
> "Rovers: W. Green; D. Greenwood, J. Haworth; F. Hargreaves, R. Duckworth; J. Duckworth, R. Birtwistle, J. Lewis, W. Standing, W. Duckworth, G. Avery"
> *Blackburn Times* (Feb. 22nd 1879)

Some notes about selected members of the Rovers team:

Fred Hargreaves: just over a year later he would be an England player, one of the first from the provinces to be so honoured (and soon followed by younger brother John). A hard-working, speedy midfielder, and a solicitor by profession;

John Lewis: a founder of the Rovers, he would go on to be one of the game's most respected referees and FA committeemen. He was co-owner of a coach-and-horses business in the town;

Richard Birtwistle: a forward of some ability, and son and grandson of cotton magnates;

Doctor Haydock Greenwood: sturdy, powerful full back, also on his way to gaining an England cap, and original member of the Corinthians club.

Rovers, then, could boast the influence and the pedigree. No doubt defeat at the hands of the young pretenders concentrated the mind wonderfully. So, from the quiet beginnings of a natural rivalry between the two clubs, the struggle for supremacy – and ultimately, survival – was set in motion.

By now Olympic were well enough supported to cater for a successful reserve side, which was to prove a vital nursery for the first team. Recorded results for the 2nd XI in the 1878-79 season were:

v. St George's Res.	W 1-0	(at Roe Lee)
v. Enfield Res.	W 2-0	(at Roe Lee)
v. Haslingden Grane Res.	W 1-0	(at Roe Lee)
v. Parish Church	W 3-1	(at Roe Lee)
v. St Mary's	W 5-0	(at Roe Lee)
v. Christ Church Res.	W 2-0	(at Ewood)

Looking a few years into the future, one circuitous claim to fame of the reserves would be a victory over Newton Heath, an earlier incarnation of Manchester United.

The week after the match with Rovers, on a field adjacent to the Cattle Market on what is now Galligreaves Street, the replayed Blackburn Association Cup Final took place. Clearly inspired by their win against the Rovers, the relative newcomers overwhelmed the Queen's Own side.

Westwell hit the opener for Olympic after just five minutes, and relentless pressure from the same team brought the second, after a series of corners, from Askew's boot. Another corner was cleared as far as Beverley, who after some nifty inter-passing with other forwards, scored the third before half-time. The second half began with the Queen's Own intent on at least damage limitation, but because of the heavy pitch and the indomitable defending of the victorious team, there was no more scoring until the final minutes when Askew bagged his second, making the final score a conclusive 4-0. Olympic duly carried off the "heavy silver cup and medals".

Up until the end of March in their first full season, the team's recorded results make impressive reading:

P	W	D	L	F	A
15	10	4	1	33	4

But then came a rude awakening. After defeating a Blackburn Select XI 6-0 (Beverley scored 4) at their temporary home of Cob Wall Cricket Club, Olympic fought out a creditable 0-0 draw with Rovers on the same ground. Then they took on the team of the moment, Darwen. Fresh from their epic, nationally recognised struggles with Kinnaird's Old Etonians, the Darreners agreed to meet the nominal champions of Blackburn at Barley Bank on Easter Monday. This would perhaps indicate how close the newcomers were to mixing it with the heavyweights. Would they prove themselves ready for the lions' den of the FA Cup?

On the Saturday before this match, Darwen had invited the Rovers to play at Barley Bank. Joe Beverley guested, and Rovers, to general surprise, won 2-1. Did Olympic have a chance then?

Much was made of the discrepancy in experience. Established outfit Darwen had encountered "Metropolitan and Scottish teams", whilst Olympic were a "Junior club of 18 months' standing".

The home side scored first, then Beverley equalised. Despite having "a more scientific knowledge of the game than Rovers", Olympic were mauled by a far heavier, physical side. The beefiness of Darwen's approach would later become a subject for satire as town rivalry reached its height in the 1880s. For the moment, the slighter team had no answer to it, either on the pitch or in the newspaper columns. 1-5 down at the interval, Beverley's team eventually succumbed 2-8.

A return match the following week at Christ Church's ground at Ewood was also lost, 1-3. In this more closely contested game Beverley scored first, a lead which was held until half time. This player's throw-ins were causing the opposition some problems, and it took all of the great Glaswegian Fergie Suter's wits and bulk to repel boarders. It was a Suter free kick that led to the equaliser, after which Darwen had the better of it, with Scot Jimmy Love and future England international Thomas Marshall hitting further goals.

Consolidation before ambition then: as the Queen's Own folded, its playing resources swallowed by the voracious Rovers, their ground at Hole-i'th'-Wall at the top of Shear Brow became available. Olympic moved in for the next season, when they would set out to retain their hard-won Blackburn Association trophy.

2: BALANCE OF POWER

> The comparison is now before the public, and it is for the latter
> to say whether Darwen have been pursuing a foolish and empty phantom,
> or that they have gallantly endeavoured to lay before the football world
> that there is some cause to treasure up ambition in their hearts.
> *Cricket and Football Times* (Mar 22nd 1879)

> Each team strived their utmost to score a goal, showing some very
> good passing, especially on the part of the Olympic, and good long and
> steady kicks on the part of the Rovers.
> *Blackburn Times*, after Olympic 0, Rovers 0, at the Cob Wall Cricket Field (Mar 22nd 1879)

In order to appreciate Olympic's achievement fully, we should remind ourselves of the kind of place England was in mid-Victorian times.

It was a society of deep and inflexible divisions (some said divinely imposed) in which everyone knew their place, and until the upsetting of a few apple-carts courtesy of the Hole-i'th'-Wall gang, these divisions were by and large reflected in the world of football.

At grass roots so to speak, you had the local teams of journeymen players who were never realistically going to compete beyond the home parish. They were the pub, church or workplace sides, the Livesey Uniteds and the Furthergates of Blackburn.

A level higher were the provincial teams with the financial backing, the connections and the ambition to assume local supremacy, and from there to target the County Championship, and even the FA Cup. Theirs would be a predominantly middle class input, and as we approach 1880, Blackburn Rovers could be considered to be at this level – but rising.

There were a few sides who could consider themselves a cut above such as the Rovers, and the results proved it. The top Sheffield and Nottingham clubs, with their rich traditions in the sport and their more populous catchment areas, were challenging for national pre-eminence. Darwen too (at least before Suter's decamping to Rovers) had their significant fifteen minutes of fame.

And finally the élite: the sides consisting of privileged metropolitan gentlemen, mostly old boys of the Public Schools, who had won the FA Cup since its inception, and who were expecting to hang on to it for the next generation or so. These were the men who, besides playing football supremely well and supplying the England team with most of its players, were to go on to become academic, legal or economic pillars of the establishment and the Empire. The two such teams that Olympic met in their 1882-3 FA Cup run – the Old Etonians and the Old Carthusians – would supply the following:

> JPs and MPs;
> solicitors;
> peers of the realm;
> a Director of Barclay's Bank;
> a leisured landowner;
> a Maharajah's tutor;
> a chairman of a Bombay trading company;
> a University Professor (and one-time tutor to the Duke of Clarence);
> an infantry Captain;
> Managing Director of a brewery;
> Senior Judge in Southern Rhodesia[1]

which made up a sizeable chunk of *Who's Who* and *Debrett*.

It is no exaggeration to say that football at the time helped to emphasise the social divisions. We need look no further than the England trial match at Bolton in March 1882. The "Probables" – mostly Old Carthusians, Swifts, Pilgrims etc., from the privileged set – were pitted against the "Improbables", a Lancashire select XI containing five players from Blackburn Olympic:

Beverley, Matthews, Warburton, Gibson, and Cunliffe. The supposed sparring partners showed that they packed a surprise punch, and the result of an exciting game was 4-4, Cunliffe hitting a hat-trick. The after-match comment in the *Blackburn Times* speaks volumes:

> "The Blackburn Olympic earned the gratitude of the Lancashire Association by putting off an advertised match in order to play a practice game with the "Probables", and they earned the dislike of the "Probables" by not letting them win. The Probables actually hadn't the courage to turn up at dinner after the match, but decamped to Manchester by an early train. Some of them were such "swells" they came on the ground with linen shirts and gold sleeve-links, and would not deign to speak to their opponents."
> (March 11th 1882)

A game of football was presented as a minor skirmish in the class war, in which there was no question of a truce.

In a world of engrained attitudes many of those who took on teams from a higher social milieu were beaten before they kicked a ball. Before the 1883 Cup Final, assessing the chances of victory of an unsung north country "village side", a number of provincial newspapers expressed the feeling that it was "now or never". The correspondents were apparently assuming that, give or take the odd blip, the gentry would continue as English Champions until kingdom come. Even the Blackburn pundits gave Olympic little chance, especially after Rovers' defeat to the same opposition, the Old Etonians, the previous year. You didn't beat these fellows, certainly not on their home ground. It simply wasn't done. This, then, was the mountain to climb, as Olympic negotiated the foothills of 1879.

It was in the first three months of that year that the football *status quo* was shaken to its foundations. We have seen the defeat of Blackburn Rovers by the emergent Olympic. It was also the time of Darwen's heroic clash with the Old Etonians in the quarter-final of the FA Cup.

The full story of that valiant, ultimately doomed battle has been told elsewhere. Suffice it to say that the first symptoms of Cup fever were brought back to Lancashire from Kennington Oval by the Darreners on a cold February day in 1879. Trailing by five goals the northerners had staged one of the most stirring fight backs in the history of the game, playing the Old Boys off the pitch in a whirlwind second half before emigrant Scot Jimmy Love hit the equaliser with a minute or so left. In those days the playing of extra time was a matter for discussion between referee and captains, and the exhausted Etonians declined the invitation to play on. It was, as the *Athletic News* was to point out quite reasonably, "a one-sided proposition", given the physical condition of the teams at the end of ninety minutes. Maybe so, but it didn't gain the Old Boys too many friends across the country, especially as, according to the competition rules then in force, Darwen were obliged to return to London at great expense for the replay.

On this occasion extra time was played, but still it was a draw, 2-2, at the end. So the Darreners made the trip to the Oval for a third time a week later. Now they found their opponents in better condition, and, carrying a couple of injured players themselves, finally succumbed 2-6. The Etonians, captained by the indomitable Rt. Hon. Arthur Kinnaird, went on to win the trophy.

Nevertheless, besides enjoying a profit of over £56 (at the time over a year's wages for a workman) from the adventure, the Lancashire club had served as an inspiration to every up-and-coming provincial team. In the next few years Nottingham Forest (twice), Darwen again, Sheffield Wednesday and Blackburn Rovers were to reach the FA Cup semis, even though victory in the Final still went to the gentlemen players of the capital and home counties.

In neighbouring Blackburn, the repercussions of Darwen's exploits were huge. Suddenly football took centre stage, supported and financed by the town fathers. After the damaging cotton mill strike of the previous year, the new upsurge of popular interest in soccer was a godsend to the bosses. Here was something the workers could believe in passionately without any obvious threat to production. Not only did it deflect attention from issues of pay and work conditions, it went a long way to providing a "fit, deferential and grateful" workforce that was a long-term economic asset. Small wonder then that the town bigwigs (most of whom owned the factories and the mills) gave such substantial backing to the new game.

This was reflected by the sudden increase in the newspaper coverage. From an obscure occasional mention on the back page (or shoehorned into the Local News section if there was room) football now had a column or two to itself, with specialised commentaries. Match reports became fanatically detailed, sometimes giving a ball-by-ball account. Advertisements for games appeared on the front page.

Attendant industries were born, and flourished. Players now wanted proper leather footballs, decent boots and customised gear. An eye-catching advertisement on the front page of the *Blackburn Times* of Jan 3rd 1880:

> W. Hayhurst
> Shirt and tie shop
> 13, Northgate
> is now showing a splendid selection of football suits:
> caps, jerseys, trousers, stockings and belts,
> in any colours required.
> We supply football clubs at most reasonable prices.

Moreover, playing areas had to be rented, and sooner or later transport to the more distant away games had to be organised. Lunches and refreshments were usually provided for teams visiting from out of town. "Must-have" miracle tonics and embrocations appeared on the market. None of this came cheap, but once again to a large extent it was philanthropic bosses who footed the bill. It was the thin end of the wedge of professionalism, theoretically banned by the iron rule of the FA, but already open to dodges and loopholes. (For example, Blackburn Olympic's extensive – and expensive – preparation for the 1883 Cup semi and final stretched the bounds of current legality, or at least ethics. And were Jack Hunter and George Wilson, importations from Sheffield, professionals? It depends on where you're standing. The issue will be looked at later.)

Besides, from the point of view of the sponsors, there were political as well as economic advantages from financing the development of football in the borough. To be sure, there was a genuine interest in the sport, in that it wasn't merely a means to an end, but it certainly didn't harm the political careers of, for example, future MP Henry Hornby and Councillor Boothman (both mill-owners) to be seen as generous supporters of the Rovers.

Olympic had their guardian angel too, in the shape of Mr. Sydney Yates, owner of the iron foundry of Messrs W. and J. Yates, later known as the Canal Engineering Works, on Birley Street. His financial contributions towards what from his point of view can only be seen as a hobby would soon prove to be indispensable. It's a sobering thought that the FA Cup run of 1882-3 would have rendered the club bankrupt if not for him.

So far the demands on the club's purse were modest enough. The major expense for 1879-80 would be the renting of the pitch behind the pub at Hole-i'th'-Wall, Olympic's home ground for the rest of the side's existence.

---

[1] *I am indebted to the research of Keith Warsop (see bibliography) for the compilation of this list.*

3: HOLE-I'TH'-WALL

> The way in which [the Olympic Club] have clung together when they
> might have been swallowed up in the Rovers FC is very creditable to them, and
> it is to be hoped that they will try their fortunes in a wider sphere next year.
> *Blackburn Times* (Feb. 28th 1880)

> In due time I arrived at the bottom of that awful Alpine roadway, the
> ascent of which can only be accomplished by *shear* sweat of the *Brow*.
> *Football Field* (Oct. 30th 1886)

The name of the pub was derived from the days when bootleg booze was actually sold from a hole in the wall alongside the Pleckgate Road. These days the interior is welcoming and plush, and the inn serves a fine pint and tasty meals.

Just along from the bar there is a framed photograph of the 1883 Cup-winning team, and a painting of what the pub must have looked like in the days of Blackburn Olympic. Out the back, beyond the beer garden area that used to be the bowling green, the pitch is still there, now part of the playing fields of the adjacent St Mary's College.

The terrain was originally owned by a brickworks, who had planned to dig it up for clay. Then the Queen's Own rented it for their football games, and this was where the Olympic came in.

Climbing Shear Brow to watch a match must have seemed a bind after Cob Wall Cricket Club in the valley, but healthy-sized crowds still came. Olympic could now attract some of the "name" teams of the moment: Darwen, Accrington, Eagley, Sheffield Zulus (more of them later), and the emergent Bolton Wanderers. And Hole-i'th'-Wall was nearer the centre of town than the club's other temporary residence: the Roe Lee pitch out at Pleckgate, on the northern edge of the borough.

The terrain had a slope, minor but noticeable, with the southern goal lower than the north. This idiosyncrasy wasn't uncommon at the time, especially in towns that skirted the Pennines. Jack Hunter's team Heeley in Sheffield had a pitch that was once memorably described as having "one goal in as it were a coal pit, and the other on the summit of Snowden"!

The drainage of the Hole-i'th'-Wall terrain sometimes left a lot to be desired. Indeed, visiting teams were known to blame their sluggish performances on the frequently quagmire conditions. Visiting Scottish Champions Dumbarton, after their 3-4 defeat in February 1884, blamed the state of the pitch: "The ground was an inch deep with mud, which nullified dribbling capabilities." (*Dumbarton Herald*, Feb 27th 1884) (That the complaint should come from Dumbarton, whose home ground of Boghead was at the time, apparently, aptly named, has a measure of irony.) For a while, Olympic's home results were appreciably better than their away ones, so the grumbles seemed justified. Then stunning victories were achieved away from the mud bath too (Clitheroe 5-0, Liverpool 12-0, Bootle 7-0), and the critics went home to think again.

Besides, heavy conditions are supposed to favour bigger and stronger players with a blood-and-thunder approach to the game. Theoretically Olympic's lightweight, cohesive style should have foundered in their own gluey back yard. This was evidently not the case. In the first season based in their new home (1879-80), Olympic were to lose just four games, out of the nineteen that were recorded. These were to the Rovers (twice), to the Suter-enhanced Darwen at Barley Bank, and to another of the strongest Lancashire teams of the day, Turton.

The 0-2 home defeat to Turton in November highlighted another of the early shortcomings of the pitch. According to the *Bolton Evening Guardian* the terrain was "long but very narrow, giving little opportunity for wing play". (Nov 25th 1879). It was a far-seeing move of the Olympic to widen the pitch considerably the following summer.

Accrington, who were to go on and secure the Lancashire County Trophy that season, were played twice. Encouragingly, both games were won 2-1. In the February game at Hole-i'th'-Wall the home side's "passing and combined play were greeted with applause". *(Blackburn Times)*

The defeat at Darwen in October was a vastly different affair from the 8-2 drubbing of just six months before. Westwell scored for Olympic after just one minute, a psychological body-blow from which the home team did well to recover. For the first ten minutes the visitors' rapid inter-passing had the Darreners scurrying back in defence. At one point Suter himself, facing his own goal, was obliged to kick over his own crossbar to relieve the pressure. The home side's counter-attacks, however, did the business: Darwen's renowned ability to convert free kicks (usually placed with devilish accuracy by Suter) bagged them three goals before the interval. In the second half the Blackburn side hit back through Gibson, and although the final score was 4-2 to the home team, the winners knew they had been in a fight.

The return game at Hole-i'th'-Wall the following January gave notice that Olympic were a force to be reckoned with. The deployment of both Gibson and Beverley in the attack announced from the outset that this was one game they were aiming to win. Gibson, enjoying his position on the right wing, embarked on some early probing runs that tested the opposing defence. Then, with the perfect riposte to the visitors' skill with free kicks, Beverley launched one of his howitzer throw-ins into the goalmouth, and Askew latched onto it to hit the opener. Within minutes Darwen had equalised, and play was even until half time. After change of ends Olympic gradually gained the upper hand. Gibson sent in a precise cross for Hanson to convert with a header, and the 2,000 crowd roared their appreciation of what turned out to be the winning goal. It was a stirring, talismanic victory. The celebrated Darwen – Suter, Brindle, Love, Marshall and all – had succumbed to the comparative newcomers.

The victorious team, which would change out of all recognition in the next couple of years, was: W. Baldwin; W. Traynor, T. Taylor; A. Astley, A. J. Brown; T. Gibson, J. Bradshaw, J. Beverley, W. Askew, R. Westwell, W. Hanson.

Elsewhere in that month of January 1880 we hear news of future Olympians. Arthur Matthews is scoring regularly in the reserves, for whom William Astley, Alfred's younger brother, plays half back; Jack Hunter is seen at Accrington, captaining the Sheffield Association team that beats Lancashire 7-1; a "J. Crossley" (this is almost certainly Jimmy Costley) is hitting goals playing as outside-left for Brookhouse Rangers; the precocious fourteen-year-old James T. Ward makes the odd appearance for Little Harwood; and an "A. Warburton" is playing full back for Cob Wall. This last can only be the future captain, six weeks or so before he teamed up with Joe Beverley and Tommy Gibson to play in the Blackburn Association Cup semi-final.

Olympic's progress as they attempted to retain this trophy appeared easier this year – at least until the final, when "Blackburn Perseverance" lived up to their name and took the Hole-i'th'-Wall side to a replay.

In the earlier rounds Blackburn Park Road were disposed of 5-1, in a game played on the Cattle Market field. Mackereth scored after three minutes, after which it was almost complete domination by the victorious team. The one blip was Baldwin's fumbling of a cross: he dropped it, and the referee adjudged that it had fallen over the line before the 'keeper could kick clear. This made it 2-1, but the superior Olympic attack carried the day.

St Mark's, who had taken Beverley's side to two replays the previous year, were easier meat this time around. As ever the captain's throw-ins created havoc in the opposing defence. Midway through the first half one such missile struck a bemused St Mark's defender on the head and was deflected into goal. In the second the winners' sharp and productive inter-passing was captured by the *Standard*'s report:

> "Askew next seized it and passed it to Mackereth, who kicked it to
> Bradshaw, who forwarded it to Hanson, and Hanson shot it through."
> (Feb. 28th 1880)

Thornber made it 3-0, after yet another devastating Beverley throw.

The team was strengthened yet further before the semi-final by the inclusion of one S. A. Warburton. Tall and strong and a capable sprinter, the twenty-four-year-old had yet to reach his full potential in the football arena. He partnered Beverley at full back, allowing Gibson to give expression to his marauding right wing skills.

Details of the semi have so far proven elusive, owing to blanket newspaper coverage of the 1880 General Election, throughout March. It is known, though, that this was Warburton's debut. And the result must have been a win for Olympic, as they appeared in the final the following month.

The team for the Blackburn Association Cup Final: W. Baldwin; S. A. Warburton, J. Beverley; A. J. Brown, A. Astley; T. Gibson, J. Bradshaw, A. Mackereth, W. Askew, R. Westwell, W. Hanson

The Perseverance team: H. Walsh; E. Warburton, J. W. Pickup; A. Wilson, C. Ramsbottom; G. Hacking, T. Smith, T. Hacking, J. Butterworth, L. Marchbank, G. Holt

The Perseverance central attacker doesn't seem to be Thomas Hacking, future Olympic goalkeeper, for reasons given in the next chapter. This "T. Hacking" was essentially a useful striker, who would turn out for the Blackburn Select XI as well as Olympic reserves within the next year or so. Marchbank, however, was to switch to the Hole-i'th'-Wall the following season, finishing one of the top scorers alongside Beverley, Matthews and Yates.

The final took place once more on the Cattle Market field. Despite its central position this terrain was still at times open to some high winds. One such was blowing from goal to goal on the day of the final. Olympic opted to play with the wind at their backs for the first half, reasoning that their superior fitness (already a trademark attribute) would come into its own after change of ends.

For a while it appeared to be working. The holders exerted enormous pressure almost throughout the first half. Askew struck home early on, but was given offside. But soon after that Beverley hurled a throw into the goalmouth, and Hanson headed in. The same tactic brought further profit: Mackereth shot, and Walsh the Perseverance 'keeper caught the ball. Under pressure, though, he threw clear without too much thought, and an alert Gibson latched onto the loose ball and drove in the second.

With a two-goal lead, Olympic began the second half with confidence, even though they were playing into the wind. Westwell came close twice. Then Perseverance launched the expected fight-back. First Bradshaw in attempting to clear put into his own goal, then T. Hacking tried his luck with a shot from some thirty yards. Carried on the wind the ball eluded an earthbound Baldwin and produced the equaliser. Westwell hit the crossbar with two minutes left, but that was that: despite having had most of the play, Olympic had to fight another day.

The replay, strangely for a final, was at Hole-i'th'-Wall the following Saturday. It was perhaps for this reason that Perseverance, feeling that they would be up against it on the opponents' ground, opted for a more physical approach this time. It certainly evened things up for a while, as the lighter Olympic team (minus Warburton) were hustled and charged and unable to play their normal game. Beverley cast caution to the winds and joined the attack. The gamble paid off, as the captain headed a goal. Back came Perseverance, and it was T. Hacking again who gave the first half a more representative scoreline by making it 1-1.

With no high wind this time to distort strategy, in the second half Olympic were irrepressible. Their supremacy produced just the one goal, however: Brown sent in a shot which the 'keeper could only parry, and the lurking Beverley, reacting quickly, headed his second. It was the winner.

As the Blackburn Association folded at the end of that season, becoming part of the Lancashire Association, Olympic were allowed to keep the trophy in perpetuity. After all, theirs was the only club name ever to appear on it!

Across town, Rovers were continuing on their own steady road to glory. Their first ever FA Cup run showed glimpses of the bonanza to come in the mid-eighties. Victories over Tyne Association (5-1) and bitter rivals Darwen (3-1) led to a tie with Nottingham Forest, away. Here the road ended, emphatically: Forest were clear 6-0 winners. The Midlands club progressed as far as the 1880 semi, where the *status quo* was confirmed with a narrow 0-1 defeat at the hands of Oxford University. (This was Forest's second successive losing semi-final. The insurmountable hurdle the previous year had been the Old Etonians. It must have seemed that some sort of force field was protecting the select few.)

Olympic and Rovers were to meet twice before the summer. The first game, at Alexandra Meadows, was largely flippant and freakish, the 8-2 scoreline in favour of the home side obscuring the fact that the visitors had dominated proceedings early on, running up a 2-0 lead. It was 2-2 at half time, but then:

> "The latter portion of the game partook almost of the character of a
> farce, the Olympic team appearing to play with the greatest indifference."
> *Blackburn Times* (Mar, 20th 1880)

Rovers "scored heavily in the last few minutes." Perhaps Olympic felt that they had proven their point with their early superiority, and with nothing at stake save pride, had lapsed into ineffectiveness in the final throes of the game. In any case, back at Hole-i'th'-Wall a fortnight later, Joe Beverley's team had the last word, with a 1-0 win.

Just before the beginning of the next season (1880-1) there was an item about Olympic in the "Local News" section of the *Blackburn Times*. It was reported that about £100 had been spent on pitch refurbishments at Hole-i'th'-Wall. Over the summer the drainage had been improved, and the slope in some measure rectified. The playing area had been widened, creating a pitch measuring a sizeable 120 yards by 80.

The light blue team shirts first become the official club colours this season. New Secretary William Bramham had arranged games with such illustrious clubs as Sheffield Wednesday, Welsh Champions Wrexham, Turton, Liverpool, Preston North End ... and of course, local adversaries the Rovers. Transport to away games, if not by train, was supplied by local cab proprietor Robin Walker. The Olympic had also decided to compete for the two most prestigious pots available to a Blackburn club: the Lancashire Association Challenge Trophy, and the English Cup, otherwise known as the "Little Tin Idol", or the "National Tankard", or the FA Cup.

It was a bold move from a club with limited resources, and whose players were so far drawn solely from the mills and factories of the town. In the FA Cup first round they found themselves up against the powerful Sheffield Association team, away. How would they fare against such an experienced outfit?

HOLE-I'TH'-WALL, THIS DAY,

OLYMPIC v. ROVERS.

Kick off at Three p.m. prompt.
Admission, 3d and 6d.   Ladies free.   Season tickets, 5s.

Saturday Next,
OLYMPIC (2ND) v. TURTON (2ND).
Kick off at Three p.m.   Admission 3d.

October 1880. A crowd of 7,500 came to watch Rovers win this one 2-0. This was a ground record at Hole-i'th'-Wall until November 1884, when fully 10,000 crammed into the ground for the game with Preston North End, also lost 0-2. The largest crowd for an Olympic game was the 16,000 at Trent Bridge, Nottingham, for the 1884 FA Cup semi-final.

The Hole-i'th'-Wall pitch, 2006. Olympic would have played the full length of the field, and the original grandstand – the one destroyed by a gale in February 1884 – would have been at the far (southern) end, in front of the line of houses. These houses had not been built in Olympic's day.

Robert Pate's painting of the Hole-i'th'-Wall Inn as it would have appeared in Olympic's day.

4: BAPTISM OF FIRE

> After about half an hour's play the game came to an abrupt
> termination, owing to a petty quarrel.
> Report on Druids vs. Olympic: *North Wales Guardian* (Feb. 19th 1881)

> The score stood – Sheffield five goals and Blackburn four, there being
> yet a few minutes to play. The visitors played up as strong as lions to the finish,
> and were twice within an ace of scoring.
> FA Cup Round One: *Sheffield Daily Telegraph* (Nov. 1st 1880)

At the same time as all this, on the other side of the Atlantic, Billy the Kid was robbing banks, and Geronimo was still waging his guerrilla war with the US government.

This sideways glance may help us to focus on one aspect of football around 1880: despite the supposed *pax Victoriana* and the ministrations of the London committeemen, the game was still riddled with uncertainties and unresolved disputes, often culminating in an English sporting equivalent of lawlessness. If ever there was a soccer Wild West, this was it.

Ideally a decision on the pitch was adhered to if upheld by the referee (neutral) and at least one umpire (one supplied by each club). It seems a reasonable rule of thumb, but passionate support for either team, along with some grey areas in the written rules, tended to blur the issues. Match officials were openly challenged by players, often verbally abused or threatened by all and sundry, and on the rare occasion, chased by an irate mob as far as the railway station. If general agreement could not be reached on the field of play, one possible tactic was for an entire team to return to the pub or pavilion in a communal sulk. This withdrawal of labour sometimes persuaded the referee to reverse his decision, sometimes not. "Disputed goals" or "match abandoned" (and not because of the weather) occur in reports with depressing frequency.

Moreover, the accepted rules didn't always travel well. Officially the Sheffield and London codes had been brought together under the unifying FA banner in 1877. Unofficially, local variations lived on.

Blackburn Olympic discovered this when they travelled to Ruabon to play North Wales Champions the Druids, in February 1881. Olympic had beaten them 3-0 at Hole-i'th'-Wall a fortnight before, outsmarting the burly Welshmen with a neat display of inter-passing. There was naturally great interest in the return game at Wynnstay Park, Ruabon. Despite the pouring rain, there was a crowd of "a large number ... some of whom had assembled from a considerable distance", but they were to be disappointed. The first twenty minutes or so appear to have been spent arguing about the rules and playing a bit of football in between. The *North Wales Guardian* gives a commendably balanced description of the flashpoint incident:

> "The Olympic umpire [a Mr. Whiteside] blew his whistle owing to 'hands'
> or some other cause, when the ball continued to roll, causing the dispute. The
> Blackburnites argued that when the umpire 'whistled', the ball should at once
> stop, but this, the Druids replied, was not in their rules, and that as they were
> playing on their (the Druids') ground, they would have to comply with their rules
> and play to them. 'Harangues' ensued upon 'the rules', and after some minutes'
> lively discussion the Olympics hurriedly left the ground."
> (Feb. 19th 1881)

This is possibly a rudimentary version of the advantage rule. But in any case it's difficult to criticise Olympic's decision to leave the field, as continuing under such conditions, whereby a match official's whistle may be ignored according to some unfamiliar ruling, would have made play very difficult, if not impossible. Joe Beverley was captain, and given his great love of the game, it may be concluded that the decision wasn't taken lightly.

The two teams weren't to meet again until two years later, in a match of immense significance.

The Olympic had had a similar experience earlier that season when playing Lower Chapel of Darwen, in the Blackburn club's first ever tie in the Lancashire Cup. This time, with progress in the competition at stake, the matter could not be left hanging fire.

Lower Chapel, with a thumping 9-2 win over fancied Eagley to their credit, were never going to be pushovers. The Darwen team had been trumpeting their likely victory in the tie ever since the draw had been announced. Matters weren't helped by the fact that Beverley decided to absent himself for the day, "from a cause which is not considered satisfactory". This was perhaps the first inkling of the captain's temporary, though crucial, switch of allegiance to the Rovers. There certainly seemed to be a clue in an item in that morning's *Blackburn Times*:

> "Councillor Boothman took out ten of his workpeople, including Suter and Beverley, on Wednesday, to play a match against eleven workpeople from Messrs. Meadows' Bridge Mill, on the Olympic ground. The jovial Town Councillor was to be seen keeping goal for his side, arrayed in velvet knickers and waistcoat, with a Turkish cap to crown all, and although he did let the ball pass through his posts once, he had the satisfaction of knowing that the game resulted in a victory for his side by two goals to one. Dinner was afterwards partaken of at the George Inn."
> (Nov. 15th 1880)

All very jolly. But three days later Olympic had to climb to the exposed, snow-laden plateau of Knowl Meadow and take on this free-scoring side without their captain and best utility player. The *Standard* correspondent predicted a lottery of a match, due to "the rushing, whirling power which upsets our best new chimney pots on a miry day", i.e., the wind.

And so it proved. Despite Olympic's strategy of playing the ball close and low, the game was as wild as the high wind that roared down from the Pennines. Yates, whose dribbling skills came into their own on the snow-hard pitch, was still haphazard in his shooting, with a couple of good chances going astray. Eventually it was Matthews on his first team debut, bearing down on the Chapel 'keeper Haworth after a Brown corner, who bundled man and ball over the line for the first goal. (Until the arrival of George Wilson, this was an unusual way for the slightly-built Blackburn team to score.) The home side equalised before half time. It was Yates again who set up Westwell for his side's second goal during a twenty-minute period of domination in the second half. Then during a brief silly session towards the end Chapel, against the run of play, hit two past Baldwin. It was right wing Lever who rescued matters with a late, late equaliser.

Olympic were quite happy with a replay at their place a fortnight later. Not only did it mean extra revenue from what was sure to be a good crowd, they were now of course quite confident of progressing to the next round. Beverley was back, apparently without hard feelings on either side.

It was a throw-in from the errant captain after ten minutes that led to the first goal. The usual distance and accuracy on the throw created panic in the opposing goalmouth, and Westwell scored with a "grand low shot". For most of the first half it was all Olympic. Despite the waterlogged pitch, the home side's dribbling and passing skills completely bamboozled the Chapel defence. Askew hit a shot between the 'keeper's legs as he came out to challenge, but the ball stuck in the mud just before the line. Since the home team were overly committed to attack, the visitors managed one breakaway, from which they equalised. Amazingly, given the run of play, it was 1-1 at half time.

Lower Chapel had turned up late at Hole-i'th'-Wall, so darkness was descending as the game neared its end. Given subsequent events, one wonders if the late arrival had been part of a deliberate ploy on the part of the visiting team. In the gathering gloom the side from Darwen launched a desperate, massed attack. The ball landed in front of the Olympic goal, and the backs found it difficult to clear. There ensued a free-for-all, one of those up close and personal situations a yard or so from the goal line that contemporary reports called a "scrimmage". At one point in the random hacking and kicking the Chapel forwards roared "Goal!", throwing their arms up in celebration. The referee, unsighted and several dozen yards off the play, duly gave it.

Nobody else who was within sight of the incident thought that the ball had crossed the line. Olympic, of course, protested. Since the referee, a Mr. Rostron of Bolton, refused to relent, Beverley's side once more left the field. After about twenty minutes in the pub, during which time, we may be sure, the issue was warmly debated, they decided to come back out and finish the game. It was perhaps agreed that any moral high ground would have been forfeited by abandoning matters. This was a Cup match, after all, and not some prosaic "friendly".

So they returned to the fray, but to encounter a problem: they had no opponents, and the referee had gone home! In what must have been pretty well total darkness (apart from the lights from the back of the pub), Olympic kicked off and "scored". They were obviously aware that the "goal" would be disputed, but would maintain that one disputed goal apiece made matters even. Over to the Lancashire FA committeemen.

The first decision from the Lancs. FA offices was that the tie should be replayed. Lower Chapel's furious response was that that was effectively to invalidate the referee's ruling, and therefore to cast doubts on Mr. Rostron's probity or competence. They categorically refused to play again. After long deliberation the Lancs. FA surprisingly reversed their decision, opting to support their local referee by awarding the tie to Lower Chapel.

The defeat may be seen as prophetic. The Lancashire FA Trophy was the only major available cup that Olympic were destined never to win, despite some agonising near misses.

There is also possibly a degree of relevance in the following postcard sent by Rishton FC to the Football Association offices the following season, the week before a Lancashire Cup tie:

"Will you please appoint a Referee for our match with Bolton
Wanderers on Saturday, at Bolton. We would rather not have a
Member of the Lancashire FA, they are so one-sided."
The History of the Lancashire FA 1878-1928

It wasn't always the team who walked off the pitch when matters reached a head. Later in the same season as the Druids and Lower Chapel shenanigans, Olympic travelled to Bolton to play the aforementioned Wanderers. It was always going to be one of those days: Gibson and Westwell missed the train, and were left behind at Stoney Butts station, Blackburn.

In the game itself, Beverley was fulfilling his new role of libero-cum-sweeper (see next chapter), and the Wanderers, unable to adapt to what was essentially a one-back defence, kept on falling for the offside trap. (Before 1925, to be onside an attacker had to have at least three, and not two, players between him and the goal at the moment the ball was played forward to him.) There is little more frustrating for a forward to be repeatedly caught out this way. Towards half time Wanderers had a goal disallowed. Nailor, the Bolton captain, could take no more, and went up to the referee and warned him, loud enough for all to hear, that any more decisions like that against his team and he (the ref) would have to leave the field. The official duly left the field.

He returned after some persuasive talk from the visiting team, who obviously didn't want to have travelled to Bolton for half a game. Then in the second half, with the score at 1-1, Wanderer Sharples forced Beverley to handle the ball in an attempt to forestall him. The captain ran back to defend, and as all his team were expecting a free kick, Sharples was ignored as he ran forward with the ball. Here again it seems that some sort of advantage rule – even though theoretically it didn't yet exist – was behind the ref.'s thought processes. Sharples ran on to put the ball past new 'keeper Hacking, and great was Olympic's surprise when the goal was allowed to stand.

Once more the pitch became a debating area, and the outcome was, to use the *Standard's* words: "As neither side would agree, the game was not played out."

The 1880-1 season generally, though, was a successful one for Blackburn Olympic. Tommy Gibson was selected to represent the North of England against the South, over at Bramall Lane. For the team, high-scoring wins were registered (Witton 8-0, Church 9-1, Liverpool 12-0 and 7-0, Bootle 7-0, Staveley 7-1, Blackburn Park Road 6-1). Defeats were few and far between, and usually away from home. Two of the teams who bested them – Turton and Wrexham – were beaten in the return match at Hole-i'th'-Wall. The one side proving impossible to defeat were Rovers. In the three matches played between the two teams that year the scores were: 0-2, 0-4 and a thrilling 2-3 on Alexandra Meadows. These games will be described in more detail in Chapter 5.

One of the defeats was no disgrace: the baptism of fire in the FA Cup first round, a tough away fixture with the Sheffield club. The previous season the Yorkshiremen had progressed to the fourth round, where they had succumbed to the mighty Notts Forest (6-0 conquerors of Rovers), and that only on a technicality after a 2-2 draw, at Nottingham.

On the Sheffield team, Thomas Heathcote Sorby (of the celebrated local footballing clan) had received an international cap the previous year; his brother R. A. Sorby (goalkeeper) and half back F. H. Marsden were to represent the North against the South – alongside Tommy Gibson and Jack Hunter – the following February; and W. Beardshaw, soon to be a youthful FA committeeman, would be a founder member of the Corinthians. This was the team's eighth season in the FA Cup, as opposed to their opponents' first. By rights, Olympic should have been put to the sword.

Moreover, for a visiting side that had rarely travelled far from their own muddy hilltop, and never further east than Accrington, Olympic's crossing of the Pennines and their arrival at the splendid Bramall Lane ground must have highlighted the size of the task before them.

At the time owned by the Duke of Norfolk and leased out to sporting interests, Bramall Lane, the home ground of the Sheffield Association, was basically the terrain of the town's Cricket Club. The northern half of the playing area was roped off to cater for games of football, an arrangement which was brought to an end as late as 1973. The ground had seen baseball and lacrosse matches, although the more plebeian pursuits of "rabbit coursing,

Bramall Lane cricket ground in the 1880s. This is the northern half of the terrain, where football was played in the winter months.

pigeon shooting, or race-running for money" were banned. It had been the site of the world's first ever floodlit football match, in October 1878, at about the same time Olympic had been struggling to beat St Mark's in the Blackburn Association Trophy.

The Sheffield – Olympic FA Cup tie was a cracker, the rain-softened turf and slippery conditions scarcely detracting from a spirited, skilful tussle. The scarlet-clad home side won the toss and opted to play with the low wintry sun at their backs for the first half. Both teams were committed to attack from the off: a couple of Beverley throws were cleared by a well-regimented trio of backs, then Sheffield forced two corner kicks at the other end. Wake took both corners: the first was headed clear, then the second landed on the Olympic crossbar. From the rebound Bradbury was first to the loose ball, and a fine drive opened the scoring for the home team.

Scenting an easy victory, Sheffield took the game to their opponents. For about ten minutes it was mainly Joe Beverley who held the fort, his tackling and clearances doing the necessary. But not even he was prepared for the grotesque piece of ill luck that led to the second goal. Lever had run back to help the defence, and as he turned to face the opposition he was temporarily blinded by the sun. A hopeful lob struck him on the back of the head and looped past a bemused Baldwin into the goal. Shortly afterwards it was 3-0. T. H. "Heathcote" Sorby ran up to join the attack and scored, latching onto a precise high cross from the wing.

Recovering from such early traumas is the mark of a great side. The Light Blues fought back, Gibson initiating a typical combined move which ended in Beverley shooting just wide of the posts. Then, after the home side had twice come close to hitting a fourth, Lever, finding himself with some space around twenty-five yards from goal, hazarded a shot. The Sheffield 'keeper appeared to have the ball easily under control, but it somehow eluded him and passed between his legs. A fluke, maybe; but it cancelled out that earlier bit of bad luck, all the more satisfying as it involved the same player.

Nettled by these upstarts actually taking a goal off them, Sheffield were determined to have the last word before the interval. When E. Barber restored his side's advantage to three, the home contingent were no doubt convinced that the game was as good as won. Another unkind twist: at half time the sun dipped below a bank of cloud, so even that advantage was denied to the visitors after change of ends.

Olympic went for broke. One of their now frequent attacks resulted in a throw-in. Beverley sent in one of his specials, and a harassed defender headed through his own goal. Against the run of play Sheffield hit their fifth goal which even the local newspaper described as "somewhat a fluke". But it was clear that, despite their 5-2 lead, the home side were now a spent force. Just as Sheffield had dominated the game in its early stages, now it was Olympic's turn to call the shots.

Within a minute, the Blackburn side had retaliated. Tommy Gibson was now lending his presence to the forward line, and the home side were defending desperately. Following a corner Beverley headed his side's third. With around five minutes left, Yates cracked in one of his "screw shots" from some distance and the ball found its way past the home 'keeper. Olympic, who were by now running rings round their opponents, felt certain of at least a replay. Into the final minute: in an atmosphere of intense excitement, with even the sporting home supporters applauding the visitors' efforts, Askew fired in a shot which the opposing 'keeper pushed round the post. Olympic threw everybody forward for the corner kick. The ball was half cleared as far as Beverley, whose thundering shot hit the bar ... and dropped safely behind. The final whistle blew, and all the heroics had been for nothing. The teams were:

Sheffield Association: R. A. Sorby; T. H. Sorby, W. R. Wake; W. Beardshaw, F. H. Marsden; J. H. Barber, E. Barber, W. A. Matthews, W. Bradbury, H. Barber, W. Rodgers
Olympic: W. Baldwin; J. Beverley, S. A. Warburton; T. Gibson, A. Astley; A. J. Brown, A. Lever, J. Yates, R. Westwell, W. Hanson, W. Askew

Sheffield lost 1-5 to Darwen in the following round.

That season saw the arrival of four key players who were to figure in the 1883 FA Cup run. The slimly built John Yates came from Accrington to Blackburn to work as a weaver. As a player, although not in his element against heavier opposition, he added some skill and mettle to the left attack. His shots at goal tended to be hit-and-miss, but when he got his "screw shots" right, the results were often spectacular. (Not to be confused with James Yates, who played for Accrington in the earlier 1880's. The two namesakes were to meet each other in the 1883 FA Cup match.)

From the reserves there emerged Arthur Matthews, a right-sided attacker renowned for his spirited runs and thrilling goals. He hit the target for the first team on ten recorded occasions in his debut season. His actual total was almost certainly higher, but goalscorers' names weren't always given in the reports. Matthews was a picture framer or gilder by profession, and a member of the Blackburn Presbyterian Church.

Also from the reserves, Alfred Astley's younger brother William came to prominence as a left-sided halfback. When Olympic switched to 2-3-5, and with Hunter and Gibson as his midfield partners, he would fit the bill perfectly. For a while Alf and Will played in the same team, before the elder brother took up umpiring and refereeing, and succeeded Edmonson as treasurer.

Tracing the playing background of "very sharp and active" goalkeeper Thomas Hacking is beset with difficulties, especially as the family name occurs with surprising frequency in Blackburn at the time. Indeed, the England international 'keeper John Hacking (Blackpool and Oldham Athletic) was born in Blackburn in 1902. There doesn't seem to be any direct lineage from Thomas, as this latter's children were two daughters, so obviously any direct descendants wouldn't have kept his name. However, there were at least three other Hackings playing football in the town during Olympic's lifetime.

Blackburn Perseverance had a G. Hacking and a T. Hacking playing in their attack (see previous chapter), and another one, initials J. P., played in goal for Cob Wall behind Warburton, and once for Olympic, against Wrexham the October before Thomas' debut. A lot of the potential confusion is lifted by the following detail from the *Blackburn Times*' pen pictures of the team after the 1883 FA Cup Final:

> "Thomas Hacking, goalkeeper, is by occupation a dentist, and first entered the football arena towards the close of the season 1880-81. He has never filled any other position but that of custodian of the goal, and made his debut in a match against the Turton club."
> (April 7th 1883)

Turton, one of the stronger Lancashire sides of the time, were beaten 2-1. The *Standard* sang the praises of the new 'keeper, who had been enlisted the evening before the match: "Hacking, in the absence of Baldwin, rendered good service at the goal, and effectively maintained his post." (Feb. 26th 1881). Willy Baldwin, despite his general competence between the sticks, had for some time been guilty of errors of handling, letting in saveable shots. The newcomer was comparatively small and slight, but more than made up for this with his mobility and sureness of hand. Amazingly, he had never played in goal before, and had but a scant knowledge of the rules of football, but immediately impressed. (He would be picked to represent the North v. the South in a trial match in Olympic's cup winning season, but an injury, sustained when he fell from a train at Blackburn station, meant that he was unable to play, and his chance of international selection would be lost.)

The results for the rest of the season, with Thomas Hacking in goal, were:

P	W	D	L	F	A
12	10	0	2	48	12

This included five clean sheets. Olympic had found their goalkeeper.

The second FA Cup, identical to that won by Olympic. This one was used after the original was stolen from a Birmingham shop window. It was presented to Lord Kinnaird when a new trophy was designed, and was recently sold at auction.

5: THE SHAPE OF THINGS TO COME

> The game began to be played substantially in its present form, and 'passing on' completely superseded dribbling about the same time that the great provincial centres suddenly came to the front, about 1878 or 1879."
> Montague Shearman: *Athletics and Football* (1887)

> Who that have seen this light brigade-like team [Olympic] in the full display of its genius but have been charmed with their mode of action? Once they were a lot of untutored random kickers of a ball, neither graceful nor charming in their movements ...
> *Blackburn Standard* (Sep. 24th 1881)

Blackburn Olympic form a crucial link in the chain that runs from the rollicking, violent free-for-alls of mediaeval folk football to the sophisticated team deployments of modern times.

The celebrated Wanderers, as they made their way to five unbeaten FA Cup Final appearances in that trophy's early years, developed from a 1-1-8 formation to the accepted template of 2-2-6. Teams with eight forwards apiece suggest scores more reminiscent of table tennis than football, but it was not unknown for entire teams to funnel back into defence if need be. This was total football with a vengeance. The drain on players' energy, and the realisation that some form of zone defence was more efficient than a rugby-like "chasing the game", led to the two backs, two half backs and six forwards arrangement. The point of the six forwards was to cater for the classic paired runs at goal, in which one attacker put his head down and set off on a heroic dribble into the heart of the opposing defence, with a colleague following him as a back-up in the event of a tackle.

But if soccer is seen as essentially a team rather than an individual game, then a natural corollary of that approach is to place a pivotal figure in the centre of the field, one whose constructive job is to control and direct the flow of play. The textbook manoeuvres now would be the through or high ball to the nippy or bustling striker, or the weighted pass out to the wings. Either way, the new attacking role of the three halfbacks was established.

There is some controversy as to when the 2-3-5 system first appeared, and as to who can claim to be the pioneers. Cambridge University, Turton, Wrexham and Nottingham Forest have all put their case forward, and, as we shall see, teams in Sheffield can quite justifiably be considered too. The journey to the source of 2-3-5, as interesting as that might seem, is beyond the scope of this book. We are simply concerned with how the shifting formations influenced Olympic's development.

For the Hole-i'th'-Wall side there was no obvious watershed moment, recognisable as when a definitive switch was made to the new system. Over a couple of years, several team formations were tried, and there was much shuffling around of individual players. But a seed was surely planted back in December 1880, when Sheffield Wednesday came to Alexandra Meadows to play the Rovers in an FA Cup tie. Olympic didn't have a game that day, so it's more than likely that some of the team went to watch. They no doubt noted the Wednesday line-up with three halfbacks (one of whom was Jack Hunter), and were perhaps stunned by the 4-0 dismissal of the Rovers. It must be admitted, though, that the severity of the defeat wasn't entirely due to relative merit or team deployment. The day was freezing cold, and the pitch icy. Wednesday had taken the precaution of attaching leather strips to the soles of their boots to aid their grip. The unprepared Rovers slipped and floundered on the ice.

Then Wednesday brought much the same team (without Hunter) to Hole-i'th'-Wall a couple of weeks later, and in less extreme conditions won fairly easily 3-1. Tinkering with 2-2-6 seemed to be a profitable exercise, then.

Olympic set to thinking: given the present line-up, if you could spare one forward from uniquely attacking duties (a) who would it be? and (b) where would you most usefully deploy him?

The startlingly innovative answer was to play Joe Beverley as *libero*, thus:

> "Goal: W. Baldwin
> Backs *(sic)*: J. Beverley
> Three-quarter backs: T. Gibson, S. A. Warburton
> Halfbacks: A. Astley, A. J. Brown
> Right wing; A. Lever and A. Matthews
> Centre: W. Askew
> Left wing: R. Westwell and J. Yates"
> *Blackburn Standard* (Jan. 29th 1881)

This was some sixty or seventy years before Swiss, then Italian, coaches reinvented the wheel. Olympic weren't particularly trying to start a fad; they were simply playing to strengths. Their captain was a mobile, multi-skilled presence, equally happy breaking up opposition attacks as making and hitting goals himself. His tackling ability had received much praise:

> "Beverley coolly waited until the ball was within a few yards of him,
> when he ran forward and wrested it from his man, and sent it flying down
> the field."
> *Blackburn Standard* (Feb 26th 1881)

His reading of the game and athleticism were such that a trademark move would be for him to win the ball in this way and start a counter-attack, then arrive in the opposing goalmouth in time to hit the goal, or at least provide the crucial assist. With his greater mobility, he would have been a real headache for a defender to mark. With a single back, it was also easier to catch opposing forwards offside, under the old "three defender" rule.

As with any new regimen, there was a settling-in period. Olympic played Accrington twice within the space of a couple of weeks in that crucial month, January 1881. The first match with the new system, away, was lost 1-4. The *Accrington Times* claimed a 5-1 win, and a supporter was inspired to write a dialect poem in celebration. A sample stanza or two:

> "Last Saturday aw went to watch
> A celebrated futebo match,
> 'Twixt Accrington and 'Lympic boys,
> Eh dear o me ther war a noise.
>
> "... When time wur coed an' t' game wur done,
> The noble Reds stood five to one;
> Un' t' team ut Lympic Club had sent
> Went quietly up to t' dressing tent."
> *Accrington Times* (Jan 15th 1881)

Within a fortnight Accrington came to Hole-i'th'-Wall, and the home team deployed the 1-2-2-5 formation once more, but this time with more assurance and flair.

There was a crowd of over a thousand. Part of the interest was that "large sums of money were laid against the Olympic team". Clearly the general opinion was that the Blackburn side were on a hiding to nothing. Accrington were to win the Lancashire Cup that year, and were to score an impressive 112 goals in 28 games.

Beverley was inspired. An impregnable rock in defence, he moved upfield to score the first, a craftily placed free kick that struck a defender's leg en route to the goal. Five minutes later Yates delivered one of his banana shots to make it 2-0, and Matthews hit the third before half time. There was no more scoring in the second half.

The *Standard* was ecstatic: "Never before this season have we seen the Olympians play together so well." The one blemish was the shooting: Yates, for one, could still be haphazard with the final strike.

The 1880-1 season finished on a high note. With the arrival of Yates, Matthews, Will Astley and the ebullient Hacking in goal, the Olympic put together a run of eight consecutive wins throughout March and April. The club's fame was spreading: Partick came from Glasgow, and despite the visitors' typically Caledonian array of cohesive skills they were defeated 3-0, Beverley once again playing his new role to perfection. It was on Shrove Tuesday that they met the Rovers for the third time that season, in a thrilling tussle on Alexandra Meadows.

Rovers had been strengthened by the defection of Fergie Suter from Darwen. Fred Hargreaves and young Jimmy Brown had just represented England (Doc Greenwood would receive his cap the following year), and the Scot Hugh McIntyre played alongside Jimmy Brown in a devastating central attacking partnership. Olympic had lost the two previous encounters 0-2 and 0-4, so to many the result was a foregone conclusion.

The teams were:

Rovers: A. Woolfall; F. Suter, D. Greenwood; F. Hargreaves, A. Blenkhorne; J. Duckworth, J. Douglas, J. Brown, H. McIntyre, G. Avery, T. Jefferson
Olympic: T. Hacking; J. Beverley; S. A. Warburton, T. Gibson; A. Astley, A. J. Brown; A. Matthews, T. Strachan, W. Askew, J. Yates, R. Westwell

On a day of high wind and swirling snowflakes, Olympic opted to play against the elements in the first half. This appeared to be no disadvantage, as after ten minutes a Matthews pass found A. J. Brown, who opened the scoring. Rovers, realising they had a game on their hands, hit back through McIntyre. Then Matthews, giving another of his eye-catching dribbling displays, found some space and centred to Askew. His fierce shot hit the crossbar and was fumbled by Woolfall, who allowed the ball to drop over the line for a goal.

So, against all expectation, Beverley's team were leading 2-1 at half time. Soon after the restart Jimmy Brown went on one of his elusive, jinking runs and equalised for Rovers. Then Olympic, with the wind at their backs, went all out for the winner. Shot after shot hit the woodwork or went close. In the dying seconds Jefferson embarked on a breakaway, and finding just Hacking to beat in the opponents' half, with the last kick of the match hit the decisive goal for the home side. The *Standard* described the game as "one of the most exciting witnessed in Blackburn this season".

Whilst Rovers kept stubbornly to their tried-and-tested 2-2-6, their rivals continued to experiment. In March 1881 (a month after playing Turton who had deployed the extra half-back) Olympic played host to the Bootle team, and fielded their first ever recorded 2-3-5:

                            Hacking

          Warburton   W. Astley

   Beverley   A. Astley   A. J. Brown

Matthews   Mackereth   Askew   Westwell   Yates

Even without Gibson, the Light Blues made short work of their opponents, who were briefly enjoying their role of the best team in the city of Liverpool. The score was a convincing 3-0. Perhaps this three-halfback business was worth using again?

Not for the moment: it took a shock FA Cup defeat some six months later to persuade Olympic to give it another go.

Worthy of note that spring was Beverley's goal with an overhead kick against Bolton Wanderers; Yates' swerving shot from near the corner flag that scored against the same opposition; and Matthews' hat-trick in the Liverpool match. Elsewhere Jack Hunter was captaining England against Wales on Alexandra Meadows, and in Brookhouse Rangers' 16-0 obliteration of St John's, one Jimmy Costley featured significantly on the score sheet.

Perhaps the most outstanding result of that season was the 7-1 drubbing of the powerful Staveley, at Hole-i'th'-Wall on the last day of April. The visitors were a tough mining community side from Derbyshire who were to take Sheffield Wednesday to two replays in the next year's FA Cup. A close match had been predicted, but Olympic's attack was unstoppable. Interestingly, Staveley had opted for the same deployment as their opponents, with cover goal, two three-quarter backs and two halfbacks. It was a clear enough demonstration that the system alone maketh not the men; rather, it was the capabilities on offer that dictated the winning system.

An in-depth report in the *Standard* included brief assessments of the players. Hacking was described as "a very sure goalkeeper, and if once the ball gets near his hands he never fails to drive it away". Warburton, who would be representing Lancashire before the end of the year: "He can dodge his opponents well, and does not often miss a kick." Gibson was simply hailed as "the best man the Olympic possesses". Matthews was " a good screw kicker, and, fearless, can often take the leather from an opponent". Yates' dribbling skills and accurate crosses from the left wing also received praise. So half the 1883 team was already in place, and clicking.

In August 1881 the Olympic hosted a "Grand Athletic Sports" at Hole-i'th'-Wall. The events were running, five-a-side football, and Cumberland style wrestling. There were 180 entrants, not including the footballers, and the Temperance Brass Band enlivened the afternoon. The pub landlord, a Mr. Catterall, supplied the refreshments.

> THE BLACKBURN OLYMPIC FOOTBALL CLUB and TEMPERANCE BRASS BAND.—GRAND ATHLETIC SPORTS will be held on the ground of the Olympic Club, Hole-i'th'-Wall, on Saturday and Monday, August 27th and 29th, 1881, and will include Flat Races, Sack Races, Wrestling, Football Contest, and a grand One Mile Flat Race for professionals.
> Forms of entry can be had from the Hon. Sec.,
> Mr. JOHN EDMONDSON,
> 55, Altom street, Blackburn.

It was also an excuse to draw attention to the new grandstand, a forty-yard long structure built at the cost of £100. Once again the club were stating their intention to go places. The grandstand, unusually, was situated behind the southern goal, "at the bottom of the slope".

Albert Warburton won his heat in the 100 yards handicap, as did Rovers' Jimmy Brown. In the final the handicap no doubt worked against experienced sprinter Warburton, as he was unplaced, Brown finishing second.

The prizes on offer for this event give some idea of the flavour of the proceedings:

"1st: alloyed gold watch, value £1 10s;
2nd: a case of electro-plated fish carvers, value 10s."

Jimmy Brown's team won the five-a-side, and carried off £5 cash! There were over a thousand spectators, so at either a shilling or sixpence a head, the Sports were financially a great success too.

Despite ventures such as these and Sydney Yates' sponsorship, Olympic were ever in the shadow of debt. The arrival of "name" teams at Hole-i'th'-Wall seemed to coincide with vile weather, thus decimating potentially large crowds. When Partick Thistle came from Glasgow to play a widely advertised game in November 1881, the freezing horizontal rain literally put a dampener on the event. A 4-4 draw, an attractive proposition under normal circumstances, was the result of a 35 minutes each way game, watched by a comparative handful of dedicated souls. On one occasion the team travelled at great expense to Bramall Lane, Sheffield, supposedly to play a lucrative game against the Exchange side, only to be told on arrival that the pitch was in an unplayable state. Their ambitious moves seemed dogged by bad luck.

And bad weather too. Over Christmas 1881 Olympic embarked on a Scottish mini-tour, based in the Glasgow region. On Christmas Eve they played at Thornliebank, in those days a village a few miles south of the city. The idea was to play the first half under Scottish rules, and the second under English – at the time a common practice for such games. The home side were no slouches, holders of the Renfrewshire Cup, and had been Scottish Cup Finalists in 1880, losing to the all-conquering Queen's Park. They opted to play the first half with the icy wind and rain at their backs, and began the game with a will, peppering Hacking's goal with shots, all of which the Blackburn 'keeper held or fisted clear. It was 0-0 at half time. Then five of the home side, morale sapped by Hacking's saves and the thought of playing into the subarctic blast for all of the second half, refused to play on. According to the *Glasgow Herald*, "The elements proved an insurmountable obstacle." The persuasions of supporters were to no avail. So the visitors kicked off against six men, Beverley scored a token goal, and the remaining players decided to call it a day. A visit to the newly built Turkish baths nearby was a no doubt more attractive proposition.

On Boxing Day, in far better weather, the opponents were Partick, at the Inchview ground. This was a separate club from the Thistle, there being two main teams in that area of Glasgow until amalgamation in 1885. On the day the Scots were clearly superior, winning 3-0, thus cancelling out their 0-3 defeat at the Hole-i'th'-Wall the previous April. In mitigation, the Light Blues were playing without Will Astley and A. J. Brown in midfield.

Olympic's fame continued to spread. The team travelled to the Drill Field, Northwich, for the return match against the Cheshire Champions. No less than ten local clubs had cancelled their games so they could go and watch. The *Blackburn Times* claimed that the attendance was the "largest ever seen in Cheshire", estimating "several thousand". In an exciting match Matthews hit the winner with a minute or so left, giving the visitors a 3-2 win.

Typical of the "so near and yet ... " dramas was the first round FA Cup match with Darwen, down at Barley Bank. The 1-2-2-5 system was still being used, but this time with Warburton as cover goal, allowing Beverley more freedom to push forward. Olympic expected to come away with at least a draw, but the 3-1 defeat was to highlight the vital flaw in the "cover goal" arrangement.

A huge crowd, estimated at 6,000, made the journey to Barley Bank, whether by train, the new steam tram, or on foot. A group of Olympic supporters piled into a horse-drawn waggon, which set off down the Darwen Road at around midday. They got as far as Hollins Grove when the waggon took a tumble into a ditch. No one was hurt, and the passengers were in no way deterred from walking the extra half-mile to the match.

The game was every bit as close as predicted. After a goalless first half, Darwen's lead was rubbed out by Wensley. Matters were even until the last ten minutes, then the home team launched a series of ferocious attacks. For a time Warburton and Hacking were the heroes of the hour, equal to everything the Darreners could throw at them. It took a dreadful stroke of ill luck for the wall to be breached: a viciously kicked ball struck Warburton between the legs, and down he went. Whilst he was recovering Darwen scored twice. Obviously heaping so much responsibility on the shoulders of a single back had its potential problems. The winners progressed to the fourth round, where they were dismissed 5-1 by Rovers.

The 1-2-2-5 deployment was now for the most part shelved. A string of early season high-scoring wins (Enfield 9-2, Witton 7-2, Northwich Victoria 9-0) wasn't enough to persuade that this system worked against the very best. Rovers, in their smart new Leamington Street home, beat them easily 4-1.

The logic and stability of the third halfback clearly appealed to Olympic now, as just one week after the Darwen defeat, in a home match against Wrexham, the published team was:

Hacking, goal; Beverley, Warburton, backs; A. J. Brown, W. Hargreaves,
Gibson, halfbacks; Marchbank, W. Astley, Matthews, Yates, Wensley, forwards

The result was an 8-0 stroll. The team was kept unchanged for the following week's game with Cowlairs. Cowlairs were another of the batch of teams from the Glasgow area that appeared in the late 1870's. This one was to last until 1896, when Celtic – plus one or two English clubs – were to benefit from the club's demise.

Scottish teams were always good box-office south of the border, since at the time they had a reputation as sophisticated exponents of the game. The national team was regularly scoring five, six or seven goals against England, so to some extent the reputation was deserved. And on this occasion the Lancastrian weather was mild enough, so a healthy crowd of over 2,000 climbed Shear Brow to watch the game.

Early on it was Cowlairs' neat man-to-man passing that caught the eye, but gradually, through Hargreaves' marshalling of the play, Matthews' vigorous runs, and the forwards' shooting, Olympic took control. Wensley hit a hat-trick, and Matthews had a goal disallowed through a careless handball. The final score was 3-1 to the home side.

Centre-half W. Hargreaves was no relation to the brothers who played for Rovers and England. A. J. Brown was tried out in the central midfield position too, in a winter of shuffled line-ups and chequered results. It would be another five months before Olympic's permanent centre-half arrived at Hole-i'th'-Wall, and he would fit the role to perfection.

Olympic's progress in the Lancashire Cup of 1881-2 reflected the season's ebb and flow of fortunes. A trip to Astley Bridge near Bolton in October, with Warburton still playing as solo stopper, resulted in a clear 5-1 win. The opposition had no answer to the speed of Yates and Matthews, even though this latter had just recovered from an illness. Yates hit a hat-trick, and would be top scorer that season with 29 recorded goals in 43 games.

Padiham came to Hole-i'th'-Wall for the next round, and despite the occasional defensive misunderstanding with the new 2-3-5, the home side were well worth their 3-1 win. The match was rough and bad-tempered, and at one point, according to the *Blackburn Times*: "One man ventured on the field with the avowed intention of turning off the referee." For Olympic Will Astley shone, scoring twice. Padiham's goal was instructive: Hacking had a shot well covered, but Warburton intervened, and in trying to head out for a corner, put through his own goal. At one point Hacking slipped and fell, allowing a Padiham forward an easy chance to score. Fortunately Gibson was at hand to clear off the line. Teething troubles, and not enough to dissuade the winners from their new formation.

The third round against Enfield from Clayton-le-Moors needed three bites at the cherry. Fielding a depleted line-up, Olympic did well to hold their opponents to 1-1 at Hole-i'th'-Wall. It was a well-contested, skilful game, despite the poor conditions: "not a single player left the field that had not tasted of the mud" *(Accrington Times)*. The reason for the weakened "mixed bag" team was that the club played two games on the same day: the Lancashire Cup match in the morning, then a promised friendly (won 4-1) away against Church in the afternoon. Matthews and Yates played in both games, and lanky forward Tommy Dewhurst, a regular scorer in the reserves, took the field against Church. Dewhurst had made his first team debut the previous February.

Five days later, in the Lancs. Cup replay over at Enfield, the Light Blues were back to full strength. Yates and Beverley were the driving force behind an attack that ran up three goals by half time. In the second half the home side fought back, penning the visitors around their own goal for all of twenty minutes, but Hacking was in brilliant form, bringing off some agile saves. Three decisive counter-attacks towards the end of the game, results of Hargreaves' intelligent distribution, put the issue beyond doubt, and the Blackburn team, even though without Warburton on this occasion, finished six goals to the good.

Unfortunately, it was to no avail. Enfield protested about the inclusion of Sharples, claiming he was a Rovers player and therefore ineligible for a Cup match. The Lancashire Association upheld the complaint, and the teams had to face up again. This time Warburton and Beverley excelled themselves in defence, and Will Astley was a more than adequate replacement for Sharples at halfback. Olympic won fairly easily 3-1.

It was back to Bolton for the quarter-final, to take on Great Lever. In another tetchy game Olympic allowed a 2-0 lead to be nullified deep into the second half. But the six forwards, including Beverley, took control in the last ten minutes, and the final score was 4-2. Beverley hit a hat trick.

The prospect of an all-Blackburn Lancashire Cup Final disappeared when the town's two major teams were drawn against each other in the semi. It took place at the Hole-i'th'-Wall in late February, just four weeks before Rovers, unbeaten for well over a year, were due to play the Old Etonians in the Cup Final.

Olympic were 0-2 down after 26 minutes of the first half. Beverley cast caution to the winds and left his designated role as full back to join the attack. Within a matter of minutes he supplied the pass for Matthews to reduce the arrears, but Howorth in the Rovers goal was in top form, and wasn't beaten again. The Rovers attack took advantage of the threadbare opposing defence, and ran out 6-1 winners. A commentator in the *Times* rather meanly wondered if the Olympic had been joking when they had predicted they would win this one.

The 1881-2 season, then, had appeared to put Olympic in their place. They could claim to be one of the best teams around on their day, but they were still chasing the pack of the near-élite: Rovers, Darwen, and the top Nottingham and Sheffield clubs.

One of the problems in the second half of the season was finding a good enough replacement for the temporarily absent Hacking in goal. Even Beverley and Warburton had been tried out, once each, in the position: the former had shown that his skills extended even to the role of custodian; the latter, deployed between the sticks for the first game after his return from illness, was obviously happier as an outfield player. Hacking pleaded work commitments and poor health to explain his absence. There is, however, more than a suspicion that a lengthy spell of foul weather may have played a part in his decision to stay away!

With no trophies to play for, Olympic's drive appeared to slacken towards the end of the season. After the 1-1 draw with Witton the *Blackburn Times* stated that their play "lacked dash and inspiration". When Kilmarnock Athletic came to the Hole-i'th'-Wall at the end of March and won 4-0, the Light Blues had to play without their captain. Beverley, without giving any notice of his intentions, had taken the midnight football special down to London to watch Rovers in the FA Cup Final!

A supporter's letter printed in the *Standard* criticised the players who were "continually trying to dribble the ball the length of the field", with "not a pennyworth of real football science shown". There was a hint that one of the reasons behind this regression was that certain players were betting on themselves to score the first goal. The writer of the letter came to the damning conclusion:

> "Selfishness and sulkiness will have to be things of the past, or they
> will never get beyond their present position in the football world."
> (March 18th 1882)

The arrival of former England captain Jack Hunter in April (see next chapter) didn't seem to make much difference at first, apart from a temporary boost to morale. On his debut there was a pulsating 4-4 draw with Darwen at Barley Bank, but an end of season 12-1 drubbing by Rovers seemed to scotch any serious hopes of a challenge to Fred Hargreaves, Suter and Co.

The two Blackburn rivals were due to meet again in the final of the East Lancs. Charity Cup in August. Hunter and the team had just twelve weeks to orchestrate a miracle.

Barley Bank, Darwen's home ground until 1899, and the scene of many exciting encounters with Olympic. Hollins Grove is the area on the left in the middle distance, around the chapel building (see chapter 5). The picture was taken in 1897 by a member of the Darwen Camera Club.

6: MR. HUNTER CHANGES TEAMS

> HUNTER, J., Blackburn Olympic. A brilliant half-back, very strong;
> a sure kick with either foot; is also clever with his head.
> *Alcock's Football Annual 1883*

Jack Hunter was born in Crookes, Sheffield, in 1852, and started playing for the Heeley club at aged sixteen. It was around this time that the Wednesday club was formed, and that football was making its first steps away from the primeval rugby hybrid with its rouge flags, fair catches for outfield players, and possible touchdowns.

Hunter was around to witness the birth of the modern game. He represented the town when the Royal Engineers came to play a friendly in 1874, and there was some astonishment amongst the military that the northerners actually headed the ball as well as kicking it! When he played alongside the Clegg brothers in a Sheffield v. Birmingham charity match in November of the following year, an observation from the *Sheffield Daily Telegraph* ran: "The old system of changing ends after every goal is now very properly abolished." He took part in the world's first floodlit football match, at Bramall Lane in October 1878.

During the course of his long playing career Hunter would see immense changes and significant innovations in the game: definite roles in attack and defence, a workable offside rule, the corner kick, the referee's whistle, the crossbar, the two-handed throw-in, the FA Cup, and a consistent set of rules across the country.

Jack Hunter looked all set to play out his time with honour in the cutlery city. He would alternate between the town's two strongest clubs – Heeley and the Wednesday – and would be natural choice for captain of Heeley, the representative Sheffield Association team, the North, and eventually England. He would receive seven international caps. The team he led won the Wharncliffe Charity Cup and the Sheffield Association Challenge Cup on numerous occasions.

He was also a strong runner, collecting a total of fifty-six prizes at various games during his time in Sheffield. His speciality was the quarter mile, and he won a few hurdle races too.

Despite the severe demeanour which comes across in most photographs, he was a popular and good-humoured character. There are records of his taking part in benefit games for injured Sheffield players. In April 1880 fellow footballers presented him with a commemorative watch and a purse of fifty gold sovereigns, as a tribute to his immense contributions to football in Sheffield.

To one of such perennial strengths and great-hearted loyalty, the respect of his lords and peers, and the glittering prizes. But that was before the Zulus affair.

It was a Mr. Brewer of the Sheffield Guardians who suggested the idea of charity football matches in aid of the widows and orphans of the soldiers killed in the Zulu Wars. The famous defence of Rorke's Drift, featured in the film *Zulu*, took place in April 1879. In November of the same year a team of local footballers, including Jack Hunter, took the field dressed as Zulu warriors, complete with blacked-up faces, shields, beads, feathers and assegais, and played a match with a Sheffield Association XI. Each of the supposed Africans took on a name from the Impi tribe: the role of the chieftain Cetewayo was taken by team captain T. Buttery of the Wednesday, and Hunter's *nom de guerre* was one Dabulamanzi. Team colours were black shirts and stockings.

It was an early combination of football and showbiz, backed up by a worthy cause of topical interest, so the venture couldn't fail to be popular. A 5-4 victory over the Sheffield XI at Bramall Lane was followed by wins at Chesterfield, Barnsley, and Edinburgh. There was a rare defeat at the Hole-i'th'-Wall on Easter Monday the following March. It wasn't just the novelty element that drew the crowds: the football was of a high standard too. The charity coffers were swelled as the thousands paid their entrance fees.

Money-generating enterprises in the world of football were bound to attract the scrutiny of the FA, and in this case their minions in Sheffield, led by the Secretary, William Pierce-Dix. We are still five years or so away from the legalisation of professionalism in English football, and the line taken by the FA at the time was that payment of any sort for playing the game was "an evil" which had to be "stamped out". When it came to light that some of the gate money was being diverted into the players' pockets as "expenses", the Sheffield Association at once issued an edict that banned all Zulu games.

Pierce-Dix, whose path crossed Hunter's on a number of occasions in those years, was a respected administrator and match official. He umpired at international level, and was chosen to referee the 1881 Cup Final between the Old Carthusians and the Old Etonians. He was responsible for a brief change in the rules for the duration of season 1881-2: namely, that a deliberate handball by an outfield player preventing a goal was punishable by a "penalty goal", along the lines of a penalty try in rugby. (The practice was dropped after one year, but it was to be another eight years before the satisfactory solution of the penalty kick was introduced.)

However, some of Pierce-Dix's antics had a tendency to irritate the rank and file. He once refereed a Lancashire Cup Final, played in torrential rain, wearing a top hat and frock coat, and with an umbrella up, scarcely moving from the centre throughout the game. He later defended himself by saying that he hadn't brought a change of clothing, and justified his lack of mobility by stating that he didn't want to be guilty of getting in the way of play! His involvement in the Zulus episode didn't gain him too many friends either.

It got worse. The Zulus ignored the edict and played another game, at Chesterfield again, in November 1880. Pierce-Dix promptly suspended all eleven players – and once again this included Jack Hunter. So the upcoming Wharncliffe Charity Cup semi between Wednesday and Heeley had to be played between two weakened teams. Supreme irony: it was Pierce-Dix himself who refereed the game. Unsurprisingly, the official was "hooted and jostled" by sections of the crowd.

The affair was given a superficial respite when the eleven banned players were reinstated, but only on condition that they write a letter of apology concerning their membership of the Zulus. It was a case of attending to the symptom, rather than addressing the fundamental issue of professionalism; but that would come in a few years' time.

In the meantime the Zulus business had thrown more sharply into relief the differences in attitude between the Lancashire and Sheffield Associations. Traditionally much closer to London in football terms, Sheffield had always taken the resolute amateur line. In Lancashire, the clubs saw nothing wrong with inducements to lure decent players, notably Scotsmen, to swell their ranks. As Fergie Suter once famously put it, at the Rovers you went and had a chat with the treasurer as occasion demanded, and were suitably looked after. It was this realism that eventually persuaded Jack Hunter that he would be better off across the Pennines.

He had met Tommy Gibson in the North v. South match at Bramall Lane in February 1881, when the Zulu suspensions were still raw in the memory. Also in the North team that day were Marshall and Rostron of Darwen. One topic of conversation must surely have been a comparison of the Lancashire and Sheffield approaches to pay for play.

Hunter's growing impatience with the Sheffield straitjacket reached critical mass towards the end of the following season. Heeley, town champions after the 5-0 victory over Pyebank, went to Blackburn to play the Olympic in mid-April, and came away with a 2-1 win. Only 500 turned up to watch, and the home side fielded an apprentice goalie in Fearsley. Olympic's slide from grace appeared to be continuing.

Then an unexpected twist: the very next Saturday Hunter took the train across the Pennines again, and guested for the Olympic against Darwen, down at Barley Bank. It began well: a pass from Hunter set up Yates, who opened the scoring. In a thrilling tit-for-tat battle Matthews gave the visitors a 4-3 lead with a few minutes left, before Darwen equalised with their last attack. The *Standard* was suitably impressed with the newcomer's contribution, in the pivotal role of the central half-back:

"J. Hunter, who had been engaged for the occasion, was the star of the
Olympic team. He seemed ever to be at the ball, and he did about as much work
as two men."
(April 29th 1882)

By September Hunter was accepted as an Olympic player, and so smooth was the transition that there must have been considerable preparation behind the scenes. The exact point at which Hunter made his decision to cash in his chips and cross the Pennines is unclear, but sometime in early summer 1882 looks probable.

He was able to take up proprietorship of the *Cotton Tree* pub on Birley Street, probably during the summer close season. No questions were asked about his playing for Olympic in FA Cup games that autumn, so residence and employment in Blackburn must have been firmly established by then. The link between club and brewery was possibly benefactor Sydney Yates. His iron foundry was just down the street from the pub, and it is noteworthy that the club excursion to Mytton (see next chapter) led and organised by Mr. Yates, set off from the *Cotton Tree*. So it seems likely that the foundry owner had some sort of relationship with the brewery that ran the pub, and was able to recommend Hunter as landlord.

A famous footballer running a hostelry made sense, whichever way you looked at it. Hunter, approaching the end of his long career, was looking for the means to earn his living after hanging up his boots. And from the brewery's point of view, having an ex-captain of England behind the bar would work wonders for custom. It was said that the word in Sheffield after Hunter's move was that he was only good for "lounging behind the bar of his pub". But the remark was surely more redolent of sour grapes than fresh ale. The emigrant player was to achieve spectacularly more than loaf around in a cosy corner.

The 1881-2 season had witnessed another development in Sheffield football. Although less of an attention-grabber than the Zulus spat, it was to prove just as significant a catalyst in Olympic's progress. It was the growth of the "Sheffield New Association", whose original aim seems to have been the bypassing of the closed shop elitism of the town's few dominant clubs. A crop of minor teams joined the New Association, which published its own Guide Book, complete with fixture lists and cup competition rules. Representative matches were organised against other Associations. The otherwise nondescript Kilnhurst FC had a half-back known as George Wilson, an energetic, attack-minded presence who was good enough to be selected for a number of these representative games.

By October 1882 Hunter, having spotted Wilson's potential as a centre-forward, had persuaded him to abandon the relatively low-key New Association and join him in Blackburn. The latest acquisition was to develop with startling rapidity into a top-class striker. But before all that, Olympic had to play the all-conquering Rovers in the East Lancashire Charity Cup Final at Ewood Park.

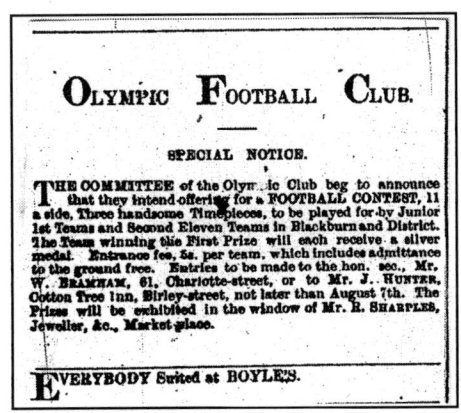

August 1882: front page advertisement for Hunter's
football tournament at Hole-i'th'-Wall (see next chapter).
Note the reference to Boyle's Clothing Store on Penny Street,
in whose front window the FA Cup would be on display the following April.

35

7: CUP FIGHTERS

> Olympic vs. Accrington – the last named should win.
> *Blackburn Standard* (Nov 4th 1882) – before FA Cup Round 1

> It is too much to prophesy any further victories for the Olympic.
> *Blackburn Times* (Feb 10th 1883) – before FA Cup Round 4

> It is said that "history repeats itself", and on that basis we may fairly assume that the Blackburn Olympic Football Club will not win the English Association Challenge Cup.
> *Blackburn Times* (Mar 10th 1883 – one week before the semi-final)

Summer 1882. Jack Hunter, ex-captain of England, must have wondered what he had let himself in for. He had joined a side bristling with talented individuals, but whose team performance was haphazard. Their insistence on chopping and changing their line-up in an incessant search for the magic formula had done them no favours. Their spirit and will to win were as the visiting moon. His feelings, as many of those around him threw in the towel in the 12-1 debacle against Rovers in May 1882, are probably best left unrecorded. He was at least able to salvage some personal pride from the wreckage, as it was he who scored the goal.

It was on August 7th, the Bank Holiday Monday, that Olympic faced Rovers for the fifth time since the previous September, in the final of the inaugural East Lancashire Charity Cup. The venue was Ewood Park, which would of course become the Rovers' permanent home nearly a decade later. Olympic's games so far that season with their closest rivals weren't too inspiring:

P	W	D	L	F	A
4	0	0	4	3	25

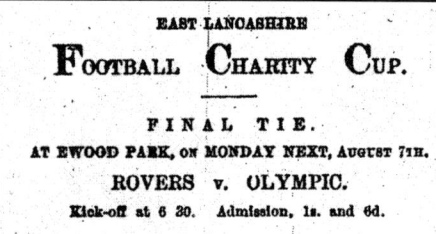

They had reached this far only on a technicality, having lost to Accrington in the semi. But it was noted that Accrington had fielded a ringer, and the Blackburn club's protest to the Lancs. FA was successful. "Th' Owd Reds" refused to replay the game, so Olympic had enjoyed a free pass to the final. Hunter was ineligible, not having been resident long enough in Lancashire, but we can assume that he was responsible for fine-tuning the 2-3-5.

The teams were:

Rovers: Howorth; Suter, Greenwood; McIntyre, F. W. Hargreaves; Duckworth, Douglas, J. Hargreaves, Avery, Strachan, J. Brown

Olympic: Hacking; Beverley, Warburton; A. J. Brown, W. Astley, T. Gibson; Dewhurst, Matthews, Cunliffe, Yates, Wensley

Rovers deployed a strong, seasoned eleven, containing ten of the team that had lost – narrowly, and to widespread northern shock – to the Old Etonians in the Cup Final. Olympic, wearing their alternative dark blue kit so as not to clash with Rovers' colours, looked firm in defence, but were taking a risk by fielding the relatively inexperienced Tommy Dewhurst, a youngster from the reserves.

Kick-off had been set for 6-30 pm on the balmy summer evening, but there was a delay owing to an accident on the tramway just outside the ground. There was one fatality and over thirty injured, but given the crowds that were amassing for the game, it was a miracle that the casualties were so few. The official paying attendance was around 2,000, but a "still larger number" were watching the game from the nearby slopes.

Half an hour later than scheduled, the game began. Rovers, confident of victory, attacked relentlessly from the off. An early "goal" was disallowed for offside, and the returning Hacking was kept busy. Fortunately his lay-off seemed to have invigorated him, and he brought off several fine saves.

His clean sheet lasted just seventeen minutes: J. Hargreaves opened the scoring, and Rovers supporters sat back in anticipation of a rout. The pounding continued, and once more Olympic had Hacking to thank for a sterling display between the sticks.

Then a touch of good fortune: Dewhurst had wandered upfield in the wake of a rare Olympic attack, and was hovering hopefully as Howorth took a swing at the ball in an attempt to clear. The ball struck the youngster and rebounded into the goal. They all count, and the underdogs responded well to the lucky break. Suddenly their attack clicked into gear, and the half-backs' passing manoeuvres began to get somewhere. Yates, running in to goal, just failed to make contact with the ball as it flew past the post. But the half ended as it had begun, with Rovers' supremacy being held in check mainly through Hacking.

And so it went on. Jimmy Brown's dribbling tied the opposing defence in knots, and McIntyre hit the crossbar. It was midway through the second half when Strachan finally beat Hacking with a ferocious shot from the left. Joe Beverley's lot had shown their usual resilience, but now it was time for them to follow the accepted script, and roll over and play dead.

Dewhurst, no respecter of reputations, had other ideas. There now followed a delirious fifteen minutes, in which Olympic, individually and collectively, played out of their skins.

Two goals in four minutes, both courtesy of the young winger, gave the supposed makeweights the lead for the first time. Whilst Rovers were still reeling Beverley ran up to join the forwards, and bagged the fourth. Yates hit number five just before the final whistle.

"The winners were heartily cheered on leaving the field, and in driving
through the town in their jerseys a little later."
Blackburn Times (Aug 12th 1882)

So the Hole-i'th'-Wall club were the first ever winners of the East Lancashire Charity Cup, "the handsomest in England", according to *Football Field*. Thanks to the tournament as a whole, the Blackburn Infirmary was £40 better off that summer. (See Appendix V.)

At the end of the month sponsor and club president Sydney Yates showed his appreciation of the victory by taking the players and their families to Mytton, a bucolic beauty spot some six miles to the north of Blackburn on the River Ribble. The *Standard*, without a trace of irony, called the outing a "treat", laid on by the foundry owner. It's interesting that a whole near-feudal society can be suggested by the one word.

Still, the beneficiaries weren't complaining. The day was enlivened by a game of football, a picnic, some speeches and toasts, and a players' sing-song in the evening. The past is indeed another country!

As further evidence of the social dimension to the club, the following advertisement had appeared on the front page of the *Blackburn Times* in May:

OLYMPIC FOOTBALL CLUB TRIP TO
BLACKPOOL ON WHIT-MONDAY

THE BEST TRIP OF THE SEASON

More advantages by this trip than any other at the same fare.
Intending excursionists are requested to purchase their tickets at
once, as
the number is strictly limited.
For full particulars see window bills.

Two of the ticket outlets were given as Alf Astley's newsagents, and "S. A. Warburton, 42 Earl-Street".

Hunter's arrival had had a knock-on effect throughout the club and the town. That summer he organised a football tournament for Junior and reserve clubs. It took place at the Hole-i'th'-Wall, and offered "three time-pieces and twelve medals" as prizes. Fifteen teams entered, including of course Olympic reserves. The wily Hunter was using the competition as a means of talent spotting, and of induction of promising youngsters into the club, from under Rovers' noses, as it were. On several levels, the tournament was a brilliant idea.

Brookhouse Rangers won it, and that was how the Rangers forward, twenty-year-old Jimmy Costley, came to the notice of the Olympic club. By September he would be playing for the reserves at Hole-i'th'-Wall.

There were a number of innovations for the new season. The grandstand was given an overhaul: " ... more comfortable and better protected from rain than previously." The main entrance from Shear Brow had been enlarged, and now boasted a ticket box and turnstile, facilities paid for by Sydney Yates. In an attempt to cure certain players of sloppy timekeeping and turnout, prizes were offered for punctuality to games and smart presentation! The 1882-83 campaign was embarked upon with great enthusiasm, and with a feeding frenzy of goals: Park Road were demolished 11-0 in the opening home game, and the attack ran up thirty-two goals in the first five weeks. Witton, who had drawn 1-1 with the Light Blues not so long ago, sent a team boosted by three Rovers players, including Jimmy Brown. They were sent packing 4-1. Prolific scorer was George Wilson, the half-back turned centre-forward newly arrived from Sheffield.

The signals were clear: Olympic were planning for the future, and were stating their intention to be here to stay. The Rovers, naturally, drew the sword.

Joe Beverley, whose feet had already shown signs of wandering towards the Rovers, dropped a bombshell that autumn. Although still wishing to consider himself a Hole-i'th'-Wall man, for that season's FA Cup he committed himself to playing for Rovers. He obviously felt that the previous year's losing finalists had every chance of going one better – certainly this seemed a far more likely bet than Olympic doing the same. There were rumours of under-the-table inducements. The following January the *Blackburn Times* postulated:

> "A few people who seem to be behind the scenes try to make it
> appear that Beverley's fickleness is due to certain payments which he has
> received as a kind of retaining fee to one club or the other. Is it coming to this?"
> (Jan 6th 1883)

Yes, it was coming to this. And this was one of the many reasons why a regulated form of professionalism, tying a player to one club per season for all games, had to be not far away. In any case, by Christmas "Bev" was playing regularly in friendlies for his first club once more, since the Rovers had surprisingly been knocked out of the FA Cup by Darwen. At the same time Olympic were preparing for their fourth round match with Church, but of course without their past captain. The cup-tied Beverley had backed the wrong horse.

Incidentally, one of Beverley's specialities, the devastating one-armed throw-in, would no longer have been part of his armoury, as from September 1882 the rules were changed to make the modern two-handed ("Scottish style") throw-in compulsory.

His replacement at left back was the seventeen-year-old James Ward. Ward, a weaver by profession, was a big, ebullient, occasionally hot-headed lad, who had shone in the reserves. He was the perfect foil to the elder statesman Warburton, who now took over the captain's role. Despite his youth, Ward was fearless in the tackle, and possessor of a walloping kick. He used to take bets on his athletic prowess, usually at a fiver a time: winning a 100 yards sprint, and jumping across the Leeds-Liverpool canal were two of his lucrative exploits. He won a long jump challenge against the celebrated athlete Aulty at Witton, again for £5, and collected a cool £25 (a four-figure sum in today's money) for flooring a professional wrestler in a local-style bout.

Victory followed victory in that free-scoring autumn. Sixty-five goals were chalked up by mid-November. Flies in the ointment were the usual defeat at the hands of the Rovers, and a hotly disputed 0-1 against the high-flying Notts Forest (billed as the "match of the season") at Trent Bridge. This match was George Wilson's debut. On the same day Joe Beverley played his first FA Cup game for Rovers, as full back alongside Fergie Suter in the 11-1 win over Blackpool St John's.

One week later, in the Lancashire Cup first round, Olympic's opponents were Padiham Church. The result, pretty much as expected, was an 11-0 landslide. Just one problem: major contributor to the goalfest was new boy George Wilson, who scored five. Padiham did their homework and questioned Wilson's eligibility for a competitive match. He was seen as quite clearly an importation, and the Lancs. FA awarded the tie to Padiham. The *Blackburn Standard* leader was incredulous:

> "The conduct of the Olympians in playing Wilson against Padiham is
> more than I can comprehend. They know he was not qualified to play for the
> county cup, nor will he be for nearly two years."
> (Oct 28th 1882)

If the idea had been to give the new striker a run out and a chance to find his shooting boots, though, the venture was a signal success. There were just two weeks to go to the FA Cup first round tie with Accrington.

Accrington, of course, were going to win. Even the Blackburn newspapers gave Olympic little chance. Form was against them: as people were constantly reminded, the Hole-i'th'-Wall team had progressed in the East Lancashire Charity Cup some six months ago only by virtue of a legal loophole. In reality the score had been 3-1 to Accrington, whose whirlwind attack, it was predicted, would this time make short work of their opponents, with no questions asked. The teams were:

> *Olympic*: Hacking; Warburton, Ward; Astley (W.), Hunter, Gibson; Dewhurst, Matthews, Wilson, Yates (John), Wensley
> *Accrington*: Chew; Whittaker, Hindle; Bryce, Hargreaves; Wilkinson, Brown, Eastham, Bamber, Yates (James), Hindle

The Reds pushed forward right from the off, but the home defence remained steady. One of the tactics introduced by Hunter was the quick and purposeful break from deep. Instead of clearing the lines with a bludgeoned kick directed more by beef than brain, the trick was if possible to locate a man in a likely looking forward position, thus shifting the focus of play upfield with unexpected speed. After that, a long pass from wing to wing (or a vigorous run at goal) would, it was hoped, further perplex the opposition.

Just such a move led to the first goal. An Accrington offensive was cleared to Dewhurst, who sent in a long cross-pass through the stretched opposition defence. Wensley, running in from the left, scored a cracking goal.

It was Wilson who had the field day, though. Five minutes later Yates sent in a precise cross and the big centre-forward claimed goal number two. Soon after that Wilson profited from a misunderstanding between the visitors' 'keeper and his defence and bundled in the third. Then it was the centre-forward again, with a fine header from another spot-on centre from Yates. "Wilson pounces like a hawk", enthused one reporter.

4-0 after thirty minutes. This was looking set to be a clobbering. But you underestimated Accrington's forward line at your peril. Their first goal was a cautionary tale: Ward, always keen to be in the thick of things, wandered upfield hoping for some pickings from an Olympic attack. A swift break from Bryce caught him out, as Accrington winger Brown set off on an unchallenged run for goal. Hacking was well beaten.

There still seemed no cause for alarm, but suddenly the visitors began to get a grip on the game. Bryce started to play a more dominant role in midfield, and before too long another quick manoeuvre found Bamber unmarked in front of goal, and The Reds bagged another.

Slack marking was to blame for Accrington's third: a swiftly taken throw-in into James Yates' stride, and the winger thumped in number three. Symbolically, the rain started to patter down.

Half time was gratefully reached. At that moment in time, it must have seemed that the Olympic had reached a crossroads in their destiny. After all, they had never won an FA Cup match before. Did they have the self-belief to pull this one out of the fire? Victory meant progress, and ultimately taking on the best in the kingdom. Defeat meant bowing to the pundits, and being satisfied with a weekly fare consisting mostly of local teams. Defeat meant waiting at least another year for a similar chance.

The second half began with an onslaught by the visitors, inspired by their three quick goals just before the break, and now playing down the slope. Ward and Warburton covered and tackled well, and Hacking showed his equal to any shots that sped through to him. There was one heart-stopping moment when a smart move involving several Accrington players resulted with the ball landing on the goal line with two forwards charging in to apply the *coup de grâce*. The famous Hole-i'th'-Wall mud came to the rescue, holding the ball just long enough for Hacking to pop up and boot it to safety. An equalising goal was surely not long in coming.

Yet Olympic found their second wind. An hour into the game the siege was lifted, swiftly and marvellously: John Yates set off on a gallop down the left wing, cut inside through a stretched defence, left his marker Whittaker chopping at fresh air, and whipped in a centre which Wilson converted.

This was the goal that doused the Accrington fires. From now on there was only one team in it, and Yates himself added number six towards the end. The *Accrington Times* declared itself mystified by the shell-shocked state of the team in those final minutes: "We are only at a loss to understand the paralysed state of the visitors, who seemed to make no effort whatever." (Nov 11th 1882). Olympic had arrived on the FA Cup scene with a flourish.

Two minor teams from Darwen were dismissed without too much trouble in rounds two and three. Lower Darwen, confidence boosted by a recent win over Enfield, came to Hole-i'th'-Wall expecting to do a Lower Chapel and discomfit their hosts. Olympic, though, by now were gathering momentum, and won at a canter, 8-1. Wilson bagged four.

A week later it was the turn of Darwen Ramblers. Hacking and Gibson were absent, playing for Lancashire against Sheffield. No matter: a win of 8-0 was registered, Matthews helping himself to a hat-trick. But complacency was outlawed in the Hunter camp: from now on it was going to get difficult.

And it didn't get any easier when Warburton seriously injured himself at Partick during the New Year mini-tour of Scotland. He would miss the next round, and wouldn't play again until the end of February, against the Druids.

In the topsy-turvy world of that year's FA Cup, Darwen had beaten Blackburn Rovers – at Leamington Street – and Church, the hitherto unsung side from a satellite of Accrington, had defeated Darwen by two clear goals at Barley Bank. Logic suggested that the Olympic would find Church an insurmountable hurdle.

Many modern-day records state that this fourth round tie between Olympic and Church took place at Hole-i'th'-Wall. This wasn't the case: the match was fought out at the "soup bowl" pitch off Pickup Street at Spring Hill, Accrington. As a Blackburn wag pointed out: "I allus thought it were a sin to go to Church an' play football!"

Olympic were still without the services of Warburton, his place being taken by Crook. The replacement's comparative lack of experience was perhaps highlighted by the fact that he was injured early on in the game, and spent most of the ninety minutes a hobbling non-participant. Up front, newcomer Jimmy Costley (named erroneously as Crossley in most reports around this time) had been introduced as a left wing partner for John Yates.

Costley was small and wiry, fleet, and in that time-honoured phrase, "he knew where the goals were." A Liverpudlian by birth, he had travelled up the Leeds-Liverpool canal with his family looking for work. He had found a job as spinner in Hornby's mill at Cob Wall, Blackburn. He claimed never to bother with training, as working in the mill kept him fit! He had been out of his class at Brookhouse Rangers, for whom he regularly hit double hat-tricks. Since the previous September he had been seeking out new challenges with Olympic reserves, and would relish the showcase of the FA Cup.

The game with Church, though, had little of the pyrotechnics of the Accrington tie. Crook's incapacity was partly the reason for that, with one or more of the half-backs (usually Hunter) restricted to covering the gap. Play was even until midway through the first half, when Wilson latched onto a wayward Church clearance, found some space beyond the opposition midfield, and scored with a speedy ground level shot. Apart from this goal, there was little to choose between the two teams for much of the game. The Light Blues' defence was hard pressed at times, but Ward and Hacking were in dominant form.

It took a tenacious piece of work from Dewhurst deep into the second half to put matters beyond doubt. A kick clear by Horrocks the Church 'keeper only got as far as Hunter, who set up another attack. As the Olympic vanguard swarmed forward, a defender managed to squeeze out another half-clearance ... as far as the marauding Dewhurst, for whom the ball fell nicely enough for a successful pot at goal. An eerie silence fell over most of the ground, as the Blackburn contingent celebrated.

The rest of the results from the fourth round, which was still being played according to regional divisions, were as follows:

Aston Villa	2	Walsall Town	1
Sheffield Wednesday	1	Notts County	4
Druids	2	Eagley	1
Marlow	0	Hendon	1
Old Carthusians	6	Royal Engineers	2
Old Etonians	2	Swifts	0
Clapham Rovers	–	bye	

The draw for the quarter-finals was:

Blackburn Olympic v. Druids
Hendon v. Old Etonians
Notts County v. Aston Villa
Old Carthusians v. Clapham Rovers

At this stage of the competition, of course, there were no easy ways to progress. The Druids had won the Welsh Cup for the past three years, and their team contained several of the internationals from the team that had recently beaten England. Much was made of their intransigent defence, led by the Powell brothers, "bulwarks of the principality", who very rarely leaked more than a goal a game, if that. The *Blackburn Times*, once again, appeared to have little confidence in Olympic's chances: "With such a team as they have the Welshmen ought to strike terror into the hearts of all their opponents."

Sporting all-rounder A. N. "Monkey" Hornby had offered his services to the Olympic cause. Usually associated with the Rovers, the adept footballer, cricketer, rugby player and boxer had partnered Costley on the left wing in a 5-1 win over Heeley. Wisely, it was decided not to disrupt what was clearly a winning combination, and Yates was retained for Cup matches.

The Druids came to Blackburn on the 24th February for the quarter-final. Warburton was at last back from injury, and both sides were at full strength. For the first ever time, Olympic fielded what was to be their FA Cup final team:

Olympic: Hacking; Warburton (capt.), Ward; W. Astley, Hunter, Gibson; Dewhurst, Matthews, Wilson, Yates, Costley
Druids: H. Adams; J. Powell (capt.), R. Roberts; A. Powell, J. Davis, W. Williams; J. Lloyd, S. Roberts, E. Bowen, A. Jones, J. Vaughan

Adding a touch of spice to the tie – if it were needed – was the aspect of unfinished business. It will be remembered that when these two teams had last faced up, at Ruabon two years before, Olympic had left the pitch in protest at the referee's interpretation of a rule. For the Blackburn team there was now something to prove. The FA, perhaps mindful of the tie's history, sent Sheffielder David Haigh to referee. Haigh was an experienced official and an esteemed FA Council member, forward-looking enough to be elected to the committee of the Football League a decade or so later. It did the trick, as the closely fought match was memorable for its football rather than any disputes.

It took just ten minutes for the myth of Welsh impregnability to be given a severe jolt. After a few early forays from Olympic, Matthews found enough space for a shot. J. Powell, captain of Wales, headed clear, but only as far as Yates, who scored with a fine swerving volley. The Druids retaliated with an aerial bombardment, which was dealt with by Hacking without too much trouble. Just before the half hour the visitors tried another tactic, which immediately bore fruit. Lloyd set off on a run down the right wing, leaving Ward floundering in his wake. The winger hit a stinging shot which Hacking parried but was unable to hold, and in the resultant melee Bowen equalised.

The Druids now enjoyed a period of domination, but the home defence held firm, with Hunter in the thick of it and Warburton gaining in confidence after each successful tackle. Shortly before half time Olympic broke the siege, and Wilson scored with a fast low shot into the corner of the goal.

Theoretically the heavier-built Welshmen would perform better playing down the slope in the second half, but instead, as was often the case, the home side's fitness began to tell. Just before the hour Wilson capitalised on a goalmouth scramble to bag the third goal. Four minutes later Hunter booted a free kick at the defensive wall, and the indirect award was made to count as it struck an opponent's shoulder on the way in.

Three goals in the clear, the Light Blues refused to rest on their oars. Costley put a shot over the bar, and Matthews twice went close. On the final whistle, the home side's supremacy was total. A great cheer greeted the victory, which put Warburton's team into the last four of the competition.

The semi draw pitted the Hole-i'th'-Wall side against the Old Carthusians, FA Cup winners two years previously. Olympic were playing with the big boys now.

The East Lancashire Charity Cup. Olympic were the inaugural winners in August 1882.

8: TO THE SEASIDE FOR THE SEMI

> The very prevailing opinion is that the Old Charterhouse boys will win
> *The Sporting Chronicle* (Mar 17th 1883)

> No better advertisement for a health resort could be wished for.
> *Blackpool Evening Gazette* (Mar 23rd 1883)

Meet the Old Carthusians XI, FA Cup semi-finalists, 1883 vintage. Only five of the Cup-winning team of 1881 survived, but the Charterhouse Old Boys who turned out for the semi against Olympic were still a formidable outfit, especially in attack.

R. P. Thompson was the safe and alert 'keeper whose speciality was reaching and clinging to the thunderbolt shots from afar. At right back was Walter Norris, the *wunderkind* not yet out of his teens, member of the Cup-winning team of 1881, and said to be a "capital back" with a "strong, cool, kick". Alongside him was Andrew Amos, also nineteen, who was later to be capped for England as a capable midfield link man.

South African-born halfback Joseph (later Sir Joseph) Vintcent would have made a perfect centre-half if the line-up had been 2-3-5. He was tall and mobile, and a skilful header and distributor of the ball to his forwards. "One of the best half-backs in England ... rarely makes a mistake" was a contemporary assessment of his play. His midfield partner was relative newcomer W. A. Evelyn; not the strongest in the team, his shortcomings were nonetheless usually more than made up for by Vintcent's brilliance.

The Carthusian ace, though, was the skill and power of the forward line. Their six front men seemed to have brought the classic "paired" attacking style to its zenith. William Cobbold, only just turned twenty, would become a star England forward of the 'eighties, with nine caps and four international goals to his credit. His partner on the left wing was Walter Hansell, a quick-moving dribbler who had already hit the target in the FA Cup. There was central attacker Edward Parry, a prolific scorer with fifteen recorded Cup goals already, plus three England caps. He had appeared in two Cup Finals: on the losing side with Oxford University in 1877, and then scoring in the 3-0 victory over Old Etonians four years later. Inside-forward Lewis Richards, ex-Cambridge University player, was another fine dribbler, in his third Cup campaign and a regular scorer for his team. The remaining two forwards were A. J. Last and E. T. Hardman. Whilst not quite attaining the glamorous status of their fellows, they were nonetheless vital components of that 1883 forward line, and both skilful dribblers – it would take a capable defender to stop them.

The Cup run, littered with destroyed opponents, says it all:

Round 1: Pilgrims	W 6-0
Round 2: Etonian Ramblers	W 7-0
Round 3: Old Westminsters	W 3-2
Round 4: Royal Engineers	W 6-2
Round 5: Clapham Rovers	W 5-3

The scalps included two former winners of the trophy. Had the Olympic much cause for optimism? Not according to the vast majority of the predictions that appeared in the newspapers on the morning of the match. Even the Blackburn publications hedged their bets. On the other hand, all the Carthusian Cup matches so far that year had been played at Charterhouse School, in Godalming, Surrey. Travelling up to Manchester for the semi was a new experience for them, as far as competitive matches went. Previously, their furthest Cup excursion had been to Saffron Walden. Olympic would be playing within their own county, with massive support.

Of possible concern to the Olympic – or at least to one of their number – was the fact that the referee would be Mr. Pierce-Dix, the gentleman who had orchestrated the witch-hunt that had provoked the departure of Jack Hunter from Sheffield. It would be the first meeting of official and player since the parting of the ways the previous year.

The three weeks between the victory over the Druids and the semi were ones of quiet but thorough preparation. Preston North End were taught a thing or two over at Deepdale (4-1, even though Joe Beverley was helping out), and then the team raised a few eyebrows by taking a week's training at Blackpool. This was obviously one of Hunter's ideas, and it was generally met by a mixture of incredulity and amusement. Olympic's policy of actually training for games had been looked upon as unusual enough to warrant some gently satirical, though admiring, scrutiny:

> "As to the match at Church, which made the Olympians the cracks of
> the district, I can speak in very high terms concerning the winners, who seemed to have been generalled with as much cleverness as many an army has been in victorious wars. That good generalship was not alone displayed in the actual battle, but it was manifested previous to the match, and like all big encounters under such fine management this contest morally was won before it was fought. It was a miniature Tel-el-Kebir affair. Silent night marches (training walks) during the week brought the light blues nearer coign of vantage (condition of form) and the repose of the Church players was suddenly disturbed by the bold and accurate onslaught of the Olympians, who were supposed to be far away – in form."
> *Blackburn Times* (10th Feb 1883)

The idea of training walks, besides helping to keep the players in trim, no doubt also helped, as would any social activity, to foster a team spirit. The Olympic were also renowned for their adage: "Keep teetotal until after the match". A team spending the week at Blackpool, however, was another matter entirely: logistically demanding, and startlingly new.

Firstly, it had to be paid for. Sydney Yates' generous contribution of £100, and sundry additions from supporters, helped considerably towards meeting the bill (although Olympic would finish the season over £32 in debt). Secondly, players had to gain permission from employers to take a week off work, and in most cases, still to receive their wages. Starting a precedent which was to have enormous repercussions later, the bosses, mindful of the kudos that victory would bestow on the whole town, agreed.

So on Saturday, 10th March, just one week before the encounter with the Old Carthusians, the Olympic contingent took the train to Blackpool.

The week was spent following a strict regime. Alcoholic indulgence, of course, was taboo, and the following timetable is often quoted:

6 a.m.	Glass of port wine and two raw eggs followed by a three mile walk along the sands.
Breakfast	Porridge and haddock.
Dinner	Two legs of mutton (one for each end of the table).
Tea	More porridge and a pint of milk each.
Supper	Half a dozen oysters each.

The last item, incidentally, wasn't the luxury that it would become in the following century, mentioned in the same breath as caviar and champagne. It was a staple fish dish for those living on the coast.

The locals, too, were amused by the arrival in the seaside town of these out-of-season trippers. Didn't they run the risk of becoming stale before the big game, by overdoing this training business? Then someone thought up the idea of putting together a team and playing them a match. The principal club in Blackpool at the time was South Shore (Darwen had beaten them 5-2 in that year's FA Cup) but there was a cluster of smaller clubs too. A select XI met the Blackburn men on the "narrow and dry" South Shore pitch at Cow Gap Lane (now Waterloo Road) on the Monday, and to general amazement and local joy, won 1-0. The Olympic attack, underestimating the opposing defence, had tried to dribble their way through, but had met with a stubborn resistance. There was only one way forward now: the seasiders were challenged to a rematch on the Thursday. This time Olympic got it right, played their usual passing game, and demolished the home side 6-0. Except for Yates, all the forward line scored. Hunter, at least for the moment, could breathe a sigh of relief.

The Olympic took the Saturday morning train from Blackpool, and after a brief wait at Stoney Butts, continued their rail journey south to Manchester. They were followed in a football special by an estimated "few hundreds" of their supporters.

The day was fine but cold as the Blackburn side arrived at Victoria Station, Manchester. At roughly the same time on the other side of the city at the London Road Station, a train containing the Charterhouse contingent was chugging in from the south. Horse-drawn hansom cabs took the players and club officials to their destination: the Manchester Rugby ground at Whalley Range, at that time on the southern edge of the cottonopolis. With less than an hour to kick-off, the crowds were already gathering: an estimated 3,500 spectators converged on the College Road ground.

The weather was still crisp and sunny as three o'clock approached. Several of the Carthusians were already on the pitch, wearing overcoats and strolling and chatting. One or two were smoking cigars, which added to their affected air of nonchalance. They were, of course, quietly confident of winning this one by a country mile.

But first an unforeseen problem: because of the late switch of venue from Birmingham, nobody had thought on to bring an Association ball! Whalley Range being a rugby club ground, the only balls available on site were of the oval shape. A carriage was sent to Fallowfield, two miles away, to fetch one of the spherical variety. This caused a delay of around thirty minutes, during which time the sky darkened and it began to snow heavily. The shivering spectators were entertained by the efforts of a workman – presumably on referee Pierce-Dix's directions – straddling the crossbar and attempting to saw off a couple of wooden protuberances that were outside the FA canon. The ball arrived and the workman was ordered down, having made no appreciable inroad into the superfluous wood. The snow stopped, the sky cleared, and at last both sides made their appearance.

The Old Carthusians' FA Cup winning team of 1881. Standing: L.M. Richards*, W.H. Norris*, E.G. Colvin, L.F. Gillet, W.E.Hansell*. Seated: E.G. Wynyard, A.H. Tod, J.F.M. Prinsep, W.R. Page, E.H. Parry*, J. Vintcent*. At front: unknown. The players marked * also appeared in the 1883 semi against Olympic.

Olympic fielded the same team as against the Druids. The Charterhouse side was:

C. P. Thompson; A. Amos, W. H. Norris; J. Vintcent, W. A. Evelyn; L. M. Richards, A. J. Last, E. H. Parry (capt.), E. T. Hardman, W. E. Hansell, W. N. Cobbold

The immediate impression was the discrepancy in size between the two teams. The Old Boys were on average a head taller than the Olympic – whose mean height was just 5ft. 6ins. – and generally broader of shoulder. A casual observer with a limited knowledge of the forces at play in a football encounter would have agreed with the pundits, and come to the quick conclusion that the game was going to be somewhat one-sided. And so it was. In fact, it was a rout.

To nationwide astonishment, though, it was Olympic who trounced the fancied southerners. The Carthusians' lauded three-pronged attack broke down time after time against the

Blackburn half-back line. This was possibly Gibson's, Hunter's and Will Astley's finest hour. Moreover, once the ball had been won in midfield, it was the precise deliveries into the forwards' path that set the Olympic attack rolling forward unstoppably.

The first five minutes set the template for the game as a whole. Parry kicked off, and Hardman set off on a dribble that took him deep into Blackburn territory. It was a Hunter tackle that stopped him, and so was launched the first counter-attack, with Yates and Costley working the ball down the left. Yates' shot went over the bar. Back came Charterhouse with another dribble involving the central forwards, and once again the move got no further than the opposing halfbacks. Olympic forced a corner, which Hunter took. The wind caused the ball to drop on the crossbar and fall behind the goal.

Then, after five minutes, there came the first significant manoeuvre. Hansell and Cobbold were making progress down their left flank in a promising-looking move, when Tommy Gibson spotted a momentary lack of understanding between the two. Quick as a flash he nipped between them and won the ball. His pass down the right was into the path of a galloping Tommy Dewhurst, who used the sudden space to take the ball on and hit it on the run. The fast rising shot rocketed past Thompson into the Carthusian goal.

The crowd, unashamedly biased, roared their appreciation of this quite unexpected overture. Inspired, the Olympic poured forward in attack after attack. Their opponents found it virtually impossible to break out of their own half. Their forwards' usually devastating dribbles foundered on the impregnable rock of Gibson, Hunter and Astley. On the rare occasion that the half-backs were bypassed, Ward and Warburton were on hand to clear the lines "with apparent ease". Hacking was hardly ever called upon.

It was the outstanding play of Hacking's opposite number, Thompson in the Charterhouse goal, who prevented Hunter's team from hitting three or four more in the first half. That and some inexplicable misses in front of goal. It was only after thirty-five minutes that the Blackburn team scored again, this time by the bustling Wilson taking advantage of the rules of the time and bundling both 'keeper and ball over the line.

There was no complacency at half time. For all their superiority Olympic had only a two-goal lead. In the second half the Carthusians would be playing with the wind behind them, and the general feeling was that their best was yet to come. The first half had seen several missed chances by the northern team – perhaps they would regret them in the next forty-five minutes? Instead, the pummelling continued.

It was Olympic's man-to-man passing that won the day. The southerners' heavy charging and tackling were to no avail, as by the time the charge was delivered, the ball was away across the pitch at the feet of another player. The usually imperious Vintcent was rendered anonymous in midfield. The Carthusians, exhausted from chasing shadows, simply folded as the game progressed. Jimmy Costley put the ball between the posts but was adjudged offside, then Yates cracked in a shot from the wing to make it 3-0. By now the Old Boys were defending desperately in an attempt at damage limitation, but after some nifty approach work Costley stabbed in the fourth. Soon afterwards the final whistle blew, and "amid tremendous cheering and waving of hats" Olympic were declared worthy winners. Even Pierce-Dix must have been impressed.

In many ways this stunningly clear-cut win was a greater achievement than the Cup Final. Never before had one of the nation's élite teams been so comprehensively outplayed in a competitive match. The 2-2-6 system with its paired dribbling attackers and sparse midfield had, it seemed, been well and truly rumbled.

The victorious team were met at Stoney Butts that evening by a crowd of a couple of thousand. Several of the players were carried shoulder high from station to carriage (or pub). There was a double celebration in Blackburn that Saturday night, as Rovers had defeated Bolton Wanderers in the Lancashire Cup semi that afternoon, down at Darwen.

At last the nation woke up to the fact that Olympic weren't a second-class side who had wandered thus far in the competition almost by default: "The play of the Blackburn men was of the first order all through," stated *The Sporting Chronicle*, especially praising the half-back line – "a bulwark of strength" – and the winning team's physical condition towards the end: "as fresh as newly painted butterflies", whilst the Carthusians were "showing signs of fatigue".

Nine days before the Cup Final, on Thursday 22nd March, Olympic travelled to Blackpool once more. It was the day before Good Friday, and the seaside resort was boasting its new attractions of the Southern Pier (the "People's Pier", with "dancing area and steamboat traffic") and the Winter Gardens (where the "Marvellous Miltons, operatic, dramatic and burlesque artistes", were performing). There is no record of Olympic playing any football against local sides this time around, but John Yates helped keep himself in condition by refereeing a game between South Shore and Rovers reserves on the Saturday. The *Blackpool Herald* of the following week would report simply: "Olympic trained quietly one week."

The beneficial effects for athletes of a seaside stay had been given a publicity boost by the semi-final win. Blackpool newspapers weren't slow to assert that the town with its "health-giving climate" could take a lot of credit for the team's "good form". The Rovers and Darwen, who were to contest the Lancashire Cup Final on the same day as the FA Cup Final, were quick to follow suit. The Darwen team arrived in Blackpool after the Easter holidays, and the Rovers set up camp in Morecambe.

The day before Olympic set off for the south, Jimmy Ward celebrated his eighteenth birthday – discreetly, one supposes, and under Hunter's eagle eye. He would be the third youngest cup finalist at that time. As of now, he is still the sixth youngest ever.

The team made the long train journey down to Richmond in southwest London on the Thursday, allowing themselves a full day to recover. They were booked into a hotel near the Thames. The Friday was spent sight-seeing in the metropolis. The story goes that Jack Hunter splashed out on a top hat, and joined the group as they were gathered on the balcony of St Paul's cathedral. One or two of the players crept up behind Hunter and flipped the "chimbly-pot" hat off his head and down into the street below. The Sheffielder's reputed geniality must have been sorely tested. At least the team were in high spirits, and apparently not fazed by the capital or the occasion.

Well, then: now for Mr. Kinnaird and his band.

Blackpool beach in the 1880s. The Olympic team would have trodden this stretch of sand during one of their early morning training walks – although at 6 am the beach would have been considerably less crowded! There's an advertisement for Beecham's Pills on one of Mr Penswick's bathing machines which illustrates Blackpool's famed health-giving properties, a renown given a further boost by Olympic's FA Cup success.

9: LITTLE TIN IDOL

Will the Olympic win it? What a stupendous task they have set themselves to perform!
Blackburn Times, morning of the FA Cup Final (Mar 31st 1883)

The Old Etonians' FA Cup results from the First Round of 1878 until the eve of the 1883 Final make fearsome reading:

P	W	D	L	F	A
30	25	3	2	103	31

In those five years they had been Cup-winners twice and losing finalists once. Still fresh in the memory was the previous year's Final victory over the hitherto unbeaten Blackburn Rovers.

It had seemed that circumstances had been against the Rovers almost from the start. Their captain, "Doc" Greenwood, had been unable to play through injury. They had opted to make the exhausting six-hour journey to London the day before the match, possibly not giving themselves enough time to relax and acclimatise. Fred Hargreaves lost his kit bag en route, and was forced to play in new, uncomfortable boots. The Etonians took the lead in the psychological game by claiming that the Rovers' shirts of blue and white halves were a possible clash with their all-white strip. The Blackburn side, being the younger of the two clubs, were obliged to change, and played in unfamiliar dark blue and white hoops. One of their players was to say later that he had passed to an opponent by mistake, blaming the change of kit. Eton had adopted their usual ploy of keeping their opponents waiting before appearing on the field: another subtle psychological touch which didn't help the nerves of the visiting team.

The Rovers had been unbeaten throughout the season, so to both teams defeat had been unthinkable. The Old Boys had scored early on through Anderson, and had spent most of the game successfully repelling Rovers' attacks with a mixture of good luck, skill, and uncompromising tackles. Their captain the Rt. Hon. Arthur Kinnaird had celebrated the win by indulging in his party piece of standing on his head in front of the Kennington Oval enclosure. Now, one year on, Blackburn Olympic were trying to go one better than the Rovers. Very few people gave them a prayer.

True, Olympic had made short work of the Carthusians a fortnight before, but that had been up north. How would the northerners fare against an even stronger team playing on its home ground, where they had tasted defeat but rarely in their nine-year existence?

The Old Etonians would field the same team as the year before, except that Bainbridge replaced Novelli on the left wing. Herbert Bainbridge would be better known as a Surrey and Warwickshire cricketer than a footballer, but he was still a speedy, aggressive winger who made an effective partner for fellow left-sided attacker Arthur Dunn.

Dunn, a fast, incisive dribbler and an unerring marksman, was one of six of the team who had won international honours. John Rawlinson the goalie had earned just the one cap, in the previous year's 13-0 cakewalk against Ireland (in which, incidentally, Rovers' Jimmy Brown scored twice). Full back Percy de Paravicini had played in all three internationals that year. He was a two-footed defender, generally regarded as one of the finest backs of his time. Two more of the forward line had been capped for England: Reginald Macaulay, a high-scoring, speedy and industrious centre whose other area of excellence was athletics – he had won the AAA high jump, and was Cambridge University quarter-mile champion; and top scorer Henry Goodhart, who had a recorded twenty-three FA Cup goals to his credit in five years. His actual total was certainly higher, since, as we have seen elsewhere, scorers were not always named in the match reports.

Other players of note were right-sided attackers William Anderson and John Chevalier. Anderson was a founder member of the Corinthians, and Chevalier "a hard-working forward, possessing weight and pace", would be on the original Derby County first XI the following year.

Charles Foley was half back, adept at both defensive and constructive roles. Right back was Thomas French, fast and dependable, who, along with seven more of the team, was playing in his third successive Cup Final.

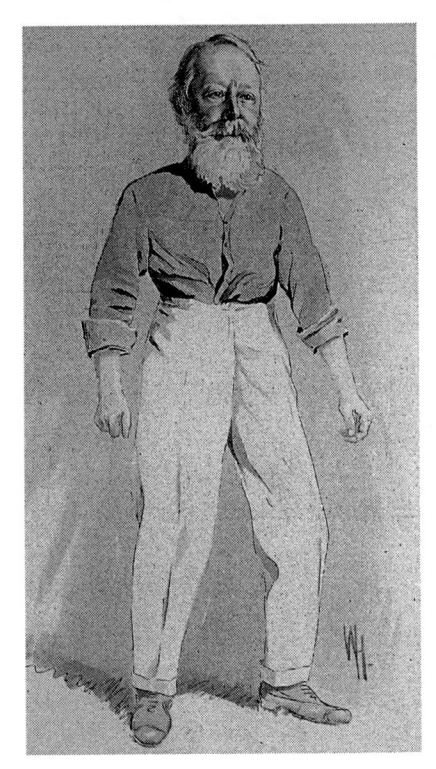

And then there was the captain, Kinnaird. A Scottish international, and instantly recognisable with his boisterous red beard, cricket whites and cap, the Rt. Hon. (later Lord) Arthur Kinnaird was, more than anyone else, the iconic player of the glorious decade of the amateurs. This would be his ninth Cup Final – five on the winning side – a record which is unlikely ever to be beaten, despite the modern-day cornering of the FA Cup market by a handful of teams. He was a ferociously competitive player, capable of bone-jarring challenges that teetered on the edge of GBH. This recalls a well-known anecdote, well worth repeating here, one of the best jokes to come out of those years. Modern research has questioned what was exactly said, and by whom, but my favourite version is the one given here. Kinnaird's mother was expressing concern about her son's involvement in such a violent game, confiding in mutual friend Charles Alcock: "If he carries on like this, I fear he may come home one day with a broken leg." "Worry not, Ma'am," came the reply. "Be assured it won't be his own." This, then, was the formidable Old Etonian team.

The Kennington Oval, home of the Surrey Cricket Club, played host to twenty out of the first twenty-one FA Cup Finals, plus two replays. Part of the terrain would be roped off in front of the enclosure, with touchlines marked by a row of small flags. Ends of the pitch were denoted by the "gasometer", and the "Crown Baths" (Harleyford Road) respectively.

A caricature of Lord Kinnaird, celebrated enough to be presented as one of the "Men of the Day" in Vanity Fair.

With hindsight, we might say that the choice of officials for the final has a kind of significance. The past was represented by umpire M. P. Betts, who had scored the first ever Cup Final goal, for the Wanderers back in 1872. Referee was Charles Crump, who was to serve on the FA Council for resolving disputes in the Football League, inaugurated just five years in the future. And the other umpire was our old friend William Pierce-Dix.

There was a crowd of 8,000, the highest at a Cup Final at the time. According to a report in *The Sportsman* the spectators were "assembled round the ropes or perched on every coign of vantage from which a glimpse of the game could be obtained". About 700 faithful had made the journey from Blackburn, catching the midnight special train from Todmorden. One of the many innovations brought from the north was the first appearance of spectators' club colours: Olympic supporters wore light blue scarves and neckties, and some clogs even had blue rivets in them!

Cricket at the Oval in the 1890s

The day was fine, with a light breeze. The pitch was dry and in good condition, promising a fast, lively game. It was a far cry from the Hole-i'th'-Wall and its frequently mudlark state, but the last three games played by the Olympic (two in Blackpool and one in Manchester) had been on a similar terrain to the Oval. The lighter Costley had been selected instead of reserve Parker, as the ex-Brookhouse player's nippy skills were deemed better suited to firmer ground.

As kick-off time approached the majority of the crowd gave a rendition of the Eton chant. This was a many times repeated, screeching, thunderous war cry that went something like:

Eeeeeeeeee – TONNNNNN!
Eeeeeeeeee – TONNNNNN!

Belted out by several thousand voices in unison, this must have sounded unnerving to any visiting player hearing it for the first time.

Olympic were first out onto the pitch, and Eton, true to form, emerged several minutes later. The teams were:

Old Etonians: J. F. P. Rawlinson; P. de Paravicini, T. H. French; Hon. A. Kinnaird (capt.), C. W. Foley; J. B. Chevalier, W. J. Anderson, H. C. Goodhart, R. H. Macaulay, A. T. Dunn, H. W. Bainbridge
Blackburn Olympic: T. Hacking; S. A. Warburton (capt.), J. T. Ward; W. Astley, J. Hunter, T. Gibson; T. Dewhurst, A. Matthews, G. Wilson, J. Costley, J. Yates

Eton won the toss, and opted to play from the Crown Baths end. Hunter kicked off, intending to set off the left wing on a run, but the ball was intercepted and returned with gusto into the northerners' half. Within the first few minutes the pattern of the game became clear: both sides were committed to attack, Eton with strong clearance kicks and penetrating individual runs, and Olympic with attempts at passing manoeuvres. Unsurprisingly, it was the home side that settled more quickly into their attacking rhythm. Dunn, then Goodhart, then Macaulay, advanced dangerously, and it took a defence in numbers to close down the threat.

Olympic countered with a smart move from Yates, who dodged Kinnaird and French and whipped in a shot that ran just wide. Wilson came close too, heading over the bar. It was a rare pot at goal from the Sheffielder, whose contribution to the final was unusually quiescent. It was revealed later that for most of the match he was carrying an injury, the result of a biting tackle. Eton seemed to have a game plan for the free-scoring centre, which involved severe shackling from Kinnaird, backed up with Paravicini's experienced reading of the play and faultless interceptions.

Play was fast and furious – sometimes violent – with Eton having the better of it. Their attack continued their incisive runs, with Dunn especially showcasing his dribbling skills. Here, though, was a possible Achilles' heel: where Dunn might profitably have ended his run with a pass to one of his team mates, he kept possession until forced out into an irrelevant position by the corner flag. It was a habit that was cruelly to backfire on him later in the game.

With twenty minutes gone, the Old Boys suddenly found a higher gear. They were attacking with panache, and forced a series of corners. Olympic were unable to clear the lines, and the siege culminated in a ferocious drive from Goodhart, whose shot sped past Hacking for the first goal. The crowd were in raptures, and for many the only surprise about the goal was that it had taken so long to breach the opposing defences.

The effect of the score, however, was to inspire the northern side. Suddenly their play started to look recognisable. Wilson may have been subdued, but Olympic found other avenues to goal. The centre-forward, playing deeper, acted as link man, finding his wings with telling passes. Yates hit the crossbar, and from the other wing a searing shot from Matthews struck a post. Generally, though, supreme defending from the Eton 'keeper and two full-backs held the fort until half time.

As the teams changed ends the opinion expressed amongst the tiny enclave of Light Blues supporters was that it was looking like "another Rovers do". The previous year, Rovers had gone behind early on, had spent the best part of the ninety minutes hammering at the gates, but had come away goalless and frustrated. How could Olympic hope to do any better?

Eton opened the second half with an onslaught, no doubt convinced that a second goal now would be enough to put these upstarts away for good. A couple of bewilderingly fast attacks ended up with first Macaulay, then Goodhart, right in front of goal with just Hacking to beat. The Olympic goalie, hero of the hour, saved both.

These were the last clear-cut chances for Eton until the final minute of normal time. Midway through the second half there was a sea change to the whole run of the game. The Old Boys were beginning to tire, and the constructive passes from the Olympic midfield were beginning to tell.

It was Wilson who set up Matthews, running into space on the right wing. Before an opposition back could get close, the forward had cut inside and hit a low-level lightning shot at an angle past Rawlinson and into the goal. There was some applause, but the majority of the crowd fell relatively silent. The blue and white-clad supporters, of course, were whooping it up. There was a cheer from the Olympic players too: at a stroke, they were now convinced that a fantastic win was very much on the cards.

As full time approached, the benefits of Hunter's training became increasingly apparent. To add to the Etonians' discomfort, Dunn embarked on another of his "tunnel vision" runs, this time to end up on the wrong end of a vigorous Jimmy Ward challenge. Dunn fell to the ground, badly injured, and could only hobble from the pitch.

Olympic pounded the ten men, seeking the winner which was surely inevitable now. But Eton, though clearly a spent force, defended heroically, and almost snatched a goal from a breakaway with a minute or so left. Kinnaird started the move, showing there was life in the thirty-six year-old yet, by dribbling the ball out of defence and exchanging passes with Bainbridge. The Light Blues had thrown men forward, and when Kinnaird delivered a pass into the path of Macaulay, clear of Ward and with an unopposed run on goal, it must have seemed that the fabled Eton luck was about to kick in again. Macaulay was a big, fast-moving fellow who relished such clear-cut chances. He took the ball on a pace or two then struck it hard and low at the corner of the goal. It looked impossible not to score. But Hacking, who had earned his mutton and oysters several times over that day, read the shot to perfection, dashed across the goalmouth and in the manner of the time, kicked the ball to safety.

The final whistle blew, and whilst a number of the Etonians profited from the lull to have a lie down on the pitch, the captains and the referee engaged in a brief discussion. Should they play on? The crowd were in no doubt: they had just witnessed a thrilling, full-blooded battle, and they wanted more.

Meanwhile, outside the offices of the *Standard* on Church Street, Blackburn, a large crowd had gathered. Bulletins from both finals – Rovers v. Darwen in the Lancashire Cup Final, as well as Olympic's progress – were posted in the window at fifteen minute intervals. Rovers' 3-2 victory was greeted with cheers. It was after five o'clock when the 1-1 result from the Oval appeared.

Did that mean that Olympic would have to travel to London again, as Darwen had done four years before? Nobody seemed to know. Still, everyone agreed: 1-1 was a tremendous achievement, and far better than most people had expected.

Warburton, one can guess, was more than happy to play extra time. The prostrate Etonians were all the indications he needed. Kinnaird, possibly concerned about public opinion should he insist on bringing the northerners up to London again, agreed to play on. As nowadays, there would be two halves of fifteen minutes each.

The game continued as before: Olympic's domination, baulked at the last by increasingly desperate, but still effective, defending by Eton. The home side held out for the first quarter of an hour. Then, three minutes into the second half, the inevitable happened. Dewhurst hooked a long diagonal pass across the field into Costley's path, and the tiny winger hared in through the statuesque Etonian defence to place his shot out of Rawlinson's reach from close in. It was the winner. Kinnaird made one abortive run into the opposition's half, but otherwise Olympic had the game by the throat until the final whistle.

For the first time the Cup was presented publicly, and soon after the end of the game. The players had time for a quick wash and change of clothing before re-emerging from the pavilion. Major Marindin, FA President, handed over the 18" high trophy to Warburton, calling for three cheers for the winning team. Most of the crowd generously applauded Olympic, but some reports tell of a background noise of hissing from a lunatic fringe. The players received their gold medals: "about the size of a sovereign, and on the front the representation of a football surrounded by a floral wreath, and on the back the inscription, 'The Football Association Challenge Cup 1882-3'" (*Blackburn Times* Apr 7th 1883).

Hunter held up his medal and, as if still unable to believe it, said: "Fifteen years at football, and got the English Cup at the finish!" Back in Blackburn, outside the offices of the *Blackburn Standard*:

> "The final result from London … created the greatest amount of interest,
> and when the news was first made known that the Olympic had won the cup it
> was received with great incredulity. As truth gradually impressed itself, however,
> the shouting was tremendous. For a long time the streets were thronged … "
> *Blackburn Standard* (Apr 7th 1883)

The crowds were nothing, though, compared to the multitude that welcomed the conquering heroes home on the Monday evening. This was celebration in style.

J Dinsdale's drawing of the 1883 FA Cup final, from the Illustrated Sporting and Dramatic News. *The section depicting Costley's winning goal contains a number of errors, not least the spelling of the scorer's name.*

10: THE ROAD TO TRENT BRIDGE

> After the disqualification of the Preston club, it is difficult to know what defence the Bolton Wanderers and Blackburn Olympic – not to mention the Rovers – could make if protests were lodged against them. They are surely 'all in the same boat'.
> *Pastime* (official FA publication) (February 1884)

> What the Olympic have to say about their defeat is that for two seasons no English club has beaten them in an Association Cup tie, and when the premier Scotch *(sic)* club came down to do it they were aided by a policeman and a crowd of spectators.
> *Blackburn Times* (Mar 8th 1884)

There is an old saying: *When you are an anvil, hold you still; when you are a hammer, strike your fill.* Olympic had struck hard to dislodge the Old Etonians from their position of English champions. Now it was their turn to be the target of every major club in the realm. But first, the festivities.

The entourage left Euston Station on the 1-30 pm on the Monday after the final. Their carriage was festooned with blue and white regalia, and at every stop on the journey crowds had gathered to catch a glimpse of the National Tankard. Arrival at Stoney Butts Station, Blackburn, was around 8 pm.

A dense crowd packed Jubilee Street, Railway Road, Salford Bridge and beyond. Somewhere in the crush, three brass bands and a line of policemen were trying to keep their dignity and a semblance of order. News of the approaching train brought on a deafening roar which all but drowned the rendition of *Hail the Conquering Hero Comes*. As the players appeared from the station entrance, trophy held high, the police line was overrun by cheering well-wishers who hoisted the heroes onto shoulders. It was cab proprietor Robin Walker who was waiting with four flag-bedecked carriages to drive the team and club officials around the town – another tradition for Cup winners started by Olympic in that year.

Salford Bridge, Blackburn at the time of Olympic's heyday. In the distance, in the centre of the picture, at the end of Railway Road, may be seen Stoney Butts station. The large corner building on the right is the White Bull Hotel, venue of many important football meetings.

The story goes that a rare dissenting voice was heard from the crowd: "Is that t'Coop? It looks like a tea-kettle!" Warburton, not usually renowned for his quick retorts, nevertheless had a nice one here: "It might well do to thee, but it's right welcome here in Lancashire, and it'll ne'er go back to Lunnon!" (Which, of course, turned out to be true, as that particular trophy, won by northern or midland clubs for the next twelve years, was stolen from a shop window in Birmingham in September 1895, and reputedly melted down into counterfeit half-crowns.)

After the tour of the town (a loop involving Church Street, Victoria Street, the Town Hall, Northgate, Church Street again, Salford Bridge, and Penny Street), the procession finished up at Jack Hunter's *Cotton Tree* on Birley Street. Everywhere they had had to struggle through cheering crowds of unprecedented number, and several times the brass bands, tenaciously following and playing as best they could, were in danger of being dispersed by the crush. Down Penny Street streamers had been hung across the way, and a firework display greeted the arrival of the carriages.

In the pub toasts were drunk, and appreciative mention made of patron Sydney Yates, unable to join in the festivities because of illness.

Each of the players was to receive a gratuity of £2 from the sponsors' coffers – but they had to pay for the inscription on the winners' medals themselves!

Blackburn's famed poetical brotherhood played a part in the lengthy celebrations. For the quietly partisan William Billington, Olympic's victory was a natural and inevitable consequence of the town's tradition of *arte et labore*:

William Billington

> *In Education, Blackburn claims*
> > *To stand on higher ground –*
> *In Authorship, to more than rival*
> > *Many times around;*
> *And now she greets her trained athletes,*
> > *Proud the Olympic corps*
> *By winning England's Challenge Cup*
> > *Brings Blackburn to the fore.*
>
> *But – "football's an unholy game –*
> > *'Tis rude – and most unmeet*
> *That England's future manhood thus*
> > *Should educate their feet.*
> *Feet foremost to their grave men go!"*
> > *Thus wiseacres deplore!*
> *But football has, at least, done this:*
> > *Brought Blackburn to the fore.*
>
> *In the good, the golden future may*
> > *Our town enjoy the taste*
> *And the talent, still increasing, which*
> > *Has glorified and graced*
> *Her cotton-kirtled daughters and*
> > *Her sons of noble ore*
> *And industry and skill will still*
> > *Keep Blackburn to the fore.*

From "Poems and Songs", first published *Blackburn Times* (Apr 7th 1883)

It's quite probable that fellow poet Thomas Chippendale, or "Chip" to his friends and fans, was at *The Cotton Tree* that evening, as he was known to be a founder member and staunch supporter of the Olympic. He was certainly present at the post-match entertainment of Partick Thistle a week or so later "being in his best form, bar a bad voice". (*Blackburn Standard* Apr 14th 1883)

The *Standard* leader sounded a note of caution about excessive celebration, warning that a community obsessing about one issue was "not in a really healthy condition". The fans, of course, were unimpressed. "J. B." of Balaclava Street countered, triumphally hammering home the point with a barrage of puns:

> *Some say we're going football mad,*
> > *With leather quite demented.*
> *Well, leather oft will save our "soles"*
> > *And "heels" when well cemented.*
>
> *... For that which ne'er before was done*
> > *And Dunn last year prevented,*
> *Is done, and Dunn is all undone,*
> > *And London is tormented ...*

Blackburn Standard (Apr 21st 1883)

Meanwhile, the Eton coterie were finding it difficult to come to terms with the loss of the Little Tin Idol. With more than a dash of bad grace (and a number of inaccuracies) the writer in the *Eton College Chronicle* gave his analysis of Olympic's victory:

> "So great was their ambition to wrest the Cup from the holders, that they introduced into football play a practice which has excited the greatest disapprobation in the South. For three weeks before the final match they went into a strict course of training, spending, so report says, a considerable time at Blackpool, and some days in Bournemouth and Richmond. Though it may seem strange that a football Eleven composed of mill-hands and working men should be able to sacrifice three weeks to train for one match, and to find the means to do so, yet when we reflect on the thousands who attend and watch the matches in Lancashire, and so swell the revenues of the Clubs, and on the enthusiasm of the employers of labour in the pursuits and successes of their countrymen, it is not so surprising."
> (April 1883)

The real target here was, of course, the looming spectre of professionalism. (And behind that, possibly, the perceived threat from the uppity working classes.) Blackburn MP William Coddington – over from Paris specially to watch the Final – had already given an adequate response to the mercenary accusations back in St James' restaurant, Regent Street, a few hours after the match:

> "You of the Olympic Club have not had the advantages possessed by the Old Etonians. You have not had their enormous leisure – you have not had their time for practice.
> ... Blackburn is a sporting place, and the people are not afraid of their money in matters of this kind; we find the means for these working men."
> (March 31st 1883)

The principal benefactor was Sydney Yates rather than "the people", but the idea of sponsorship, anathema to the amateur brigade, was being defended as right and proper.

Much was made, too, of the violent tackling that had been a feature of the game. The implication by Eton was that Olympic had started it, and were the worse offenders. After all, Dunn had had to leave the field of play after one crunching encounter. In fact, both sides were guilty of some hair-raising challenges. Wilson had spent most of the match nursing an injury sustained early on, and Matthews had a large bruise on his face as memento of the final.

The *Sporting Chronicle* was quick to point out the likely far-reaching consequences of Olympic's win for the power structure of English football. There was now a chance that the London bias that, according to the article, existed in international selection and FA committee decisions could be more successfully opposed. The writer foresaw "a more liberal dealing with the North and Midlands", and a dilution, if not dissolution, of the FA "clique" (April 4th, 1883). This would happen, but more slowly than the writer anticipated, as there were class issues that were seen as inseparable from the football matters.

The FA Cup trophy and match ball were placed in the window of Boyle's Great Clothing Store on Penny Street, Blackburn, where the display remained for a month. In the meantime, Olympic had their season to finish. Two convincing home victories over Scottish teams – Partick and Kilmarnock Athletic – augured well for the upcoming East Lancs. Charity Cup semi with Accrington. Then Hacking twisted a thigh muscle in the pre-match kick-about, and reserve C. Harrison had to take his place until the summer. The tie, at Leamington Street in front of a 4,000 crowd, was shaded 2-1, with Dewhurst bundling in the winner in the last few minutes. The Blackburn players wore black armbands as a mark of respect to Sydney Yates' wife, who had recently passed away.

After a couple of sobering defeats (Aston Villa 1-5, Park Road 1-3) Olympic ended their long season on June 2nd at Barley Bank in the final of the East Lancs. Cup. Their opponents were

Rovers, no doubt secretly smarting from their rivals' FA Cup win, and eager to make amends for the previous summer's surprise 2-5 defeat.

The Rovers were unstoppable throughout the first half, running up six goals without reply. After change of ends the Light Blues were determined to salvage some pride, and introduced a tactic of heading on from corners and free kicks. Dewhurst scored two this way, and had one disallowed. But it was a forlorn hope, and Rovers won 6-2. It was the first time that Olympic had ever been beaten in the final of any competition. It was also an indication of how tough the new English Champions were going to find things from now on.

Even before the summer was over, the vultures were gathering. By the beginning of the new campaign, a couple had already swooped. George Wilson was the first to go, lured by moneybags Preston North End. Seeing how other Lancashire clubs had profited by enlisting talented out-of-towners, manager Major Sudell had adopted a clear policy of attracting top players with promises of ample remuneration. Wilson, with his thirty-plus goals in Olympic's Cup-winning season, was an obvious target. There is an illuminating passage from the *Preston Herald* of Sep. 15th 1883, italics mine:

> "It was well known that the North End had gone in for powerful help;
> that they had secured the services of Wilson of Sheffield *(sic)* and Strachan and
> Beverley of the Blackburn Rovers ...
>   "Strachan and Beverley, *after getting paid*, and promising to turn up,
> failed to do so."

Apparently the two Rovers players were on their way to the railway station when a Rovers official waylaid them and persuaded them to stay in Blackburn and play against Accrington that afternoon instead. Wilson turned out for Preston and got injured; but he would be playing again before long, reverting to his original role of half-back. The quantity of goals was therefore lacking, but the quality was still there: he belted one in from forty yards against Bolton Wanderers.

By the end of October Wilson was proprietor of the *Black-a-Moor's Head* inn on Lancaster Road. He got married to a Preston lass the same month. The *Blackburn Times* reflected the Olympic's feelings on the loss of the striker, wondering if the club had thrown in the woman as part of the deal.

Sudell eventually got what he wanted: a team good enough to take on the best in England on an equal footing. There seems to have been little attempt to disguise the importance of money in the process, and Preston's "wage bill" for 1883-84 was to amount to an astronomical £1,200. Of course, the FA, still embroiled in its increasingly futile attempts to stamp out pay for play, intervened the following January, and disqualified North End from the FA Cup for player importations.

At the inquest Sudell came clean and admitted ploughing money into the furtherance of Preston North End's fortunes. He cited Olympic's example of the previous year: had not the Cup winners undergone special and expensive training before the semi and the final? Had they not brought in Hunter and Wilson to help their cause? Had they not remunerated players for time taken off work? The arguments expressed indicate the many grey areas surrounding professionalism, the near-impossibility of enforcing blanket prohibitive legislation, and how close the FA now were to relenting and allowing some form of pay for play.

For the meantime, though, the enquiries and punishments were continuing. Both Accrington and North End had been slung out of that year's FA Cup, and it was only a matter of time before Olympic were put under the microscope too.

For the moment, Olympic had enough troubles of their own. Warburton and Gibson fell out over something; Gibson turned out briefly for Church, and on his return to Hole-i'th'-Wall, Warburton immediately left to play for Darwen. Hunter became team captain.

Ward played for Clitheroe early in the season, but soon came home. Hacking was concentrating on his dentist's career, so the 'keeper's place was usually taken by one of two ex-Rovers: A. "Woody" Woolfall or Roger Howorth (goalie in the 1882 FA Cup Final). The rumour that Hacking had promised to turn out for Olympic's closest rivals in Cup matches seems to be untrue, as it was "Herbie" Arthur who was Rovers' goalie throughout the year. Hacking would return to football, and Olympic, but not for a while yet.

Secretary Bill Bramham had to have his wits about him. Hearing on the grapevine that Rovers had their eye on Costley, Bramham acted quickly. Whilst Olympic were on their mini Midlands tour (Saturday 13th Oct, 2-3 v. Aston Villa, Monday 15th Oct, 1-1 v. Walsall Swifts), he contacted FA Cup opponents Darwen Ramblers. Although the first round tie was due to be played early November, Bramham offered the Ramblers £10 and a money-spinner of a return match if they would agree to play the game on the Tuesday of that week! The Darwen team accepted the arrangement. The point, of course, was to cup-tie Costley and any other potentially roving players as soon as possible. The team against the Ramblers was:

W. Whitehead; W. Parker, J. T. Ward; W. Astley, J. Hunter, T. Gibson;
T. Dewhurst, A. Matthews, R. Birtwistle, J. Yates, J. Costley

In front of a paltry midweek crowd of 300, Olympic won 5-1. The second round draw was nowhere near as kind: the opponents would be Darwen, still a daunting proposition, away.

Olympic had already played the Darreners that season, back in September in an exhibition match at Dewsbury. The aim was to spread the Association gospel in the rugby heartland of West Yorkshire. Hunter and Yates scored one apiece, but this was not enough to prevent Darwen from winning 4-2. To return the compliment, a fortnight later Dewsbury played a game of rugby against Wakefield Trinity at Hole-i'th'-Wall.

The mantle of English Champions was sometimes a burden. The 1883-84 campaign had begun with an away game against Scottish Cup holders Dumbarton. The match was billed in Scotland as the "Football Championship of Great Britain" and the Scots team had gone into special training for it, clearly treating it as a Cup Final. Olympic's side was sprinkled with reserves and guests, and since it was their first game after the summer lay-off, they can perhaps be forgiven for not taking it with the same degree of seriousness as their opponents. In the rain-drenched morass of Boghead Park, Dumbarton won 6-1. A return game was arranged for the following February.

A charity match with the Rovers was played on Thursday November 8th, in aid of the newly inaugurated Blackburn School of Art. Around 1,500 turned up to watch, so a healthy contribution was made to the cause. The match itself was an infuriating (or amusing) example of the Jekyll and Hyde persona that seemed to be attaching itself to the Light Blues since their Cup final win. They were 2-0 up against the old rivals within fifteen minutes, Matthews and Parker supplying the finishing touches to some smart approach work. Rovers pulled one back, and Olympic held on to the lead until the final minutes, when Howorth scored a grotesque own goal, somehow managing to push an apparently safe ball behind him and over the line, "amid loud laughter".

Worthy of note at that time was the strength in depth of the Olympic squad. There was an unusually strong reserve side (there was one win of 23-0!) most of whom could hold their own in the first team. A sixteen-year-old by the name of Jack Southworth (see Chapters 12 and 13) began his long and lustrous career here, as a high scoring inside left.

On three occasions before Christmas the club found itself obliged to play two games on the same day. The first three rounds of the Lancashire Cup clashed with fixtures too lucrative to be shelved, so the reserve side was delegated to take on the Lancs. opponents:

Round One: Newton Heath (A)   W 7-2
Round Two: Darwen Ramblers (H) W 4-0
Round Three: Southport (A)   W 2-0

The first team won all three of their games too: Sheffield Heeley were so completely overrun (7-1) that Olympic 'keeper Howorth had time for a quiet cigarette; Edinburgh University were beaten 1-0 (after the team had had to depart Blackburn on the 2 a.m. train so as to arrive at Powderhall on time for the game); and ambitious Midlands outfit Wednesbury Town were defeated 5-2, Costley (2), Will Astley (2) and Yates sharing the goals.

A measure of the first team's potential was indicated by the November game against Notts County at Trent Bridge. Dewhurst scored after just five minutes; the powerful County side equalised, then Hunter regained the lead just before half time. A famous upset looked on the cards, then Hunter tore some ligaments early in the second half, and had to leave the field. The home side scraped a 3-2 win against the ten men. Olympic were praised for their trademark style of accurate crossfield passing. Three weeks later a worthy victory of 4-2 was registered against Oxford University, on the Merton College ground. This game was played on a Thursday afternoon, and admission had been fixed at a shilling (5p) – very pricey for those days, and possibly to discourage the townspeople from coming to watch the cup-holders. The crowd was therefore a mere couple of hundred. It was the University side's first defeat for nearly a year. Internationals R. S. King and W. Bromley-Davenport played for the University, and Yates, Dewhurst, Parker and Costley hit the goals for Olympic.

Hunter was out until January, but was still very active during his weeks of incapacity. He would station himself behind the opposition goal and shout out advice to the Olympic attack, which practice the *Blackburn Standard* believed was "almost as good as an extra player". The captain would be playing again, after a brief run in the reserves, in the big FA Cup matches to come.

Some high-scoring wins were registered in February. A Blackburn and District XI were played in a charity match for the benefit of the striking north-east Lancs. weavers. Olympic won 13-3, Costley hitting six. The Blackburn and District side contained two familiar faces: Hacking in goal, playing his first game of the season, and Warburton. Relations between the former Olympic captain and the intransigent Gibson do not seem to have improved. Warburton would return once more to the Hole-i'th'-Wall in May with Darwen, in the semi of the East Lancs. Charity Cup. This was no doubt a satisfying outing for the ex-Olympic man, as his new side surprisingly won 1-0.

Newcomer William Moss, Warburton's replacement at right back, was another ex-Heeley player brought in by Hunter. Moss had been selected to play for the Sheffield Association, but he lit the blue touch paper by turning out for Olympic in the FA Cup on the same day instead. Whether this had the effect of provoking Pierce-Dix and the other FA amateur hard-liners is difficult to say, but Olympic suddenly became the object of close scrutiny. Moss, having already served a suspension for professionalism in his native town, travelled in from Sheffield to play, usually forking out for the rail fare himself. Was he then an importation? Was he being paid by the club over and above his expenses? Poor Moss, having escaped once, must have felt himself the quarry of some avenging angel. The FA enquiry came to nothing, and the right back gave sterling service until the summer.

Representative honours were once more achieved: Gibson was made captain when Lancashire beat London 8-1, and other players to be granted county selection were Parker, Yates, Ward, Costley, and Dewhurst. The last-named was chosen to play for England against Ireland in Belfast, but after an incident in the FA Cup match with Northwich Victoria – narrated below – he was dropped, and his place taken by one of the Bambridge brothers.

Olympic were chasing three trophies again: the FA Cup, the Lancashire Cup, and the East Lancs. Charity Cup. After Christmas they started taking the Lancs. Cup more seriously, fielding the first team against Turton (W 8-0) and Darwen (W 3-1). They thus progressed to the final at Deepdale, Preston, where their opponents would be Blackburn Rovers.

In the meantime, FA Cup aspirations were proceeding more or less according to plan. Darwen were met again in round two at Barley Bank. A rare old battle ensued. Darwen scored early on, and the rest of the game saw a gradual clawing-back by an increasingly dominant Olympic side. Joseph Duckworth equalised with a header midway through the second half, then in extra time Matthews hit the winner, "amid an indescribable scene of hat-throwing, and even hand-shaking, among the Olympic supporters." (*Blackburn Standard* Dec 8th 1883)

Round three was a bye, so as to whittle the combatants down to the final sixteen. The opposition in round four were another Old Boys side, this time the less renowned Old Wykehamists. Winchester School was better known for a bizarre ball game hybrid called "Willies", practised by the select few in and around the school in the depths of Hampshire. Whether any of the skills formed by "Willies" could be easily translated into the realm of Association Football was debatable.

Certainly, the traditions of Winchester School lay elsewhere than in soccer, and the Light Blues had a comfortable 6-0 win.

Three weeks later it was the turn of perennial Cheshire Champions Northwich Victoria – Welsh Cup finalists two years before – to travel to Hole-i'th'-Wall for round five. (Olympic continued to be lucky with the home ties in the FA Cup.) This was the quarter-final, and the complete draw was:

>Blackburn Olympic v. Northwich Victoria
>Notts County v. Swifts
>Old Westminsters v. Queen's Park (Glasgow)
>Upton Park v. Blackburn Rovers

Such a line-up of teams could only have occurred in the early 1880's. Exactly half of the quarter-finalists would remain staunchly amateur after 1885: Queen's Park, and the three metropolitan sides. Upton Park (who had progressed following Preston's disqualification) would lose to the Rovers, but by 1900 would gain ample reward for their amateur ethics. In the Olympic Games soccer tournament in Paris, the "GB" team that is recorded as winning the gold medal was actually Upton Park.

Two Blackburn teams in the final eight of the premier national competition was an achievement worthy of commemoration. Once again one of the town's poets rose to the occasion. (See Appendix IV: "Our Football Teams", by Charles Nightingale Stott.)

Olympic swamped Northwich 9-1. The Cheshire side lodged a protest about the state of the pitch, but were overruled by the FA. The game was even more one-sided than the score suggests, although the Vics were handicapped by an injury to their goalkeeper. Their captain, burly Welsh international F. W. Hughes took over between the sticks, but was unable to stem the bombardment from the Olympic forwards. At one point he shoved Jimmy Costley up against a post with unreasonable force: at least, this was Tommy Dewhurst's opinion, as the youngster immediately waded in and floored Hughes with a right hook. The Welshman got up and started throwing some of the copious mud at Dewhurst, but the other players intervened before the situation could escalate further.

Officially it was this incident that led to the Olympic player being dropped from the England team a week or so before the Ireland game. One or two northern partisans, however, started wondering. Dewhurst's call-up had originally come as a bit of a surprise, and it coincided with the Bambridge brothers (of the Swifts and the Corinthians) declaring themselves unavailable as wingers for the Ireland game. Then when they changed their mind, Dewhurst was deselected. Whether there was a connection between the two is impossible to prove one way or the other, but the disgruntled northern reaction to the dropping of the Olympic winger reflected the lingering provincial mistrust of the politics of the London committeemen.

The same week that the Dewhurst news broke, another disaster struck. Early in the morning of 21st February a gale swept across the Hole-i'th'-Wall plateau, demolishing the grandstand of the Olympic ground. For a club that was struggling to keep out of debt, this was a devastating blow. The only consolation was that two days later Dumbarton came to town to play the rematch of the supposed Championship of Great Britain. Nearly 6,000 climbed the hill to watch the game, which turned to be well worth the effort and the entrance fee.

Olympic forced a succession of corners throughout the game, but despite the pressure, found themselves 1-3 down at half time. Then Dewhurst added to his first half goal, Matthews equalised, then in a wildly exciting last few minutes, Parker hit the winner. So were Olympic now the champion club of the British Isles? Or, for that matter, the world?

In the heady enthusiasm of the next few days, even the prospect of the mighty Queen's Park from Glasgow in the FA Cup semi seemed less daunting. It seems clear that Queen's Park were intending to prove beyond all doubt who was the foremost club in the kingdom. They were to win the Scottish Cup (albeit by default, as opponents in the final, Vale of Leven, failed to turn up!) and by now had found the willingness and the means to finance every one of their long trips to England, aiming to lift the FA Cup as well. Their results in the earlier rounds need little comment:

Round 1: Crewe Alexandra (A)	W 10-0
Round 2: Manchester (H)	W 15-0
Round 3: Oswestry (A)	W 7-0
Round 4: Aston Villa (H)	W 6-1
Round 5: Old Westminsters (A)	W 1-0

Even the addition of Blackburn's A. N. "Monkey" Hornby to the Crewe team was to no avail. And the convincing dismissal of fancied Villa sounded a warning throughout the land. This year, Queen's Park were the ones to beat.

The Glasgow-based side was the richest source of recruits for the Scottish national team, the one that generally ran rings round England at the time. Nine of the eleven who faced Olympic had been, were currently, or would soon be, international players. Small wonder that the virtually unbeatable Queen's Park had earned themselves the unofficial title of "Premier Association Club of the World".

The great Charles Campbell, eight times captain of Scotland, and John Gillespie, "Prince of Goalkeepers", were absent, but the line-up was still formidable. The *Scottish Athletic Journal* published sketches of the players: right back was the "faultless" Walter Arnott, dubbed by J. K. McDougall, Scottish FA Secretary: "the greatest back who ever toed a ball". The attack drew the most praise. William Anderson the "demon dodger" was a "brilliant right wing", backed up by William Watt, a "deadly shot at goal". Robert Christie led the left attack with his mazy dribbles, and his partner was David Allan, later to play for the Corinthians. Star forward was Dr. John Smith, "unequalled as passer of the ball", renowned for his long and spectacular dribbles that cut into the heart of opposing defences.

For Olympic, there was no training week at Blackpool this year. The FA had passed a legislation that effectively banned such a "professional" approach. No more than one day's wages per week could now be claimed for time lost through football. The FA was adamant: "Men taking these 'seaside trips', unless at their own expense, infringe the rules of cup competition". (FA Council February 1884)

A huge crowd of around 16,000 – a far greater number than anticipated – descended on Trent Bridge for the semi. The *Nottingham Evening Post* related:

> "A long time before the hour – three o'clock – fixed for the commencement
> of the game every point or stand from which a sight of the game could be obtained
> were occupied with enthusiastic sightseers."
> (Mar 1st 1884)

Once again a cup-tie involving the Olympic had captured the imagination of all and sundry. "The gentry of the district turned out in their carriages in large number", reported the *Blackburn Standard*. The teams were:

> *Olympic*: A. Woolfall; W. Moss, J. Ward; Jos. Duckworth, J. Hunter,
> T. Gibson; T. Dewhurst, A. Matthews, W. Parker, J. Costley, J. Yates
> *Queen's Park*: A. McCallum; W. Arnott, J. W. Holm; J. MacDonald,
> J. J. Gow; W, Anderson, W. Watt, W. Harrower, Dr. J. Smith, D. S. Allan, R. M.
> Christie

The ground was in good condition and the weather was mild and sunny. Theoretically the setting was near perfection. Within a few minutes of the start, however, it became obvious that the authorities at Trent Bridge were unable to cope with such a dense crowd pushing at the perimeter ropes. After an early spell of Olympic domination, in which Costley came close twice, the spectators behind Woolfall's goal at the pavilion end overflowed onto the pitch. For the first of several times that afternoon, the game was stopped until the crowd was shepherded back behind the ropes.

Queen's Park were awarded a free kick which came to nothing, then Olympic were back on the offensive. Costley, who was recovering from a back strain on the day of the semi, set off on a dribble before passing to Yates, whose shot was just wide. Then it was Costley himself, sending in a header which was again just off target.

Half an hour into the game Queen's Park opened the scoring. Their typical individual sorties, combined with some intelligent inter-passing, were beginning to disconcert the Blackburn defence. There was more brute force than cleverness to the execution of their goal, though, as another player was charging Woolfall as Dr. Smith put the ball between the sticks. At the time this was perfectly legal.

The score was 1-0 to the Glaswegians at half time. Given the balance of power in the first half, and Olympic's famed second half resurgences, there was some hope that the underdogs could at least run their opponents close.

Another pitch invasion, this time at the Gamston Road end of the ground, delayed kick off for the second half. It took the scant deployment of police some time to usher the crowd back behind the ropes. Play got under way eventually, and Olympic continued to press. But just five minutes into the half Queen's Park showed how dangerous a side they were, no matter what the state of play. Dr. Smith set off on a solo breakaway dribble through the stretched opposing defence, and with unstoppable speed and close control manoeuvred himself into a scoring position, giving Woolfall no chance.

It was a severe psychological blow for the Olympic side, and matters were made worse almost immediately by yet another encroachment onto the pitch, once again at Woolfall's goal. It has been suggested that these invasions were deliberate attempts by Olympic supporters to get the match abandoned, but a careful reading of all the match reports seems to indicate that the trouble originated from several different points around the perimeter ropes. This being the case, and given the relatively small number of Blackburnians in the crowd, it would seem that the crowd problems arose not from a deliberate spoiling tactic, but from over-enthusiasm and inadequate marshalling.

There were two more serious delays, one of seven minutes, in a situation that was becoming unmanageable. The crowds crept forwards once more, in one instance eight to ten yards onto the playing area. One report claims that Watt's goal – Queen's Park's third – used a one-two off a policeman's boot as part of the build-up. Dr. Smith hit the fourth with five minutes to go, after another of his bamboozling sorties up the middle. Possibly by then Olympic had resigned themselves to the farcical, and were hoping that good sense would prevail in that the Association would order the match to be replayed.

Immediately on returning to the pavilion Jack Hunter wrote a letter of protest and handed it to the referee, the famous FA committeeman and secretary C. W. Alcock. The reply from London was prompt and unequivocal: since Queen's Park were equally disadvantaged by the pitch invasions, there would be no reason to replay the match.

This was patently nonsense, as anybody with any real knowledge of football at the time could have appreciated. It was Olympic's style of play to use the wings, either with vigorous runs into space which created opportunities for shots at goal, or with their distinctive long crossfield passes. If access to the full length and breadth of the pitch is impeded by a creeping wall of spectators, then quite clearly a team that uses these strategies is going to be severely handicapped. Queen's Park's strengths lay in the more direct, centralised approach of dribbling and short passing, which can still function in more compact areas.

Blackburn Rovers scraped a 1-0 win over Notts County in their semi, and went on to win a highly controversial final against Queen's Park, 2-1.

Incredible though it may seem, apart from an easy win and a climactic struggle with the Rovers the following season, Olympic's FA Cup Odyssey was already as good as over.

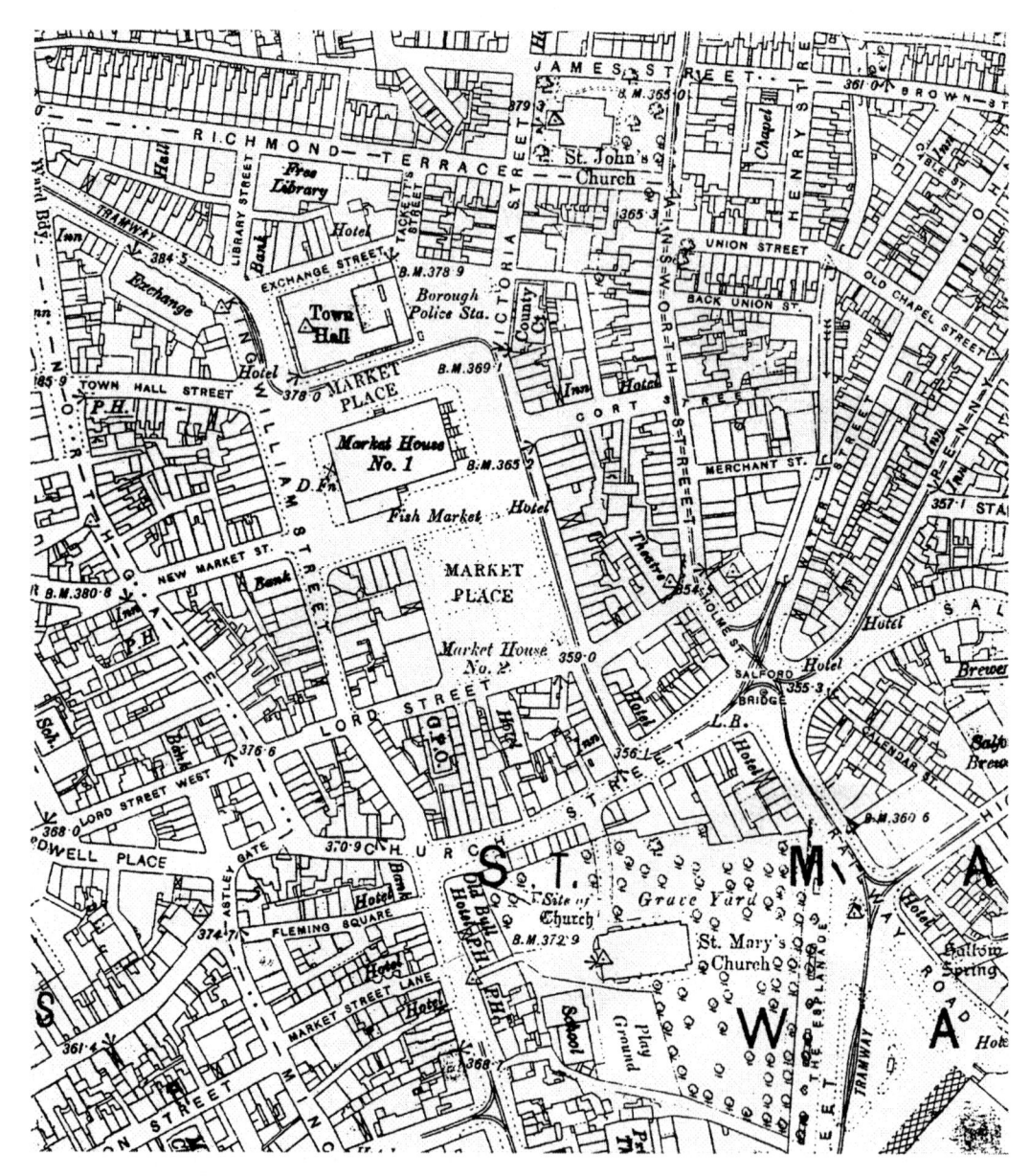

An Ordnance Survey map of Blackburn town centre, around 1890. Part of Stoney Butts railway station is visible in the extreme bottom right hand corner of the map. From here the route of Olympic's triumphal procession in 1883 may easily be traced (see chapter 10). Warburton's pub, the Dog and Partridge (not designated here) was on James Street, close to the junction with Victoria Street. The P.H. on the corner of Northgate and Town Hall Street is Hunter's Mason's Arms. The building was later taken over by the Blackburn Co-operative Society. It was more recently demolished and a section of the Town Library is now on the site.

11: SHOWDOWN WITH THE ROVERS

Go in for a win, sell yo'r soul for a place,
Oather do or be done, it's a neck and neck race.
William Billington (Blackburn dialect poet)

Dear Sir,
I am instructed by my committee to ask you to
remove our name from your list of fixtures for 1884-85.
Note from Rovers Secretary to Olympic, Sep. 24th 1884

After the defeat at Trent Bridge, Olympic were obviously keen on salvaging something from the season. One week before Rovers travelled to the Oval to face Queen's Park in the 1884 Cup Final, there was the minor matter of the Lancashire County Final. This was between the two premier Blackburn clubs, held at Deepdale, Preston in front of 10,000 largely pro-Olympic fans. The teams were:

Olympic: Woolfall; Ward, Crook; Jos. Duckworth, Hunter, Gibson;
Matthews, Dewhurst, Parker, Birtwistle, Yates
Rovers: Arthur; Beverley, Suter; Forrest, McIntyre; Douglas, Lofthouse,
Sowerbutts, Strachan, Avery, Brown

Olympic once again wore dark blue, so as not to clash with their opponents' colours. Amidst intense excitement Birtwistle gave his team the lead after fifteen minutes. Rovers possibly had their mind on the Cup Final, but the Hole-i'th'-Wall side in general, and Gibson, Duckworth and Crook in particular, were inspirational, and had the better of the play for most of the game.

Hunter's team held the lead until the final move of the match. A reporter, calculating that the ninety minutes were virtually up, sent a telegram to Blackburn, giving the result as a 1-0 win for Olympic. The referee, inexplicably adding an extra minute to the allotted span, permitted a last attack from Rovers. Lofthouse took the corner, and up rose Fergie Suter to thump a header against the bar. A slightly higher trajectory, and Olympic would have been celebrating their first ever Lancashire Cup. But the ball returned into play, falling nicely for Sowerbutts, who was able to force a shot over the line with his chest.

Emotion was running so high that the two teams didn't even take tea together after the match. Olympic, though probably knowing by now what the outcome would be, lodged a protest against the late late equaliser. The Lancs. FA ruled that the referee's word was final, so a replay it had to be. This was at Darwen, four weeks later.

In between times there was some light relief when Halliwell FC came to Hole-i'th'-Wall. At one point in the entertaining 3-3 set-to the ball was kicked over the wall into the adjacent private gardens. For some reason the visitors refused to play on with a substitute ball, so the game was halted until one of the players called round and did the "Please can we have our ball back?" number.

Back to more serious matters: battle with the Rovers was rejoined at Barley Bank. The official crowd number was around 8,000 that day, but several thousand more were thronging the nearby hillside, which afforded a free and reasonably good view of another thrilling game.

Main talking point in the Olympic camp was the return of Thomas Hacking. When Woolfall had failed to turn up against Bolton Wanderers a few weeks previously, Hacking was spotted in the crowd and persuaded to don some kit and play. He was 'keeper for the Easter games, so he naturally agreed to turn out for the old gang against Rovers. Costley was back too, taking Birtwistle's place in the left attack.

In a game of relentless end-to-end attacking Sowerbutts scored first for Rovers after twenty minutes. Ten minutes later Costley climaxed a jinking run with a fierce shot, which Arthur could only parry. Parker ran in and hit the loose ball into goal.

So it remained until the 86th minute. Olympic's approach work was as good as ever, but the failure to capitalise on several "gift" chances in front of goal proved to be crucial. It was McIntyre who broke the deadlock, giving Rovers their 2-1 win.

The teams socialised this time, sharing high tea and bubbly at the nearby New Inn. On the surface, the ill feeling had dissolved. In the long term, though, realism dictated that hostilities were resumed. There could only be one premier team in a town the size of Blackburn, and there was never any question of the two great rivals joining forces. You were either an Olympic or a Rovers man: there was no middle way.

The more discerning could see that already it was becoming a struggle not for supremacy, but rather for survival. The June 1884 AGM highlighted the gathering problems, mainly financial. As the Chairman Fred Yates pointed out, "Where there was one backer of their club, they found twenty of their rivals." They were a massive £300 in debt, and to cap it all, Fred's brother, major sponsor Sydney Yates, had sent a letter of resignation from his post of President.

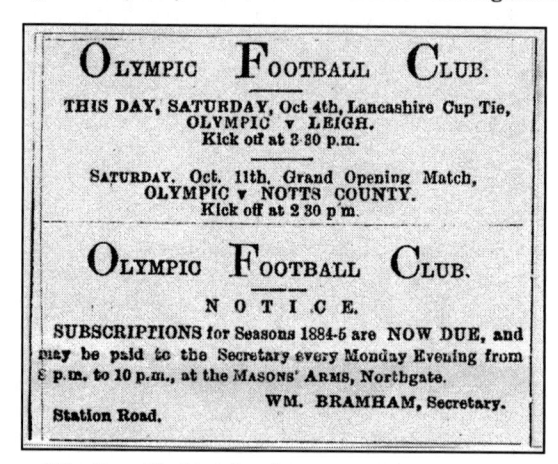

> **OLYMPIC FOOTBALL CLUB.**
>
> THIS DAY, SATURDAY, Oct 4th, Lancashire Cup Tie,
> OLYMPIC v LEIGH.
> Kick off at 3-30 p.m.
>
> SATURDAY. Oct. 11th. Grand Opening Match,
> OLYMPIC v NOTTS COUNTY.
> Kick off at 2 30 p.m.
>
> **OLYMPIC FOOTBALL CLUB.**
>
> NOTICE.
>
> SUBSCRIPTIONS for Seasons 1884-5 are NOW DUE, and may be paid to the Secretary every Monday Evening from 8 p.m. to 10 p.m., at the MASONS' ARMS, Northgate.
> WM. BRAMHAM, Secretary.
> Station Road.

The reasons for Sydney Yates' standing down were unspecified, but there are a number of possibilities. Perhaps his attitude towards public life had changed since the death of his wife the previous year. His own deteriorating health was no doubt a factor too. Perhaps he had realised how expensive the hobby of sponsoring a football club – virtually on his own – could become. There might even have been a connection with the team's decision to stage a benefit match for the area's cotton operatives during that year's eight-week strike. Was Yates unwilling to be associated with supporters of workers who withdrew their labour? Yates ran an iron foundry and engineering works rather than a mill, but it was no doubt important to show solidarity with the other bosses.

The mood of the AGM – held at Hunter's new pub the *Mason's Arms* on Northgate – wasn't all doom and gloom. Far from it: ground improvements were under way, mainly thanks to private and communal contributions. On the playing front, Hacking had returned. Best of all, despite his Cup winner's medal with the Rovers, Joe Beverley was back. In spite of the balance sheet, morale at the club was high.

There were other reasons to be cheerful that autumn. The new grandstand had been constructed, to replace the one demolished in the storm earlier in the year. It was in a different position: "with its back facing the road". This sounds as though it was now alongside the pub side touchline, rather than "at the bottom of the slope", or behind the southern goal. Skeleton stands had been erected at other points around the pitch so as to afford the spectators at least some protection from the elements on the exposed Four Lane Ends plateau.

In December 1884 a correspondent from *Football Field* sang the praises of the Hole-i'th'-Wall: "The only drawback is the difficulty of getting at the ground, but once there we find every convenience for player and spectator. The turf was in splendid order."

Jack Hunter was awarded a benefit match with the attractive fixture with Notts County in October. 4,000 came to Hole-i'th'-Wall to see the encouraging 3-0 win against the previous year's FA Cup semi-finalists. The visit of Preston North End in November attracted a huge crowd of at least ten thousand. The North End players arrived in a flash stagecoach drawn by four bay horses, another example of the Sudell razzamatazz. Former Olympian George Wilson wasn't in the Preston team that managed a 2-0 win, mainly through rough play and a strong defence. On one occasion top scorer Dewhurst found himself with four closely attentive opponents cramping his style.

Generally, scoring was phenomenally high at that time. Olympic bagged forty goals in a week: Eagley 19-0, Oswaldtwistle in the FA Cup 12-0, and Grimsby Town 9-0 away. They took four off Derby County in a seven-goal thriller at the Derbyshire cricket ground, even though the Midlands team had been boosted by two University players, a Corinthian, and old adversary Chevalier of the Old Etonians.

There was another bonanza against Leigh in the Lancashire Cup. Olympic fielded their first team this time, and ran out winners 18-0. Memorably, one of the goals was scored by Thomas Hacking (available for most cup matches) who, bored with his lonely sinecure far from the action, trotted up to join the attack. The cross came over from the wing and Hacking jumped to fist the ball between the posts. After a bemused consideration the referee had to award the goal, as at that time the 'keeper was allowed to handle the ball anywhere on the pitch! It was at this point that Strythe, the Leigh goalie, was heard to exclaim: "I wish that ball would get lost!"

The next round of the Lancashire Cup necessitated a trip to Blackpool, to play South Shore. The seaside outfit, no doubt apprehensive about the Olympic goal machine, had taken precautions to slow the visitors down. A large quantity of the famous beach had been spread on the pitch, making a layer of dry loose sand some six inches deep. Olympic struggled on the energy-sapping surface, but still managed a 3-1 win. As the *Blackpool Herald* coyly put it: "The Olympians played well, but could not understand the pitch." There was a suggestion of some transatlantic influence in the ploy: the *Blackburn Standard* reported that "a gentleman with a strong American accent" was heard to exclaim after the match that Olympic weren't that good, and that the Blackpool team could beat them on any other occasion. We can imagine the discreetly English smiles of the departing victors[1].

There are anecdotes that show the good humour and high morale of the team. On the long train journey to Grimsby the train stopped, in the British Rail tradition, in the middle of nowhere in particular. Since refreshment halts were notoriously brief in those days, one of the players left the train and nipped into a trackside pub for lunch. Luckily, the train was still there when he returned. Meanwhile the rest of the team, less daring, had noticed an orchard close by, so spent the time apple scrumping.

The results by the end of November read as follows:

P	W	D	L	F	A
15	12	1	2	102	14

But there was a dark side to the spree, mainly attributable to the envious eyes of rivals. Once again Secretary Bill Bramham showed himself to be nobody's fool. On Monday 15th September, in Paternoster Row, London, the draw was made for the first round of the FA Cup. Within a matter of hours the match with Oswaldtwistle had been arranged for that Wednesday evening. The idea, again, was to cup-tie the Olympic stars for the season. John Yates had returned to Accrington – albeit briefly – and the word was that Burnley were courting Dewhurst. Harry Kay (see bibliography) gives credence to the tale that when poachers from the Rovers came calling to try and lure Dewhurst, "the Olympic management spirited him away by the back door, and took him down a pit at Belthorne".

The team against Oswaldtwistle was:

W. Astley; J. Beverley, J. Ward; J. Hunter, T. Gibson, Jos. Duckworth;
J. Costley, W. Whitehead, W. Parker, T. Dewhurst, A. Matthews.

According to a newspaper report the following Saturday, "admirers" of the Rovers were to be seen before the game, flashing fivers in an alleged attempt to dissuade "Parker, and one or two other Olympians" from taking the field (*Blackburn Standard* 20/9/84). Whether this was true or not, the very appearance of the story illustrates the undertow of unpleasantness to Rovers-Olympic relations in those years.

The reaction of the Rovers committee was difficult to fathom. By Wednesday of the next week a curt note, the entire content of which may be read at the head of this chapter, had been sent to Bill Bramham. The cancellation of all fixtures with Olympic of course deserved an explanation of some sort, but none was forthcoming. Public speculation was rife: sour grapes at the loss of

Beverley? Anger at the allegations of attempted bribery? A low blow in the psychological war between the clubs? At a Rovers EGM in November it was stated: "There are adequate grounds for complaint, which cannot be made public". The inscrutable committee had "no explanation to make, and would offer none".

Whatever the reasons, the next twist in the plot could not have been dreamed up by the most cunning expert in hype: Rovers and Olympic were drawn against each other in the next round of the FA Cup.

In the Civil War that Blackburn football was threatening to turn into, this match was the two clubs' Battle of Naseby. To be sure, they were to confront one another on many occasions after this, but the increasingly divergent fortunes of Olympic and Rovers in the next few years can be traced back to this one epic tussle.

Fully twelve thousand came to Leamington Street, to watch the first ever English Cup meeting of the two sides, between them winners of the trophy for the past two years. A high wind and understandable nerves undermined the quality of the football, but with "feelings at fever point", a memorable game was guaranteed. The teams were:

Rovers: Arthur; Suter, Turner; McIntyre, Forrest; Lofthouse, Douglas, Fecitt, Brown, Walton, Sowerbutts
Olympic: Hacking; Beverley, Ward; Jos. Duckworth, Hunter, Gibson; Dewhurst, W. Astley, Parker, Costley, Whitehead

After just eight minutes Fecitt capitalised on a rare Ward error to put Rovers into the lead. Then Whitehead, very much against the run of play, squared matters. It was 1-1 at half time. Olympic had survived a battering, and soon after change of ends took the lead through a goalmouth melee. The underdogs were now having the better of it, with one of their typical second half rallies. Midway through the half Rovers were awarded a free kick, which McIntyre, with a high kick way above everyone's head, sent straight into goal. At least, that was what the vast majority of those present – Rovers supporters included – thought. All free kicks at the time being indirect, it was thought that a goal kick should have been the result of the shot. Then Sowerbutts – not the tallest of players – swore blind to the referee that the ball had touched his head on the way in. So vehement was his claim that, incredibly, the referee reversed his decision and awarded a goal!

The match official was Mr. Charles Crump, a highly respected gentleman of the Association game, who, it will be remembered, refereed Olympic's victory over the Old Etonians in the 1883 Final. A deeply religious man, Crump, we may be sure, didn't change his mind lightly, and must have been fully convinced of Sowerbutts' honesty. In the emotional cauldron that this game must have been, the truth was always going to be difficult to distil.

Incensed, Hunter's team started to leave the field in protest. It took a deal of persuasion from Fred Yates to bring them back and finish the game. Their heart seemed no longer in it, though, and Fecitt ended a rough and fractious game by scoring the winner for Rovers. The goal credited to Sowerbutts would be debated for many years to come.

The Rovers would go on to retain the FA Cup, beating Queen's Park again in the final, but a tad more convincingly this time.

Whilst the early rounds of the FA Cup dominated the foreground that autumn, the pro-am battle was rejoined with sabres rattling.

The FA had begun the 1884-5 season with a set of rules on professionalism and player importations that were so repressive that many considered them illegal, or at least unworkable. This time, it was felt, the amateur brigade had overstepped the mark. Thirty-seven clubs met in Manchester at the end of October with the intention of forming a breakaway organisation: the British Football Association. Amongst those represented were Bolton Wanderers, Preston North End, Accrington, and Sunderland. Perhaps wisely, given the scrupulous enquiry on Moss the previous year, Olympic kept a low profile and didn't send a delegate to the meeting.

Waiting to see which way the wind was blowing, Olympic followed the FA's directives for the vital couple of months, fielding only Blackburnians, and excusing themselves from scheduled games with the rebel clubs.

The tinderbox situation had to be resolved one way or another, and the divisive threat from the proposed BFA forced the hand of the London committeemen. A couple of the more contentious rulings were rescinded, and pay for play was back on the FA agenda. Another six months or so, and professional football would be legalised.

For Olympic and their almost completely homegrown team, the remainder of that final season of shamateurism was one of mixed fortunes.

The club performed a splendid PR job when the mighty Corinthians came to town in mid-December. Most soccer histories of the time will mention their crushing 8-1 win over cup holders Rovers, but not so well publicised was their 1-2 defeat at Albert Warburton's Darwen, nor the thrilling 4-4 draw with Olympic in the final match of their Lancashire tour. Cobbold, who had been on that Old Carthusians side beaten 4-0 in the 1883 FA Cup semi, declared that he had "never played against a stronger team in his life". The teams and officials had dinner later in the *Old Bull Hotel* on Church Street, and the occasion was rounded off with speeches and songs. The match referee was Major Sudell of the North End, emphasising the continuing good relations between Olympic and the Preston side. (More than likely, though, this was a case of "My enemy's enemy is my friend"!)

The return game with Sudell's team was in January. Not to be outdone by North End's spectacular arrival at Hole-i'th'-Wall earlier in the season, cab proprietor Robin Walker laid on two swank carriages and eight horses to take Olympic to Deepdale. The football was appropriately deft, Whitehead and Costley hitting two quick goals as an overture to a fine 3-1 win.

> **OLYMPIC FOOTBALL CLUB,**
> HOLE-I'TH'-WALL.
> THIS DAY (Saturday), January 24th,
> **OLYMPIC v. ROVERS.**
> Kick off at 2 45 p.m.
> Special Trains will run to be in time for the Match.
> The two captains, Hunter and Brown, will inspect the ground this morning, and if favourable the match will take place; if not, will be postponed.

The hatchet was buried with Rovers, and another 4-4 draw was fought out on Hole-i'th'-Wall later that month. A remarkable feature of the game was that Olympic were 4-0 up inside fifteen minutes, thanks to a Dewhurst hat-trick and a goal from the returning Yates. The long and painstaking fight back from the Rovers ended with a late equaliser from Douglas.

Another worthy draw (1-1) was achieved against Notts County at Trent Bridge. The dominant Olympians deserved to win, but the home side snatched equality with a deflected shot, literally the last kick of the match. Whitehead, who replaced the injured Matthews with some success, hit the Olympic goal. The newcomer, yet another product of the successful reserve side, was to score over twenty goals that season.

James Ward was selected for England, and played a fine game in the 1-1 draw with Wales on the Leamington Street ground in March, just a fortnight before his twentieth birthday. C. W. Alcock, in his *Football Annual 1885* noted: "Ward played well against Wales; [he is] very quick, and difficult to pass; a sure kick." Ward, Hacking, Beverley and Dewhurst had once again represented Lancashire that year.

The club lost one of its cornerstones early in 1885, when astute and capable Secretary Bill Bramham resigned. His letter of resignation stated quite simply that he was "no longer able to discharge the duties of his office". It would appear that the immense amount of work involved in guarding players from temptations to defect, the relentless liaising and bargaining with other clubs, and no doubt the feeling of being caught in the crossfire of the early season business with the Rovers, had all taken their toll. What had started as an intriguing and pleasurable hobby was fast becoming a facet of cutthroat capitalism.

Yet again, disasters at the final hurdle typified Olympic's season. Fielding a team weakened through injuries, they lost narrowly 1-2 to Rovers in the final of the Lancashire Cup at Deepdale. Yates was unavailable, and Dewhurst had broken his arm in the previous week's encounter with Darwen. During the game Beverley was accidentally kicked on the forehead by Gibson, and whilst "Bev" was off the field receiving treatment Rovers scored their first goal. During Olympic's second half onslaught reserve Slater reduced the arrears to 1-2, but after that Suter, in brilliant form, marshalled his defence to perfection. Not even the return of Matthews to the forward line could bring any joy to the "determined, but disorganised" team. (*Blackburn Standard*, April 25th 1885)

There were no excuses when Accrington were met in the final of the East Lancashire Charity Cup at Leamington Street a fortnight later. Olympic gave a woeful performance, losing 0-4 to the "Owd Reds". It was as if they could sense the approaching storm.

[1]*It is quite possible that the "gentleman with a strong American accent" was US-born Hiram Stevens Maxim, a prolific inventor (and renowned prankster) who was to design a "captive flying machine" for Blackpool Pleasure Beach. His other inventions included the Vickers machine gun and the mousetrap.*

Pike's Lane, Bolton Wanderers' home venue in the 1880s. Olympic played Church here in the Lancashire Cup semi-final of 1885, a match the Blackburn team won 4-3, with Costley scoring a hat-trick.

12: THE JACK SOUTHWORTH AFFAIR – AND OTHER TRIBULATIONS

> After being knocked about like merchandise for a good many days
> most of the professionals of Lancashire at last settled down by playing for the
> clubs which have made them the best offers.
> *Blackburn Times* (Sept 12th 1885)

> We were kept waiting a long time, because the Olympic goalkeeper
> did not turn up. A lot of people commenced chaffing, and said he was at home
> drawing teeth, so I concluded he was a dentist.
> *Football Field* (Oct 24th 1885)

In the summer of 1885, then, professional football in England was legalised at last. For Olympic, it turned out to be the best of times, and the worst of times.

The first few days of September saw a scramble to sign on the best players. It was the FA Cup-style wheedling all over again, but with greater intensity and significance, as this time a player was "fixed" to one club for all games throughout the season, if that club were paying him.

Witton came to Hole-i'th'-Wall on August 29th, and there was "some amusement and indignation" at the efforts of the home club to lure Whitehead (ex-Olympic forward) from Witton, and at the "equally persuasive arguments of the villagers" to hang on to him. Whitehead didn't switch allegiance, but the first professional line-up deployed by Olympic after the 1st September deadline was good enough, with Dewhurst and Beverley especially putting loyalty before lucre:

> Leigh; Little, Beverley; Gibson, Hunter, W. Astley; Matthews, Dewhurst,
> Bell, Slater, Costley

As was perhaps to be expected, the choicest fun and games in the rush to fasten players surrounded Joe Beverley. *Football Field* gave an account of the machinations, without naming too many names, possibly with one eye on the libel laws:

> "Beverley was interviewed by the Rovers, and carried off to the Isle of Man,
> and it is said that his wife was adorned with a new dress at the expense of a noted
> Blackburn club."
> (Sep 5th 1885)

The snippet goes on to suggest that Olympic then hid Beverley in Blackpool until it was time to play him in a game which would ensure he remained at Hole-i'th'-Wall for the coming season.

The twenty-year-old James T. Ward joined his colleagues one week later, taking Bell's place as centre forward. The Cup Final left back had been offered the proprietorship of the *Pack Horse* in Astley Bridge, as an incentive to add his talent to the burgeoning Bolton Wanderers. The matter was settled, though, when Ward travelled to Anfield in mid-September and turned out and scored for Olympic in their 3-2 win over Everton.

At first the Light Blues had no professional goalkeeper in their ranks, Hacking preferring to remain amateur. Leigh, his replacement, has received criticism for his performances; he was certainly no first team player, and many of the goals conceded in the first few months of that season were down to him. It's true he played in trousers and walking shoes once against Accrington, but this was because Hacking, unusually, had let the team down that day by not turning up as he had promised. Leigh had brought no kit, but offered to play between the sticks anyway. Olympic lost that match 3-4: it was their sixth defeat in a row.

The problem of goalkeeper was apparently solved with the return of Jack Southworth. He had once been a free-scoring forward with the reserves, but a knee injury caused him to adopt the temporary role of 'keeper. He had spent the summer and early autumn working in a theatre in Chester, as besides possessing immense footballing talent he was also an accomplished musician.

He had a younger brother, James, a talented sprinter who had played full back for Chester and a couple of minor Blackburn teams. And thereby hangs a tale.

Olympic were drawn against old rivals Church at home in the first round of the FA Cup. Jack Southworth was in goal. It was a thrilling encounter, worthy of the cup-ties of Olympic at their zenith. Smith scored for Church after three minutes, but within one more minute Yates (who had turned down a good early-season offer to join Accrington) had equalised. Hunter, Costley, and then Beverley, playing at centre forward that day, added to the tally, and the result was a convincing 4-2 win. The word was that second round opponents Third Lanark were likely to scratch, so a free passage to the third round looked likely. Despite the dire results elsewhere, things were looking rosy again in the English Cup.

Or were they? Church started ferreting around and discovered that a "J. Southworth" had played professional football for Chester earlier in the season. If this turned out to be Jack, then Olympic had fielded an ineligible player for the Cup match, so by rights should be disqualified. A Mr. Gregson of the Lancashire FA conducted a preliminary enquiry, at which Jack protested his innocence, claiming that the Chester player had been his brother James. The London FA bureaucrats, clearly not wishing any sort of loophole to be fashioned so early in the professional game, added their weight to the investigation. Their conclusion was that Jack had tried to pull a fast one, and declared him guilty, suspending him for four months. Olympic themselves were found innocent of any attempt at deception. Church, perhaps justifiably, still demanded their pound of flesh. The FA declared the Cup result void, and ordered the match to be replayed, back at Pickup Street, Accrington.

So, three weeks after what had seemed a conclusive victory, Olympic faced up to their adversaries once more. The Blackburn team performed heroically that day, their resilient backs withstanding an almighty second half battering from the opposition attack. Bruised but unbowed, Hunter's team came away with a worthy 2-2 draw.

Back to it, then, one week later at Hole-i'th'-Wall. Dewhurst hit the opener, and the home side looked likely to grind out a win. Then just before half time Will Astley had to retire injured, and the balance of the team was destroyed. The ten men were now struggling to impose any sort of pattern to the game, and Church gradually gained the upper hand. Three second-half goals were enough to secure the win for the Accrington side.

This new professionalism with its set of straightjacket rules had already caught out Olympic. Coupe, a forward who had already signed for Nelson, turned out for the Blackburn team a couple of months later. Although the club were unaware of the Nelson connection, they were suspended for a week, with resultant loss of revenue.

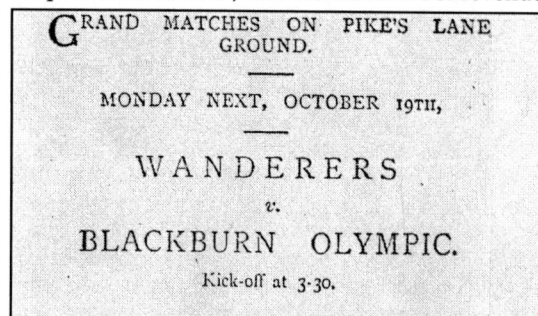

> GRAND MATCHES ON PIKE'S LANE GROUND.
>
> MONDAY NEXT, OCTOBER 19TH,
>
> WANDERERS
> v.
> BLACKBURN OLYMPIC.
>
> Kick-off at 3-30.

Fortunately, for one of the rare periods of the Olympic's existence, they weren't in the red at the time. A combination of good crowds for 1884-5, plus the reduction in travel and accommodation expenses, had left them with £46 profit at the end of the season, a healthy turn-around after the massive debt of the previous year. Sydney Yates was back as President, signalling his return with a generous gift of £5 for the club coffers.

There were other positive signs. Warburton had finally made his peace with Gibson, and had returned from Darwen. This was permissible, as the former captain had not as yet signed on as professional for any team. He didn't need to, as he now owned a popular beerhouse, the *Dog and Partridge* on James Street, Blackburn, as well as earning his keep as a master plumber. So the team fielded against the Corinthians just before Christmas had a stirring resemblance to the crowd-pulling line-ups of old:

Hacking; Beverley, Ward; Warburton, Hunter, Gibson; Yates, Costley, Dewhurst, Bell, Brown

Although the Corinthians with their team of amateur *galácticos* of the day won this one 4-1, in the same month the Light Blues enjoyed a rare win against Rovers in a 4-3 thriller at Leamington Street, and Derby County were trounced 3-0 at Hole-i'th'-Wall. The club could afford two trips to Middlesbrough early in 1886. Olympic's share of the revenue from a New Year's Day gate of 6,000 helped pay the rail fare, and an exhausting eleven-hour round trip meant there was no hotel bill. Both matches were fighting draws.

It couldn't last. It took just six months for the wage bill to become an intolerable burden. In February 1886 the club executive took the drastic step of reducing players' wages to 10s. 6d. (52½p) per match. As a comparison, Preston North End were paying their players £2 10s. (£2.50) a game. Immediately Yates, Dewhurst and Beverley withdrew their labour. All three had turned down tempting offers from other clubs at the beginning of the season. There was some talk of the club committee being in breach of contract: weren't there some bits of paper somewhere binding the club to pay the wages agreed at the beginning of the season? The executive replied that no such written agreements had been drawn up, and that it had just been a "verbal contract" between management and players. (And we all know the paper value of verbal contracts.)

> BLACKBURN OLYMPIC FOOTBALL CLUB.
>
> GRAND MATCH on the HOLE-I'-TH'-WALL GROUND, SATURDAY NEXT, October 24th,
> BLACKBURN OLYMPIC
> *v.*
> BURNLEY.
> Kick-off at 3 o'clock. Admission 4d. Stand extra.

The players, of course, without even the beginnings of a union in the brave new world of professionalism, were over a barrel. Their only weapon was simple refusal to play, with no accepted channels of negotiation. Yates and Beverley were never to return, although Dewhurst came back into the fold towards the end of the season. Yates went back to Accrington, and thereafter his star was to continue in the ascendant: in 1889, by then transferred to Burnley, he was to gain an England cap. Beverley went back to the Rovers, to partner Suter once more at full back.

Olympic, though, were never really to recover. Other Lancashire clubs – the better-off ones – had done supremely well out of the infant business of football. Bolton Wanderers inflicted two harsh defeats: 7-0 and 11-2. The latter was in a Lancashire Cup match at Pike's Lane. Bolton went on to win the Lancashire Cup that year, beating Blackburn Rovers in the final. Preston North End, who were to overcome Olympic three times that season, were just three years away from their double of FA Cup and inaugural Football League Championship. The times they were a-changing.

Yet real change, such as the mending of social divisions, was still a long way in the future. The pro-am divide was emphasised with a couple of "Gentlemen v. Players" games. In the second of these, played at the Oval in March, Jimmy Costley was selected for the professionals, and with a touch of *déjà vu*, he scored the winning goal in his team's 2-1 win. The *Times* praised his dribbling and shooting skills.

It was a rare high spot for any of the Olympic team. Towards the end of the season, even hero Jimmy Ward clearly had his mind on other things. For the away game with Church he turned up fifteen minutes late, with no kit. He started to play in trousers and clogs, until an opponent objected to the rock-hard footwear. Ward completed the game in walking shoes lent to him by another player. Olympic lost 1-3. Ward might have claimed mitigating circumstances: recently married, he had taken over proprietorship of the *Prince of Wales* on Harwood Street, Blackburn. Domestic concerns were perhaps taking precedence over football.

That game with Church also marked the return from suspension of Jack Southworth. Amongst the many who had taken over between the sticks in Jack's absence had been Albert Warburton, showing a good deal of improvement in this position since the last time he had played there.

There were still signs of spirit and enterprise within the club. Olympic were one of the very first football outfits to organise a prize draw. (The Rovers followed suit almost immediately.)

Around 30,000 tickets were sold, and the winning 100 numbers were picked out of the drum after the game with South Shore on 13th March. There was a good crowd at Hole-i'th'-Wall that day, but it seems more than likely that a good proportion of those present had come to see if they'd won a prize. The band of the Blackburn Ragged School supplied the music, and the football was cut to sixty minutes: "The game flagged towards the finish, everyone appearing anxious to witness the Draw." The total value of the prizes was £170, and the most expensive items were:

		£	s	d
1.	House of furniture, value	50	0	0
2.	Harmonium	12	12	0
3.	Lady's and gentleman's easy chairs	5	10	0
4.	Three pictures	3	3	0
5.	Gentleman's silver watch	3	3	0
6.	Lady's silver watch	2	2	0
7.	Portrait of winner (enlarged) in gold frame, and twelve carte-de-visites.	2	0	0

The first and second prizes had been on view in the shop window of "Mr. J. Dewhurst, Cabinet Maker, Fish Lane, Blackburn". To put these values into perspective, a decent middle of the range house cost around £150 at the time.

Beyond the first few items in the list, there didn't seem to be a lot of logic to the order. Prize no. 100 was £1 worth of coal, and the lucky winner of no. 46 could rejoice in the possession of a scrubbing brush.

The first prize was won by a Mr. Nathan Denham, a bookseller and stationer of King William Street. Annoyingly to some, he was a staunch Rovers supporter!

The first of these ventures – there was another the following autumn – generated considerable capital (over £227), but as far as a means of persuading the best players to stay at Hole-i'th'-Wall, it wasn't enough. Olympic's full results for that crucial season of 1885-86 were:

P	W	D	L	F	A
55	16	8	31	85	131

It was the worst record of the thirty-eight professional clubs that had played a full season. In comparison, Preston North End won 51 of their 55 games. And Blackburn Rovers won the FA Cup yet again, beating West Brom in a replay, making it three English Trophies on the bounce. One of the scorers in the Final was Jimmy Brown, who had guested for Olympic in days gone by.

Then at the beginning of the new season both Ward and Costley followed Beverley across town to sign on for Rovers.

It was a harsh irony that one of the key clubs who had helped pave the way for professionalism in English football should be the one most to suffer from its legalisation.

13: THINGS FALL APART

The Blackburn Olympic is a most unfortunate club. Perpetually
overshadowed by local rivals, suffering from chronic embarrassment on account
of poor "gates", and shaken by the defection of several of the best players, it
must needs, alas, be eaten up with internal dissensions among the committee.
Athletic News (March 27th 1886)

Here we have it in one word. The whole thing [The League] is a mere
money-making scheme, a speculation.
Athletic News (April 16th 1888)

Despite all efforts to generate and save money, at the 1886 AGM the club reported a deficit of £79. Major expenditure had been over £387 for the wage bill. The meeting itself was characterised by a certain amount of bickering, and the odd caustic personal attack. The committee was split into two cliques, roughly representing the old and new blood. There was some argument about the prize draws, but there was no denying the financial usefulness, or even necessity, of such ventures, so it was decided to organise another one for that autumn.

Sydney Yates, though by now very ill, was re-elected President. The name of the club was changed to "Olympic Cricket and Football Club". The aim of this was to pool resources, but the action was another symptom of the weakening of the football outfit. And a committee member, probably unintentionally, gave out precisely the wrong signal towards the end of the meeting:

"Mr. Chadwick said he hoped the business of the club would not be
conducted on the same lines as last year – that was by paying the players a
small fee when the funds were low, and a large fee when they had a good surplus."
Blackburn Standard (June 12th 1886)

The diaspora continued: the club had lost Ward and Beverley to the Rovers, and Costley joined them, but his play, possibly through injury, suffered a sad falling-off of quality. In a report of a late autumn game he was described as "a mere shadow of his former self, in play and appearance". He was to return to Olympic the following season.

Dewhurst now threw in his lot with Halliwell. (For a brief spell the Halliwell club from Bolton seemed set to become the premier Lancashire club; Dewhurst played a major attacking role in the 8-2 drubbing of Rovers that autumn.) Of the Olympian old guard, only Hunter and Gibson stubbornly remained. Tommy Gibson would be the only player to stick with Olympic for the entire span of the club's existence, which speaks volumes about the single-minded integrity of the man.

Arthur Matthews, who was later to emigrate to Canada to become a Presbyterian minister, had retired from competitive football to concentrate on his business. The 1891 *Blackburn Trade Directory* lists him as "carver and gilder" still working from 11 Warwick St., Blackburn.

Thomas Hacking still made the odd appearance in goal for the team. Not having signed on as a professional with any one club, this gave him the freedom to turn out for whoever he wanted – but Olympic was the only side he would consider playing for, when commitments of work permitted.

Hacking shared in one of the few bright moments of that season's gloom. He kept goal against Notts County in an inspiring 4-3 win at Hole-i'th'-Wall in October. The team:

Hacking; McLeod, Southworth; McIntyre, Hunter, Gibson; Garner,
Carlisle, J. Hothersall, Holden, Parker

There was a lot of homegrown talent here, with the comparatively strong reserve side supplying most of the attack. McIntyre guested from Rovers, and W. McLeod, a fine Scottish international fullback from Cowlairs, looked the perfect replacement for Ward. For a couple of months, the defensive bastion of McLeod and Southworth proved difficult to beat. This Southworth was James, Jack's brother, about whom there had been some confusion the previous year. Once his knee trouble had cleared up, Jack was to progress from safe goalie to high-scoring forward, hitting the target several times for Olympic in their late season mini-revival.

The patching-up was too haphazard and came too late, however, to do the team any good in that year's FA Cup. Olympic had been drawn against Partick Thistle at home, the Glasgow team containing Jarvis Suter, Fergie's brother.

The Scots settled more quickly to the task, deploying their six forwards to advantage and hitting three goals in the first twenty-two minutes. At this point the home side rallied, and most of the second half was spent bringing out the best of Duff in the Partick goal. At one point he appeared to fumble a shot and drop it behind the line, but Olympic's claim of a goal was overruled by Tom Hindle, the Darwen referee. Duff was beaten just the once: a probing cross from the right wing found Hunter unmarked, and he was able to half-volley the ball cleanly into goal.

As with the team's season, this once more proved too little, too late. Partick won 3-1, and went on to beat Fleetwood Rangers 7-0 in Glasgow in the next round. The Olympic line-up for the cup match was:

> Noble; Fletcher, James Southworth; Cook, Hunter, Gibson; Marshall, Carlisle, Parker, J. Hothersall, Gill

Left-sided attacker Jack Hothersall combined well with his younger brother Richard. On song, the wing partnership produced the goods: they shared seven of the goals in the 9-1 demolition of Denton, and were often mentioned in dispatches. Richard was described in *Football Field* as "a second Costley". (Well, not quite; but he had his moments.)

The bright spots were worth celebrating, as that winter they were few and far between. Whilst the Rovers regularly pulled crowds of five or six thousand at Leamington Street, Olympic generally drew around a third of that number, and sometimes did well to hit four figures. Poor crowds meant uncertain available capital, which in turn curtailed the number of top class players the club could afford to have on its books. (McLeod, for example, was back at Cowlairs before Christmas.) This led to indifferent results on the pitch, which contributed to the fall in popularity. It was a vicious circle, appearing to move faster by the month.

Club President and major patron Sydney Yates, who had been ill for some time, died in December 1886. He was just 39 years old. There was the first whiff of panic among the clubs' creditors. An emergency meeting was held in January at the *Mason's Arms*, at which those who had invested money in the club expressed concern about recovering any of it. Mr. Riley, solicitor, showed the meeting the accounts, which gave evidence of the current availability of a mere 6s. 8d. return (33p) in the pound. After some discussion, it was agreed to somehow make available to the creditors a dividend of 10 shillings (50p) in the pound. A bazaar, and yet another prize draw, were promised.

The committee had also adopted a policy of scouting for talented amateurs in the district (a search mostly conducted by Jack Hunter), so as to effect drastic cuts to the wage bill. The stringency worked, as the June 1887 AGM was able to report a minuscule, but significant, cash in hand of two shillings and threepence (11p)!

The late season purple patch is worth noting, as it marks almost the last flowering of any optimism that Olympic might recover the glories of old. Pleasing victories were registered over rivals old and new: Witton (twice, 6-1 and 4-2), Burnley, Church and Darwen. Major contributors to the goal tally were newcomers Garner and the diminutive Carlisle ("Lilliputian demons"), who along with the Southworth, Hothersall and Chadwick brothers formed the (mostly amateur) backbone of the team. Gibson, of course, was still there; and Hunter made the occasional appearance. Despite losses to Everton, Park Road, and Accrington in the East Lancs. Charity Cup, there was the feeling that Olympic had once more the makings of a decent team.

Alas! Come September 1887 the Southworth brothers joined the exodus to Rovers, James as defensive partner with Fergie Suter, and Jack as prolific striker. Jack was to slip into his greatest role at Rovers as team captain and centre-forward, hitting an impressive 25 FA Cup goals in six seasons, including a couple in successive winning finals. He was also to gain three England caps, scoring in all three games.

So it was perhaps inevitable that Jack hit one of the goals in the 5-1 thrashing of his old club in the FA Cup second round tie in November 1887.

A close game had been forecast, as Olympic had fought well at Leamington Street just a few weeks before, having taken a stirring 2-0 lead in the first few minutes through Carlisle and Costley, who was back for the season. Then Rovers had equalised before half time, and the visiting side, clearly out of condition, let things slip in the second half, finally succumbing 2-3.

The FA Cup game took place at Leamington Street before a crowd of 5,000. The teams were:

Rovers: Arthur; Beverley, Suter; Heyes, J. Barton, S. Douglas, Beresford, Rushton, Jack Southworth, E. Chadwick, Townley
Olympic: Barrett; Fletcher, Gill; Eckroyd, Hunter, Gibson; Garner, Fielden, J. Hothersall, Carlisle, Dickson

About the only palliative for Olympic was the general opinion that Jack Hothersall scored the best goal of the six, a well-struck shot that left Herbie Arthur standing. Otherwise, the gap in class that had been growing for some time was only too apparent. To complete the embarrassment, Gill put one past his own 'keeper. The Olympic goalie for most of that year was a Dr. Barrett, who with Fletcher and Gill made up a generally sound defence. Barrett was a 'keeper in the Hacking mould, comparatively small but lively and effective.

Indeed, some good results were recorded, especially when the forward line were clicking. In the winter of 1887-8 major scalps were Rovers (narrowly, 2-1), Church (twice) and Sunderland away. Matters may have remained in the balance, with a possible hope of a return towards former strengths, were it not for drastic developments in football's larger world.

In early 1888, realising that the game at its highest level needed a more regular competitive diet than the occasional treat of the FA Cup and similar knock-out affairs, William McGregor of Aston Villa wrote to a select dozen clubs, inviting them to create an all-play-all championship. The criterion for choosing the invited clubs was simple enough: McGregor targeted the professional outfits that enjoyed the biggest crowds. (So, despite their smattering of decent results, Olympic had little chance of consideration when set alongside Rovers.) The Lancashire teams involved were: Preston North End, Blackburn Rovers, Everton, Accrington, Burnley, and Bolton Wanderers. The Football League was about to be born.

The repercussions were immediate, and far-reaching. In April, Mr. J. G. Hall of Crewe, no doubt miffed that the Alexandra (Cup semi-finalists a month or so previously) had been overlooked, proposed a "second league", later to be dubbed the "Combination". Some eighteen clubs, including Olympic, Witton, and Darwen, were approached. Thus an unwieldy parallel to the League lumbered into motion the following season (see next Chapter).

The idea of elitism now spread to the FA Cup. For 1888-9 Qualifying Rounds were introduced, with 22 clubs being exempt from competition until the First Round proper. As the *Athletic News* put it: "Now, instead of the leading clubs being compelled to go through the ordeal of slaughtering the innocents in the initial stages, the innocents will have all the fun to themselves until Christmas ... then the real fight for supremacy will commence." (May 7th 1888)

Despite having won the thing just five years before, Olympic weren't selected to join the 22 seeds. Three times winners Rovers were of course chosen, as were local rivals Witton. This last must have been a difficult pill for Olympic to swallow, as the Light Blues had traded blow for blow with the Witton team over the past couple of years, and could be justified in considering themselves at least on a par. (It may be relevant – or at least of interest – that the exemption scheme was drawn up by Richard Gregson of the Rovers, and Blackburn Town Clerk solicitor William E. L. Gaine, who lived on the Witton side of town.)

Olympic ended their penultimate season with another East Lancashire Charity Cup tussle with the Rovers. It took place at Hole-i'th'-Wall, but as expected, home advantage counted for little. The visitors were five goals to the good by half time, and even a brief rally in the second half, with two goals in a minute from Carlisle and Jack Hothersall, wasn't enough to ruffle the composure of Arthur, Beverley, Suter, and Co. By now the Rovers were literally in a different league – or would be in a few weeks' time.

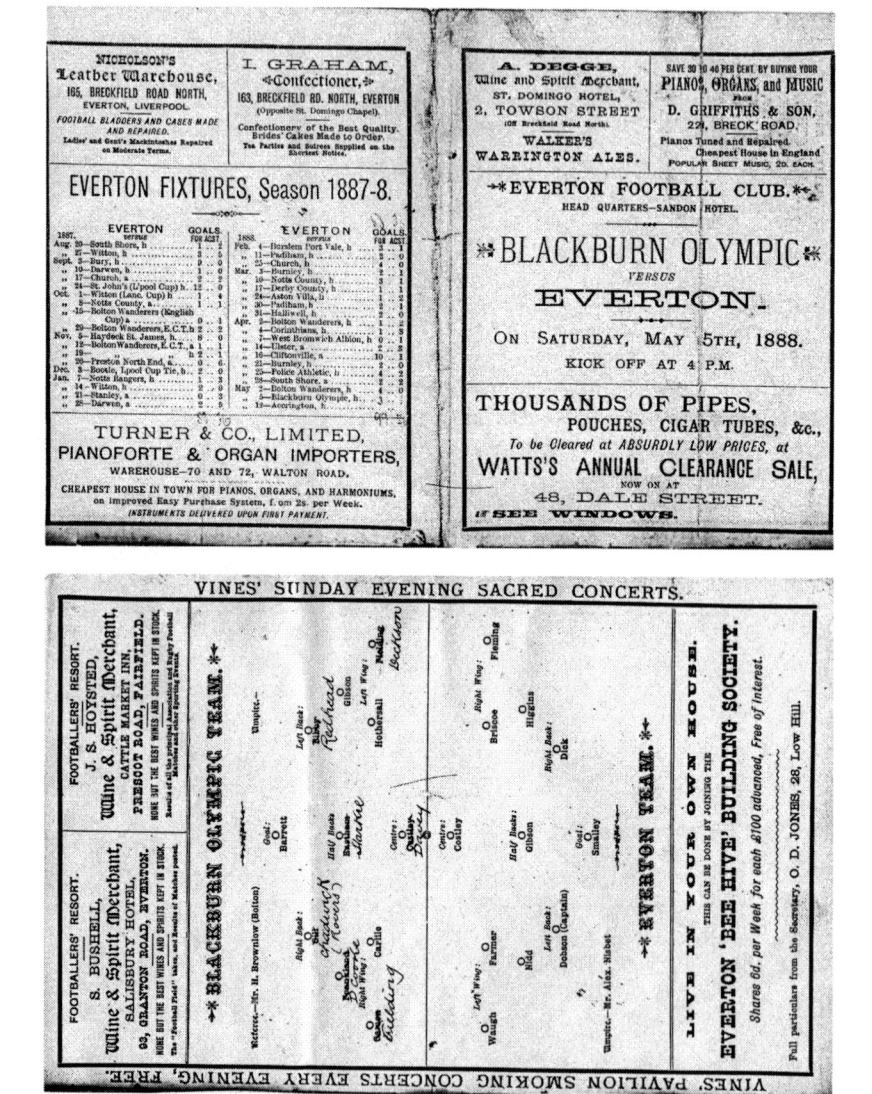

The Everton programme for the game with Olympic in May 1888.
Match result: Everton 3, Olympic 1.

14: SHADOWS OF THE PAST

> *O'er yon daisy-flecked lea, stood a sturdy oak tree –*
> *... But the lightning's fell blast struck the veteran at last,*
> *And its vigour and beauty laid low.*
> Thomas Chippendale, Blackburn poet, and Olympic supporter.
>
> This once famous club, it is to be feared, is gone beyond all recovery.
> There is no attempt to resuscitate it.
> *Blackburn Times* (Aug 31st 1889)

The Football League was launched in September 1888. For the select dozen it was a new beginning, an exciting and profitable doorway into the next century. The League was tantamount to a mutual benefit society, in which the most popular clubs played one another, cornered the lion's share of the available gate and sponsorship monies, and so reinforced their already strong position. (So, as we say nowadays, not much change there then.)

As for the rest, it was to render their position more precarious. The "Combination" or "Second League" turned out to be an insubstantial affair, and ultimately unworkable. Although composed of twenty teams, each one would play only eight games. So for most clubs there was little to hold the fans' attention after Christmas, unless they were lucky enough to be still in contention for the FA Cup.

Olympic embarked on their quest for two trophies that autumn. Firstly, in the Lancashire Cup they were drawn against tiny Higher Walton, at home. A shoo-in? Not at all. The gutsy village side adapted better to the slippery conditions at Hole-i'th'-Wall, and translated their agile skills into a 2-1 win. They then proved this was no fluke by progressing to the final, defeating Blackburn Rovers on the way. They would take Accrington to a replay in the final, eventually losing to a single, scrappy goal.

At least Olympic's tie had been conducted in a genial atmosphere and had been full of good, honest football. The FA Cup match with Oswaldtwistle Rovers, a month later, showed the other side of the soccer coin.

Olympic had enjoyed a walk-over in the first Qualifying Round, Fleetwood Rangers being unable to raise a team. "Twistle" now came from Accrington way, accompanied by a large number of raucously opinionated supporters. It was a rough, ill-tempered game, and the high wind spoiled most attempts at constructive play. The home side were a goal up after five minutes through a "scrimmage". After that the physically stronger away team took control and, roared on by their fans, ran out 3-1 winners. It was Olympic's last ever Cup match.

The Combination games raised little interest compared to the massively popular exploits of the swank brethren in the Football League. Blackpool South Shore, who had no Rovers to compete with for support, were watched by around 1,500 when they played Olympic at Cow Gap Lane in mid-December. The crowd had dwindled to 200 for the return match at Hole-i'th'-Wall later that month. Bootle inflicted two severe defeats: 4-0 and 6-0. For the first of these, because of a problem with the trains, only seven Olympic players turned up on time for the kick-off at Hawthorne Road, the deficit being made up with members of the Bootle reserve squad. When the missing players turned up at half-time, the home side already had an unassailable 3-0 lead.

Strange to relate, the playing of Combination matches wasn't compulsory, so there was no point in compiling a league table. Unsurprisingly, the rickety structure didn't survive the end of that season. It was replaced the following year by the more workable Alliance – an embryonic Division Two – too late, of course, for Blackburn Olympic to benefit from it.

Yet the season had started so well: the "other" Liverpool club of the time, Football League members Everton, had been beaten at Anfield in early September. 2,000 had turned out to watch the 3-1 win over Distillery – that season's Irish Cup winners – in Belfast, later that same month. Another trip to Belfast in early November had been the occasion of a fine 3-0 win over an Ulster XI, which team boasted several Irish internationals. Even their penultimate Rovers game, a 2-4 defeat on a Monday in December, wasn't without its positive aspect: Olympic were 2-0 up at half time.

But by the end of January, after a 1-4 defeat at Darwen, morale was at a low ebb, the coffers were empty, and the committee came to a decision:

> "An attempt is to be made to manage this club on purely amateur lines.
> The services of professionals are to be altogether dispensed with."
> *Blackburn Times* (Jan 26th 1889)

Thus at a stroke the wage bill was resolved. However, having only amateurs on the books meant that the club had no contractual hold over those players, who were free to turn out for other teams if they so wished. So the move, intended to ensure the club's survival, actually accelerated its end.

Forwards Carlisle and Dodd, and defender Frankland, left immediately for Heywood. Olympic were determined to at least survive the season, and play out their remaining games in the best of humour. Hunter took over in goal, and on occasions adopted the role of entertainer. During the match at Bootle, according to *Football Field*, he "kept a circle of gamins in a constant ripple of merriment".

Temporary financial help came from an unexpected quarter, thanks to the club's last ever game with Rovers, at Leamington Street in February. Rovers charitably allowed their former deadly rivals to take all proceeds from the gate money, thus sweetening Olympic's 1-6 defeat, and enabling the beleaguered club to soldier on through the spring.

True to form, Hunter dedicated his skills to a worthy cause. In early May the "Jack Hunter's XI" played a "Dick Whittington's Panto. Co." team, and raised £4 10s. for a local benevolent fund. It's pleasing to note that Dabulamanzi was a long time in hanging up his assegai.

After the defeats against the village sides of Irwell Springs and Farnworth Standard, the last week or so of the club's life was, despite everything, a memorable swan song. Most of the *wunderteam* of 1883 was gathered together for three final games, the aim presumably being to attract decent crowds and bridge the financial gap to the next season. Right to the end, though, the club was dogged by bad luck.

The first game, a midweek encounter with Park Road, drew a mere 500. The following Saturday torrential rain dampened the enthusiasm for their last ever home appearance, a 1-0 win against the King's Own Regiment, Dublin. The team on these two occasions was:

> Hunter; Ward, Beverley; Whiteside, W. Astley, Chadwick; Dewhurst, Matthews, Parker, Yates, Costley

Then two days later, on Monday 13th May, there was a scantily publicised game with Everton at Anfield. The *Football Field*, in an article entitled "Shadows of the Past", recorded Olympic's final hour, a 1-6 defeat against the team that would win the League Championship the year after next:

> " ... on Monday night there appeared a vision at Everton which ought to
> have been more widely advertised. Everton were down for an engagement with
> Blackburn Olympic ...
> " ... And lo! There stood Beverley and Ward, the two splendid backs that were, the veterans short of wind and stiff of joint of today. Astley alone stood in the place of yore in the half-back division, Hunter and Hacking having changed places, whilst Gibson was missing[1]. And the forwards, the buzzing, biting, not-to-be-shook-off quintette, who proved to the big burly "boys" of Eton that Lancashire pluck and indomitable spirit could rise superior to physical disparity, they were there to a man – the shadows of the past."
> (May 18th 1889)

Olympic struck first, after just two minutes, through "Tich" Parker, who was thus the scorer of the club's last ever goal. Thereafter the veterans had no answer to Everton's power play.

And so to the final act. The report of Olympic's demise in the *Blackburn Times* of August 31st 1889 was just a touch premature. A call for a committee meeting, intended to kick-start the club into a new era, had been made no less than five times. On each occasion just two people had turned up: J. E. Walmsley of the old committee, and – of course – Tommy Gibson. The *Times* correspondent therefore concluded that the dead horse was beyond flogging. But this wasn't quite the whole story.

The *Standard* was slightly more up-to-date. An article published on the same day as the *Times*' obit. note tells of a better attended, and potentially more fruitful, meeting, at which Walmsley was elected Secretary. In an attempt to generate some cash, it was decided that a trophy "value £30" belonging to the club could be put up for a town competition. This was probably the Blackburn Association Cup, won outright at the dawn of the club's existence.

Even the plan to sell off the family silver in this way, though, wasn't enough. The Football League dominated the scene now, in East Lancashire as elsewhere in the North and Midlands. With plum matches against the likes of Everton, Aston Villa, Wolves, and the double-winning Invincibles of Preston North End regularly on offer in the town, interest was bound to drift away from local competitions. No sponsor was willing to stick his neck out and back Olympic. Unable even to pay the rent for Hole-i'th'-Wall, and without enough players for a team, Blackburn Olympic finally gave up the ghost in September 1889. The ground was taken over by the football team of the Blackburn Railway Clerks. Just 11½ roller-coaster years had passed since that optimistic meeting of football enthusiasts in a back-street coffee shop.

Rival outfits weren't slow to profit from the club's dissolution. High-scoring forward Garner decamped to Park Road, and right half G. Frankland moved from Heywood to Witton, where he joined Richard Hothersall. Hunter's scouting and coaching skills were suddenly in demand at Rovers. The rest of the team either retired from active play, or returned to local amateur sides.

Thanks to various sources, we can trace the future careers of a fair number of that great team of 1883.

As already related, John Yates went via Accrington to play a couple of seasons in the Burnley first team, hitting a total of seven Football League goals. Whilst at Turf Moor he received an England cap, against Ireland in March 1889. Although he performed with distinction, scoring three goals in the 6-1 win, it turned out to be his only international appearance. He ended his playing career as an amateur, back at Accrington.

During his later years he was landlord of the *Brickmakers Arms*. The pub still exists, just along the road from the Burnley ground. Yates' house was on Mitella Street, and he died at home, from cancer, on the 1st June 1917, aged 55. His England cap was sold for £4,140 at a Sotheby's auction in May 2006. The buyer was a Burnley director, and the cap is to be part of the new club museum display at Turf Moor.

Jack Hunter became Assistant Trainer to Rovers, and for a number of years continued to scout for talented local young players. Then in 1897 began Hunter's last significant contribution to football: he was appointed coach to Cheshire side New Brighton Tower. The well-off backers of the Tower could afford to deploy a team of celebrated players of the day (many of them ex-internationals), and with Hunter at the wheel, it was small surprise when the side walked away with the Lancashire League title of 1897-8. Football League status followed, albeit for just three seasons.

The 1901 Blackburn Census records Hunter as "professional footballer and turner". He had ceased to be landlord of the *Mason's Arms* by 1894. When Hunter's

The Bricklayers' Arms, Burnley (2007), looking much as it did (minus the burglar alarm and satellite dish) when John Yates, ex-Olympian, was landlord over a century ago.

79

athletic days were behind him, his hobbies included the less energetic pursuits of fishing and shooting. His retirement was tragically short. He died of consumption on 9th April 1903, just fifty years old. At the funeral one week later, pallbearers included former fellow Sheffield and England player Willie Mosforth, and Rovers' Fergie Suter.

Jimmy Costley had signed for Everton in September 1888. He played for the Toffeemen for a season, scoring three goals in six appearances in their first ever League campaign. (But see Appendix II.) He returned to Blackburn in 1889, and was generally feted in the town. I am in possession of a letter written by Mrs. Muriel Cattow, Costley's granddaughter, in which it's stated that the former Olympian would be bought a drink wherever he went. His subsequent brush with alcoholism was brought to a healthy end when he was persuaded to join Elizabeth Lewis' Temperance Mission, and to sign the Pledge, with lasting success. He passed away in Blackburn in 1930, aged 68. The circumstances of his death are related in Appendix II.

Joe Beverley died as a result of an accident in the Albion Mill, Ewood, on the 15th May 1897. He was 39. Whilst he was repairing the mill engine the heavy cylinder top fell and struck him on his head, fracturing the skull in three places. He was rushed to the Infirmary, where he lay in a critical condition before dying from his injuries six days later.

The tracing of Jimmy Ward's post-football days presents problems. A James Ward was landlord of the *Isle of St Helena* beerhouse on Bottomgate, Blackburn in 1897. It's quite likely this was the ex-Olympic player, as Bottomgate is just round the corner from Harwood St., where Ward's first pub the *Prince of Wales* was situated. By 1900 the *Isle of St Helena* has another owner, and James Thomas Ward is nowhere to be found in the Blackburn Directory for that year, which is possibly the origin of the datum given by Farror and Lamming (see bibliography) that Ward died "prior to 1900". This would mean he died aged 34 or younger. Or does his disappearance from the Blackburn Directory simply mean that he moved elsewhere? An examination of the Deaths records for England for 1898 and 1899 reveals that in those years no James Thomas Ward in his early thirties died in Blackburn. A search of the Deaths column in the *Standard* between 1897-1900, and the relevant burial records for Blackburn Cemetery, also appears to draw a blank.

The apparent vanishing of Ward is surprising for someone who was a local sporting hero, and owner of what must have been a thriving commercial enterprise. It's hard to believe that he moved out of the borough which had been his spiritual home for virtually all his life. We then see the following entry in the 1909 and 1915 Directories:

        James Ward   vict.   *Wellington Inn*, 71 King St.

Was this the ex-Olympic player? The search for the truth continues!

Thomas Hacking remained in dentistry, his surgery on Preston New Rd. doing good business well into the next century. A humorous advertisement for his services is given in Appendix II.

By 1897 a William Astley has a stationer's shop on Whalley New Road. It is possible this is the ex-Olympian, since of course his brother Alf was in the same line, and still at 57 Church St., where the premises are now more grandly described as "bookseller, stationer, newsagent". The other possibility for Will Astley is a 1903 Directory entry which gives a William Thomas Astley, weaver, living at 95 Hancock Street. Alf, one-time Olympic player and club treasurer for many a year, died in Blackburn on 19th September 1927.

Tommy Gibson lived out his days quietly with his family on Troy St, then Tontine St, a couple of hundred yards from his place of birth. The 1900 Directory still gives his profession as "dresser", and later as "moulder". Further entries suggest that he died between 1906 and 1909.

Thomas Dewhurst remained in Blackburn, supporting the Rovers to a ripe old age. In his twilight years he supplied sports journalist Harry Kay with information on Olympic, which was used in the book *Things About Blackburn Rovers* (see bibliography). There is a photo of the elderly Dewhurst in the book.

Squire Albert Warburton applied his level-headed, dependable attitude to his business enterprises. By 1903 he is still landlord of the *Dog and Partridge* on James St., but by now he has long since abandoned his trade of plumbing, and supplements his hostelry income by buying and selling rabbits and poultry. By the outbreak of World War One he appears to have jacked in the licensing trade, being described simply as "poultry dealer".

So the team who, against all odds, opened the door to the long, long tradition of working class football teams with their dedicated, "professional" approach and modern methods of play, passed quietly into history.

[1] *The Liverpool Courier of May 14th 1889 gives the final Olympic line-up as:*
Hacking; Beverley, Ward; Astley, Hunter, Gibson; Yates, Parker, Costley, Dewhurst, Matthews.

The best-known photograph of Blackburn Olympic. This was the XI that lifted the FA Cup. Back; W Bramham (secretary), G Wilson, T Dewhurst, T Hacking, J Ward, A Astley (treasurer). Centre; J Costley, J Hunter, J Yates, W Astley. Front; T Gibson, SA Warburton, A Matthews.

APPENDIX I:

BLACKBURN OLYMPIC – THE FULL RESULTS 1878-1889

BA – Blackburn Association Challenge Cup
FA – FA Cup
FC – Football Combination
SF – semi-final
F – final
r – replay
ben – benefit match
ch – charity match

LC – Lancashire Association Cup
ELCC – East Lancs. Charity Cup
LU – Livesey United Cup
aet – after extra time
n/k – not known
w/o – walkover
og – own goal
aban – match abandoned

Some of the earliest matches may not have been recorded.
All venues are in the Blackburn district unless otherwise stated.
Occasionally, Olympic played two games on the same day.
Most attendance figures, where given, are estimates based on eyewitness reports. Scorers are given if known.

1877-78

Date		Opponents	Venue	Att	Score	Scorers
9/2/78		St John's	Oozebooth (H)		W 2-0	Askew, Beverley
16/2/78		Furthergate	Knuzden		W 2-0	J. Duckworth, Beverley
23/2/78		17th Lancers	Oozebooth (H)		W 2-0	
13/4/78	LU *F*	St Mark's	Cherry Tree Cricket Club	1,000	W 2-0	Beverley 2

1878-79

Date		Opponents	Venue	Att	Score	Scorers
12/10/78		Livesey United	Roe Lee (H)		W 1-0	Mackereth
26/10/78	BA	St Mark's	*n/k*		D 0-0	
2/11/78		Blackburn Law	Ravenswing		W 7-0	Beverley 2, Bradshaw 2, Hanson 2, Westwell
16/11/78		Enfield (Lancs.)	Enfield, Clayton-le-Moors		L 0-1	
23/11/78		Haslingden Grange	Rye Hill, Haslingden		W 2-1	
30/11/78	BA *r*	St Mark's	*n/k*		D 0-0	
7/12/78	BA 2*r*	St Mark's	*n/k*		W 3-0	
14/12/78	BA *SF*	Christ Church	*n/k*		W 2-0	
4/1/79		Darwen Grasshoppers	Roe Lee (H)		W 3-0	Westwell, Holden, Hanson
11/1/79		Livesey Utd.	Cherry Tree Cricket Club		W 1-0	
8/2/79	BA *F*	Queen's Own	Cattle Market Field		D 1-1	
15/2/79		Blackburn Rovers	Alexandra Meadows	1,000	W 3-1	
22/2/79	BA *Fr*	Queen's Own	Cattle Market Field		W 4-0	Westwell, Askew 2, Beverley
15/3/79	*ben*	Blackburn District XI	Cob Wall (H)		W 6-0	Beverley 4, Westwell, Mackereth
22/3/79	*ben*	Blackburn Rovers	Cob Wall (H)		D 0-0	
14/4/79		Darwen	Barley Bank, Darwen	3,200	L 2-8	Beverley, + 1
19/4/79		Darwen	Ewood		L 1-3	Beverley

82

1879-80

Date		Opponent	Venue	Attendance	Result	Scorers
27/9/79		Bolton Olympic	Hole-i'th'-Wall	1,000	W 4-1	Hanson, + 3
11/10/79		Darwen	Barley Bank, Darwen	2,000	L 2-4	Westwell, Gibson
18/10/79		Blackburn Rovers	Alexandra Meadows		L 1-3	
8/11/79	BA	Blackburn Park Road	Cattle Market Field		W 5-1	Mackereth, + 4
15/11/79		Accrington	Accrington Cricket Field, Thorneyholme Rd		W 2-1	Mackereth, Westwell
22/11/79		Turton	Hole-i'th'-Wall		L 0-2	
3/1/80		Clitheroe	Waterloo Field, Clitheroe		W 5-0	
10/1/80		Eagley	Hole-i'th'-Wall		2-2 (aban)	Thornber, + 1
17/1/80		Darwen	Hole-i'th'-Wall	2,000	W 2-1	Askew, Hanson
14/2/80		Accrington	Hole-i'th'-Wall		W 2-1	Hanson 2
21/2/80	BA	St Mark's	Hole-i'th'-Wall		W 3-0	og, Hanson, Thornber
28/2/80		Birkenhead	Hole-i'th'-Wall		W 6-1	Mackereth 2, Askew 2, Thornber 2
13/3/80		Blackburn Rovers	Alexandra Meadows	1,000	L 2-8	
20/3/80 (?)	BA SF	n/k	n/k		n/k	(Warburton's debut)
27/3/80		Blackburn Rovers	Hole-i'th'-Wall	2,000	W 1-0	
29/3/80		Sheffield Zulus	Hole-i'th'-Wall		W 2-0	
3/4/80	BA F	Perseverance	Cattle Market Field		D 2-2	Hanson, Gibson
10/4/80	BA Fr	Perseverance	Hole-i'th'-Wall	1,000	W 2-1	Beverley 2
17/4/80		Bolton Wanderers	Hole-i'th'-Wall	500	W 3-2	

The Hole-i'th'-Wall pub, 2007

83

1880-1

Date		Opponent	Venue	Att.	Result	Scorers
18/9/80		Witton	Hole-i'th'-Wall	500	W 8-0	(Yates' debut)
25/9/80		Church	Hole-i'th'-Wall	1,000	W 9-1	Gibson, Yates 2, Askew, Westwell 2, Hanson, +2
2/10/80		Liverpool Association	Stanley Park, Liverpool	100	W 12-0	
9/10/80		Wrexham	Hole-i'th'-Wall	3,000	W 4-1	Westwell, Gibson, Askew 2
16/10/80		Blackburn Rovers	Hole-i'th'-Wall	7,500	L 0-2	
23/10/80		Turton	Tower Street, Chapeltown, Bolton		L 3-5	Yates, Beverley, + 1
30/10/80	FA	Sheffield	Bramall Lane, Sheffield		L 4-5	Lever, *og*, Beverley, Yates
20/11/80	LC	Lower Chapel	Knowl Meadow, Darwen		D 3-3	Matthews *(on debut)*, Westwell, Lever
4/12/80	LC *r*	Lower Chapel	Hole-i'th'-Wall		L 1-2	Westwell
11/12/80		Blackburn Rovers	Alexandra Meadows	5,000	L 0-4	
27/12/80		Sheffield Wednesday	Hole-i'th'-Wall	2,000	L 1-3	
8/1/81		Accrington	Accrington Cricket Field, Thorneyholme Rd		L 1-4	
22/1/81		Accrington	Hole-i'th'-Wall	1,000	W 3-0	Beverley, Yates, Matthews
29/1/81		Druids	Hole-i'th'-Wall	1,000	W 3-0	A. Astley, Yates, Mackereth
12/2/81		Wrexham	Rhosddu Recreat'n. Ground, Wrexham		L 2-4	
14/2/81		*Druids*	*Wynnstay Park, Ruabon*		*(aban)*	
19/2/81		Turton	Hole-i'th'-Wall	1,000	W 2-1	Matthews, Beverley *(Hacking and Dewhurst debuts)*
1/3/81		Blackburn Rovers	Alexandra Meadows	2,000	L 2-3	Matthews, Askew
5/3/81		*Bolton Wanderers*	*Pike Lane, Bolton*	*1,000*	*1-1 (aban)*	*Beverley*
12/3/81		Liverpool Association	Hole-i'th'-Wall		W 7-0	Matthews 3, Beverley 3, Askew *(W. Astley's debut)*
19/3/81		Bootle	Hole-i'th'-Wall		W 3-0	Mackereth, Beverley 2
26/3/81		Enfield (Lancs.)	Hole-i'th'-Wall		W 5-3	Matthews, og, Beverley, Yates, + 1
2/4/81		Partick	Hole-i'th'-Wall	1,000	W 3-0	Westwell, Yates, Askew
9/4/81		Bolton Wanderers	Hole-i'th'-Wall	600	W 3-1	Yates, Beverley 2
16/4/81		Bootle	Marsh Lane, Liverpool		W 7-0	Westwell 3, Matthews, Mackereth, Yates, Warburton
18/4/81		Blackburn Park Road	Hole-i'th'-Wall	2,000	D 0-0	
22/4/81		Edinburgh Hibernians	Hole-i'th'-Wall	1,000	W 2-0	Askew, Beverley
30/4/81		Staveley	Hole-i'th'-Wall	2,000	W 7-1	Yates, J. Brown 4, Matthews 2
7/5/81	ben	Blackburn District XI	Hole-i'th'-Wall	2,000	L 1-2	Yates
14/5/81		Blackburn Park Road	Hole-i'th'-Wall	600	W 6-1	

1881-2

Date	Comp	Opponent	Venue	Att	Result	Scorers
10/9/81		Enfield (Lancs.)	Enfield, Clayton-le-Moors		W 9-2	Gibson, Yates 3, Beverley 2, Matthews, Wensley, +1
17/9/81		Witton	Pleasington, Witton		W 7-2	Matthews 2, Beverley 2, Wensley 2, Yates
24/9/81		Northwich Victoria	Hole-i'th'-Wall	1,000	W 9-0	Yates 5, Matthews 3, Wensley
1/10/81		Blackburn Park Road	Audley Park	2,000	W 4-1	Beverley, Yates, Mackereth, Hanson
8/10/81		Blackburn Rovers	Leamington Street	6,500	L 1-4	Wensley
15/10/81		Notts Forest	Trent Bridge, Nottingham		L 0-3	
22/10/81	LC	Astley Bridge	Astley Meadow, Bolton		W 5-1	Yates 3, Matthews, Beverley
29/10/81	FA	Darwen	Barley Bank, Darwen	6,000	L 1-3	Wensley
5/11/81		Wrexham	Hole-i'th'-Wall		W 8-0	Yates 2, A. Brown, Matthews 2, Marchbank, Gibson 2
12/11/81		Cowlairs	Hole-i'th'-Wall	2,000	W 3-1	Wensley 3
19/11/81		Bolton Olympic	Tonge, Bolton		W 1-0	Roberts
26/11/81		Partick Thistle	Hole-i'th'-Wall		D 4-4	Beverley 2, A. Brown, W. Astley
28/11/81	LC	Padiham	Hole-i'th'-Wall		W 3-1	W. Astley 2, Wensley
3/12/81		Macclesfield	Hole-i'th'-Wall		W 6-0	Marchbank, Yates 2, Matthews 2, Cunliffe
10/12/81		Lower Darwen	Hole-i'th'-Wall		D 1-1	
20/12/81		Accrington	Hole-i'th'-Wall	1,000	W 4-0	Yates 2, Marchbank 2
24/12/81		Thornliebank	Thornliebank, Glasgow		W 1-0	Beverley
26/12/81		Partick	Inchview, Glasgow		L 0-3	
31/12/81		Accrington	Accrington Cricket Field, Thorneyholme Rd		W 5-2	
2/1/82 am	LC	Enfield (Lancs.)	Hole-i'th'-Wall		D 1-1	
2/1/82 pm		Church	Pickup Street, Spring Hill, Accrington		W 4-1	
7/1/82	LC r	Enfield (Lancs.)	Enfield, Clayton-le-Moors		W 6-0	Yates, Beverley, Marchbank 2, Cunliffe, Roberts (Enfield's complaint about ineligible player upheld – see text)
14/1/82		Blackburn Rovers	Leamington Street	4,000	L 0-3	
21/1/82		Turton	Hole-i'th'-Wall	1,000	D 2-2	Wensley, Roberts
23/1/82		Queen's Park 2nd team	Hole-i'th'-Wall	3,000	W 2-0	J. Brown, Matthews
28/1/82	LC r	Enfield (Lancs.)	Hole-i'th'-Wall	1,500	W 3-1	Cunliffe, Yates 2
11/2/82		Northwich Victoria	Drill Field, Northwich		W 3-2	Cunliffe, Roberts, Matthews
18/2/82	LC	Great Lever	Woodside, Bolton		W 4-2	Cunliffe, Beverley 3
25/2/82	LC SF	Blackburn Rovers	Hole-i'th'-Wall	2,000	L 1-6	Matthews
27/2/82		Darwen	Hole-i'th'-Wall	2,000	W 4-3	Cunliffe, J. Brown 3
11/3/82		Blackburn Park Road	Hole-i'th'-Wall	1,500	L 3-4	Cunliffe 2, Yates
25/3/82		Kilmarnock Athletic	Hole-i'th'-Wall	1,500	L 0-4	
8/4/82		Macclesfield	Macclesfield Cricket Club, Victoria Road	1,800	W 7-1	
10/4/82		Notts Forest	Hole-i'th'-Wall	3,000	L 1-4	Marchbank
11/4/82		Edinburgh Hibernians	Hole-i'th'-Wall	3,000	D 2-2	J. Brown, Marchbank
15/4/82		Sheffield Heeley	Hole-i'th'-Wall	500	L 1-2	Marchbank
22/4/82		Darwen	Barley Bank, Darwen	2,000	D 4-4	Yates, W. Astley, Marchbank, Matthews *(Hunter's debut)*
29/4/82		Thornliebank	Hole-i'th'-Wall		D 0-0	*(Only 15 mins each way played, because of appalling weather conditions.)*

6/5/82		Turton	Tower Street, Chapeltown, Bolton		W 2-1	
13/5/82		Witton	Hole-i'th'-Wall	1,000	D 1-1	Beverley
15/5/82		Blackburn Rovers	Leamington Street	2,000	L 1-12	Hunter
9/6/82	ELCC SF	Accrington	Leamington Street		L 1-3	Hargreaves *(Olympic reinstated after protest)*
7/8/82	ELCC F	Blackburn Rovers	Ewood	2,000	W 5-2	Dewhurst 3, Beverley, Yates

The one that got away.... The Lancashire FA Cup, the only available trophy that Olympic never managed to win, despite a couple of close-run finals.

1882-3

Date	Comp	Opponent	Venue	Att	Result	Scorers
9/9/82		Great Harwood	Lidgett Ground, Great Harwood		W 7-1	
16/9/82		Blackburn Park Road	Hole-i'th'-Wall		W 11-0	Wensley 2, Matthews 2, Yates 2, Dewhurst 2, Cunliffe 2, og
18/9/82		Sheffield Wanderers	Hole-i'th'-Wall	1,500	W 6-2	Cunliffe, Yates 3, Dewhurst, Matthews
23/9/82		Witton	Hole-i'th'-Wall	4,000	W 4-1	Wensley 2, Dewhurst, Yates
30/9/82		Church	Hole-i'th'-Wall		W 4-1	Hunter 3, Dewhurst
7/10/82		Blackburn Rovers	Hole-i'th'-Wall	7,000	L 1-4	Matthews
14/10/82		Notts Forest	Trent Bridge, Nottingham	700	L 0-1	(Wilson's debut)
21/10/82	LC	Padiham Church	Moor Lane, Padiham		W 11-0	Wilson 5, + 6 (Olympic disqualified)
28/10/82		Turton	Tower Street, Chapeltown, Bolton		W 4-0	
4/11/82	FA	Accrington	Hole-i'th'-Wall	4,000	W 6-3	Wilson 4, Yates, Wensley
11/11/82		Birmingham Excelsior	Hole-i'th'-Wall	2,000	W 11-2	Wensley 2, Wilson 3, Yates 3, Dewhurst 3
18/11/82		Sheffield Heeley	Meersbrooke Park, Sheffield		D 0-0	
2/12/82		Great Lever	Woodside, Bolton	2,000	W 3-2	Wilson 3
9/12/82	FA	Lower Darwen	Hole-i'th'-Wall	1,500	W 8-1	Wilson 4, Wensley, Hunter, Matthews, Yates
16/12/82	FA	Darwen Ramblers	Hole-i'th'-Wall	200	W 8-0	Matthews 3, Dewhurst 2, Wilson, Wensley, Yates
23/12/82		Darwen	Barley Bank, Darwen	3,000	D 1-1	Dewhurst
25/12/82		Church	Pickup Street, Spring Hill, Accrington	2,000	W 5-2	Yates 4, Dewhurst
30/12/82		Partick Thistle	Jordanvale, Glasgow		W 2-0	Wilson 2
1/1/83		Kilmarnock Athletic	Holm Quarry, Kilmarnock		L 2-4	
6/1/83		Witton	Redlam Brow	1,500	L 1-2	Hunter
20/1/83		Blackburn Rovers	Leamington Street	3,000	L 0-3	(Costley's debut)
27/1/83		Great Lever	Hole-i'th'-Wall	200	D 0-0	
3/2/83	FA	Church	Pickup Street, Spring Hill, Accrington	5,000	W 2-0	Wilson, Dewhurst
17/2/83		Sheffield Heeley	Hole-i'th'-Wall		W 5-1	Wilson 2, Costley 2, Parker
24/2/83	FA	Druids	Hole-i'th'-Wall	4,000	W 4-1	Yates, Wilson 2, Hunter
3/3/83		Preston North End	Deepdale, Preston	2,000	W 4-1	Beverley, Dewhurst, Hunter, +1
12/3/83		Blackpool XI	Cow Gap Lane, Blackpool		L 0-1	
15/3/83		Blackpool XI	Cow Gap Lane, Blackpool		W 6-0	Costley, Dewhurst 2, Wilson 2, Matthews
17/3/83	FA SF	Old Carthusians	Whalley Range, Manchester	2,000	W 4-0	Dewhurst, Wilson, Matthews, Costley
31/3/83	FA F	Old Etonians	Kennington Oval, London	8,000	W 2-1 aet	Matthews, Costley
7/4/83		Partick Thistle	Hole-i'th'-Wall	1,000	W 3-0	Yates, Dewhurst, Wilson
14/4/83		Kilmarnock Athletic	Hole-i'th'-Wall	2,000	W 5-1	Costley 3, Dewhurst, Wilson
16/4/83		Darwen	Hole-i'th'-Wall	600	D 1-1	Matthews
21/4/83	ELCC SF	Accrington	Leamington Street	4,000	W 2-1	Costley, Dewhurst
28/4/83		Aston Villa	Perry Bar, Birmingham	6,000	L 1-5	Matthews
5/5/83		Blackburn Park Road	Audley	200	L 1-3	Wilson
12/5/83	ELCC F	Blackburn Rovers	Barley Bank, Darwen	3,000	L 2-6	Dewhurst 2

87

1883-4

Date		Opponent	Venue	Att.	Result	Scorers
27/8/83		Padiham	Hole-i'th'-Wall		W 4-0	
1/9/83		Dumbarton	Boghead, Dumbarton		L 1-6	Costley
8/9/83		Turton	Hole-i'th'-Wall	1,000	W 3-1	Dewhurst 2, Dearden
15/9/83		Darwen	Dewsbury, W. Yorks.	2,000	L 2-4	Hunter, Yates
22/9/83		Aston Villa	Hole-i'th'-Wall	2,500	W 2-0	Dewhurst, Costley
6/10/83		Blackburn Rovers	Leamington Street	5,000	L 1-3	Matthews
13/10/83		Aston Villa	Perry Bar, Birmingham	6,000	L 2-3	Matthews 2
15/10/83		Walsall Swifts	Chuckery Ground, Walsall		D 1-1	Costley
16/10/83	FA	Darwen Ramblers	Hole-i'th'-Wall	300	W 5-1	Matthews 2, Yates 2, Dewhurst
20/10/83		Accrington	Accrington Cricket Field, Thorneyholme Rd		W 3-1	Dewhurst, +2
27/10/83		Sheffield Heeley	Hole-i'th'-Wall	700	W 7-1	Dewhurst 2, Yates 3, Parker 2
27/10/83	LC	Newton Heath	North Road, Manchester		W 7-2	
3/11/83		Notts County	Trent Bridge, Nottingham	3,000	L 2-3	Dewhurst, Hunter
8/11/83	ch	Blackburn Rovers	Leamington Street	1,500	D 2-2	Matthews, Parker
10/11/83		Great Lever	Hole-i'th'-Wall	1,500	W 6-2	Parker, Yates 2, Matthews 2, Dewhurst
17/11/83		Sheffield Heeley	Meersbrooke Park, Sheffield	1,000	D 1-1	Birtwistle
22/11/83		Oxford University	Merton College, Oxford		W 4-2	Yates, Dewhurst, Parker, Costley
24/11/83		Church	Hole-i'th'-Wall	1,500	W 4-2	Parker 2, Yates, +1
1/12/83	FA	Darwen	Barley Bank, Darwen	3,000	W 2-1 aet	Duckworth, Matthews
8/12/83		Witton	Hole-i'th'-Wall	100	L 0-1	
15/12/83		Edinburgh University	Powderhall, Edinburgh		W 1-0	Costley
15/12/83	LC	Darwen Ramblers	Hole-i'th'-Wall	150	W 4-0	Birtwistle 3, Whitehead
22/12/83		Wednesbury Town	Hole-i'th'-Wall	1,000	W 5-2	Costley 2, Astley 2, Yates
22/12/83	LC	Southport	Scarisbrick New Road, Southport		W 2-0	
24/12/83		Walsall Swifts	Hole-i'th'-Wall	1,000	D 0-0	
25/12/83		Church	Pickup Street, Spring Hill, Accrington	2,500	W 2-0	Matthews, Yates
29/12/83		Blackburn Rovers	Hole-i'th'-Wall	6,000	L 2-4	Yates, Parker
31/12/83		St Bernard's, Edinburgh	Hole-i'th'-Wall	200	D 1-1	Costley
1/1/84		Blackburn Park Road	Audley Hall		W 4-1	Harrison, Yates, Parker, og
5/1/84		Darwen	Hole-i'th'-Wall	2,000	W 8-0	Parker 3, Dewhurst 2, Costley, Yates, og
19/1/84	FA	Old Wykehamists	Hole-i'th'-Wall	4,000	W 6-0	Dewhurst 2, Yates, Costley, og, +1
26/1/84		*Burnley*	*Turf Moor, Burnley*	*3,000*	*0-3*	*(aban)*
2/2/84	LC	Turton	Hole-i'th'-Wall	500	W 8-0	Matthews, Parker 3, Yates 2, Hunter, Birtwistle
4/2/84	ch	Blackburn and District	Hole-i'th'-Wall	3,000	W 13-3	Costley 6, Dewhurst, Parker 2, Matthews 2, Gibson, og
9/2/84	FA	Northwich Victoria	Hole-i'th'-Wall	4,000	W 9-1	Yates 2, Duckworth, Parker 2, Matthews 2, Hunter, +1
16/2/84	LC	Darwen	Hole-i'th'-Wall	2,000	W 3-1	Yates 2, Dewhurst
23/2/84		Dumbarton	Hole-i'th'-Wall	6,000	W 4-3	Dewhurst 2, Matthews, Parker
1/3/84	FA SF	Queen's Park, Glasgow	Trent Bridge, Nottingham	16,000	L 0-4	
8/3/84		Bolton Association	Hole-i'th'-Wall	500	W 12-2	Parker 3, Costley, Dewhurst 3, Matthews 4, Yates
10/3/84		Bolton Wanderers	Pikes Lane, Bolton	5,000	W 3-2	Yates, J. Brown 2
15/3/84		Great Lever	Woodside, Bolton	6,000	D 2-2	Birtwistle, Dewhurst

22/3/84	LC F	Blackburn Rovers	Deepdale, Preston	10,000	D 1-1	Birtwistle
29/3/84		Accrington	Hole-i'th'-Wall		W 5-1	Dewhurst 2, Parker, Hunter, +1
5/4/84		Halliwell	Hole-i'th'-Wall	1,250	D 3-3	Yates 2, Hunter
12/4/84		Edinburgh Hibernians	Hole-i'th'-Wall	800	W 4-2	Parker, Hunter, Dewhurst 2
19/4/84	LC Fr	Blackburn Rovers	Barley Bank, Darwen	8,000	L 1-2	Parker
26/4/84		Darwen	Barley Bank, Darwen	500	D 1-1	Parker
3/5/84	ELCC SF	Darwen	Barley Bank, Darwen	2,000	D 0-0	
5/5/84		Halliwell	Bennett's Lane, Halliwell, Bolton		W 5-2	Parker 2, Costley, Dewhurst, Sanderson
10/5/84		Blackburn Park Road	Audley Hall	2,000	L 4-6	Costley, Parker, Matthews, Yates
12/5/84	ELCC SFr	Darwen	Hole-i'th'-Wall	3,000	L 0-1	
17/5/84		Great Lever	Woodside, Bolton		L 0-1	

Warburton's runner's-up medal from the East Lancashire Charity Cup final of 1882-83. Blackburn Rovers beat Olympic 6-2.

89

1884-5

Date		Opponent	Venue	Attendance	Result	Scorers
6/9/84		Wolverhampton Wanderers	Dudley Road, Wolverhampton	3,500	D 2-2	
13/9/84		Eagley	Hole-i'th'-Wall		W 19-0	Parker 3, Costley 2, Yates 2, Matthews 2, Hunter, Dewhurst 2, +7
17/9/84	FA	Oswaldtwistle Rovers	Roe Greave Rd., Oswaldtwistle		W 12-0	Whitehead 3, Parker 4, Dewhurst 3, Costley, Hunter
20/9/84		Grimsby Town	Clee Park, Grimsby		W 9-0	Matthews 2, Slater, Whitehead, Ward, Costley, +3
27/9/84		Derby County	Derbyshire Cricket Ground	2,000	W 4-3	Dewhurst, + 3
4/10/84	LC	Leigh	Hole-i'th'-Wall	1,500	W 18-0	Southworth 4, Dewhurst 6, Whitehead 3, Parker, Costley, Hacking, Slater, og
11/10/84	ben	Notts County	Hole-i'th'-Wall	4,000	W 3-0	Whitehead, Duckworth, Matthews
18/10/84		Aston Villa	Perry Bar, Birmingham	5,000	L 0-4	
25/10/84		Sheffield Heeley	Hole-i'th'-Wall	1,500	W 8-1	Dewhurst 3, Southworth, Whitehead, Costley, +2
1/11/84		Port Vale	Hole-i'th'-Wall	1,000	W 6-1	Whitehead 3, Costley, Parker, +1
8/11/84		Preston North End	Hole-i'th'-Wall	10,000	L 0-2	
10/11/84		Stoke	Victoria Ground, Stoke	4,000	W 3-1	
15/11/84		Birmingham St George's	Hole-i'th'-Wall	1,000	W 3-1	Costley 2, Parker
22/11/84	LC	Blackpool South Shore	Cow Gap Lane, Blackpool	3,000	W 3-1	Parker, Costley, Whitehead
29/11/84		Sheffield Wednesday	Hole-i'th'-Wall	500	W 12-0	Gibson, Parker 4, Gregson, Dewhurst 3, Costley, Whitehead 2
6/12/84	FA	Blackburn Rovers	Leamington Street	11,500	L 2-3	Parker, + 1
8/12/84		Burnley	Hole-i'th'-Wall		L 1-2	
15/12/84		Burnley	Turf Moor, Burnley	2,000	W 3-2	Whitehead, Dewhurst, Yates
17/12/84		Corinthians	Hole-i'th'-Wall	1,200	D 4-4	Costley, Goodall Yates, +1
20/12/84		Bolton Wanderers	Hole-i'th'-Wall	2,000	W 2-1	Costley, Dewhurst
25/12/84		Church	Pickup Street, Spring Hill, Accrington		L 1-2	Dewhurst
27/12/84		Aston Villa	Hole-i'th'-Wall	2,500	W 5-1	Dewhurst, Parker, Whitehead 2, Costley
3/1/85		Preston North End	Deepdale, Preston	10,000	W 3-1	Dewhurst 2, Costley
5/1/85		Casuals	Hole-i'th'-Wall	1,000	W 2-0	Costley, Whitehead
10/1/85		Great Lever	Hole-i'th'-Wall	2,000	L 0-2	
17/1/85		Notts County	Trent Bridge, Nottingham	6,000	D 1-1	Whitehead
24/1/85		Blackburn Rovers	Hole'-i'th'-Wall	5,000	D 4-4	Dewhurst 3, Yates
31/1/85		Darwen	Barley Bank, Darwen	1,000	W 3-2	Whitehead, Dewhurst 2
7/2/85	LC	Oswaldtwistle Rovers	Roe Greave Road, Oswaldtwistle	1,000	W 5-0	Dewhurst 3, Costley, og
14/2/85		Preston North End	Deepdale, Preston	7,000	L 0-1	
21/2/85		Clitheroe	Hole-i'th'-Wall		D 4-4	Costley, Dewhurst, +2
23/2/85	ben	Blackburn Rovers	Leamington Street	1,000	W 4-1	Costley 2, Yates 2
28/2/85		Bolton Wanderers	Pikes Lane, Bolton	6,000	L 0-6	
7/3/85	LC SF	Church	Pikes Lane, Bolton	2,500	W 4-3	Costley 3, Parker
14/3/85	ELCC SF	Darwen	Barley Bank, Darwen	3,500	W 1-0	Costley
16/3/85		Great Lever	Hole-i'th'-Wall	1,000	W 6-3	Parker 2, Dewhurst, Whitehead, Yates, Beverley
21/3/85		Great Lever	Woodside, Bolton	2,000	L 1-3	Yates
28/3/85		Blackburn Rovers	Leamington Street	4,000	D 2-2	Dewhurst, Costley
3/4/85		Renton	Hole-i'th'-Wall	1,000	W 3-1	Yates 2, Costley
4/4/85		Burnley	Hole-i'th'-Wall	3,000	D 2-2	Costley, Parker

6/4/85		Everton	Anfield, Liverpool	3,000	W 3-0	Dewhurst 2, Yates
7/4/85		Port Vale	Moorland Road, Burslem	1,500	W 2-1	
11/4/85		Darwen	Hole-i'th'-Wall	1,500	L 1-2	Dewhurst
18/4/85	LCF	Blackburn Rovers	Deepdale, Preston	7,000	L 1-2	Slater
25/4/85		Burnley	Turf Moor, Burnley	4,500	D 1-1	
2/5/85	ELCCF	Accrington	Leamington Street	6,000	L 0-4	
9/5/85		Padiham	Hole-i'th'-Wall	500	L 0-1	
16/5/85		Blackburn Rovers	Hole-i'th'-Wall	2,000	L 0-3	
30/5/85	ch	Alston College	Alston College, Longridge	1,000	W 4-2	
5/6/85	ben	Burnley	Turf Moor, Burnley	2,000	L 1-2	Whitehead
25/7/85		Accrington	Hole-i'th'-Wall	500	D 0-0	

In 1908, just 25 years after his two FA Cup finals against Blackburn clubs, Lord Kinnaird came to the Lancashire town to lay this stone. It was part of the entrance to the YMCA building, situated at the corner of Tontine Street and what was then the lower end of Limbrick. The building is now the Sir Charles Napier Inn.

91

1885-6

Date	Comp	Opponent	Venue	Att	Result	Scorers
22/8/85		Bootle	Hawthorne Road, Liverpool	800	D 2-2	Slater, Costley
29/8/85		Witton	Hole-i'th'-Wall	300	L 0-1	
5/9/85		Aston Villa	Perry Bar, Birmingham		W 2-1	Costley, Bell
12/9/85		Everton	Anfield, Liverpool	3,000	W 3-2	Costley, Ward, og
19/9/85		Blackburn Rovers	Hole-i'th'-Wall	2,000	L 1-3	Costley
26/9/85		Preston North End	Deepdale, Preston	6,500	L 1-3	Costley
28/9/85		Blackpool South Shore	Cow Gap Lane, Blackpool		W 4-2	Ward 2, Coupe 2
3/10/85	LC	Great Harwood	Hole-i'th'-Wall		W 5-0	
3/10/85		Blackburn Park Road	Audley Hall	500	L 2-3	Ward, Slater
10/10/85		West Bromwich Albion	Hole-i'th'-Wall	1,000	L 2-3	Ward, Scott
12/10/85		Preston North End	Hole-i'th'-Wall	3,000	L 2-5	Hunter, Fecitt
17/10/85		Accrington	Hole-i'th'-Wall	3,000	L 3-4	Beverley 2, Costley
19/10/85		Bolton Wanderers	Pikes Lane, Bolton	2,000	L 0-7	
31/10/85	FA	Church	Hole-i'th'-Wall	1,500	W 4-2	Yates, Hunter, Costley, Beverley (result declared void – see text)
2/11/85		Great Lever	Hole-i'th'-Wall	1,000	D 1-1	og
7/11/85		Notts County	Trent Bridge, Nottingham	4,000	L 0-4	
9/11/85		Port Vale	Moorland Road, Burslem		L 2-4	Costley, Hunter
14/11/85		Halliwell	Hole-i'th'-Wall		L 1-5	Costley
14/11/85		Colne	Langroyd, Colne		L 0-2	
21/11/85	FA	Church	Pickup Street, Spring Hill, Accrington	2,000	D 2-2	Dewhurst, Beverley
28/11/85	FA r	Church	Hole-i'th'-Wall		L 1-3	Dewhurst
30/11/85		Great Lever	Woodside, Bolton		L 0-2	
5/12/85	LC	Bolton Wanderers	Pikes Lane, Bolton	2,000	L 2-11	Bell, Yates
12/12/85		Blackburn Rovers	Leamington Street	1,500	W 4-3	Costley 2, + 2
19/12/85		Derby County	Hole-i'th'-Wall	1,500	W 3-0	Costley, Bell, + 1
21/12/85		Corinthians	Hole-i'th'-Wall	2,000	L 1-4	Dewhurst
25/12/85		Hurst	Hole-i'th'-Wall		W 3-1	
26/12/85		West Bromwich Albion	Stoney Lane, West Bromwich	5,000	L 0-4	
1/1/86		Middlesbrough	Linthorpe Rd., Middlesbrough	6,000	D 2-2	Bell, + 1
2/1/86		Blackburn Rovers	Leamington Street	2,000	L 0-2	
9/1/86		Darwen	Hole-i'th'-Wall	1,000	W 1-0	Dewhurst
16/1/86		Darwen Old Wanderers	Hole-i'th'-Wall	100	W 3-0	Dewhurst 3
18/1/86		Burnley	Turf Moor, Burnley	1,000	L 0-2	
23/1/86		Preston North End	Hole-i'th'-Wall	3,000	L 2-4	Whitehead, Dean
30/1/86		Padiham	Wyre Street, Padiham	1,000	L 2-5	
1/2/86		Burnley	Hole-i'th'-Wall	600	L 0-1	
6/2/86		Notts County	Hole-i'th'-Wall	3,000	D 0-0	
8/2/86		Wigan	Wigan Cricket Club, Frog Lane	600	W 3-1	
13/2/86		Aston Villa	Hole-i'th'-Wall	2,000	W 1-0	Costley
20/2/86		Middlesbrough	Linthorpe Rd., Middlesbrough		D 1-1	
27/2/86		Church	Hole-i'th'-Wall	1,000	D 1-1	Scott
6/3/86		Church	Pickup Street, Spring Hill, Accrington		L 1-3	Dean
13/3/86		Blackpool South Shore	Hole-i'th'-Wall	2,500	W 3-2	Townley 2, og
20/3/86		Burnley	Hole-i'th'-Wall	500	L 2-3	Dewhurst 2

Date		Opponent	Venue	Attendance	Result	Scorers
27/3/86		Derby County	County Cricket Ground, Derby	1,500	L 1-2	Whitehead
3/4/86		Burnley	Turf Moor, Burnley	4,000	L 0-3	
10/4/86		Darwen	Barley Bank. Darwen	1,500	W 2-0	Whitehead, + 1
17/4/86		Witton	Redlam Brow	1,000	W 2-1	Dewhurst, + 1
23/4/86		Padiham	Hole-i'th'-Wall	1,500	D 1-1	
24/4/86		Blackburn Park Road	Hole-i'th'-Wall		L 1-2	Whitehead
26/4/86		Grimsby Town	Clee Park, Grimsby		L 2-4	Smith 2
1/5/86		Accrington	Accrington Cricket Field, Thorneyholme Rd		L 1-3	
8/5/86		Blackburn Park Road	Audley Hall	1,000	W 3-1	Smith 2, Holden
8/5/86		Everton	Anfield, Liverpool	2,000	W 4-1	Dewhurst 4
15/5/86		Great Lever	Hole-i'th'-Wall	350	W 2-1	Costley 2
17/5/86	ELCC SF	Blackburn Rovers	Hole-i'th'-Wall	2,000	L 0-2	
29/5/86		Witton	Redlam Brow	1,200	W 1-0	

1886-7

Date		Opponent	Venue	Attendance	Result	Scorers
7/8/86		Fleetwood Rangers	Copse Ground, Station Rd, Fleetw'd	1,000	L 2-4	
14/8/86		Darwen Old Wanderers	Pot House, Darwen		L 0-2	
21/8/86		Halliwell	Bennett's Lane, Halliwell, Bolton	1,000	L 0-2	
28/8/86		Bootle	Hawthorne Road, Liverpool		L 2-5	Holden 2
4/9/86		Wigan A.F.C.	Honeysuckle Field, Poolstock, Wigan		W 4-1	
11/9/86		Great Lever	Woodside, Bolton	100	W 2-0	Parker, Holden
18/9/86		Blackburn Rovers	Hole-i'th'-Wall	2,000	L 0-3	
25/9/86		Church	Pickup St, Spring Hill, Accrington	700	L 1-6	
2/10/86		Denton	Chapel Green, Denton, Manchester	1,000	W 9-1	J. Hothersall 5, R. Hothersall 2, +2
9/10/86	LC	Witton	Redlam Brow	1,000	L 0-3	
16/10/86		Darwen	Barley Bank, Darwen	1,250	L 1-7	Parker
23/10/86	FA	Partick Thistle	Hole-i'th'-Wall	1,500	L 1-3	Hunter
25/10/86		Notts County	Hole-i'th'-Wall	600	W 4-3	J. Hothersall 2, Carlisle, +1
30/10/86		Burnley	Hole-i'th'-Wall		L 0-4	
1/11/86		Burnley	Turf Moor, Burnley	700	L 0-4	
6/11/86		Newton Heath	North Road, Manchester	3,500	L 2-4	Ratcliffe 2
13/11/86		Blackburn Rovers	Hole-i'th'-Wall	1,750	D 1-1	Garner
27/11/86		Darwen	Barley Bank, Darwn	2,000	W 3-1	Parker, J. Hothersall, +1
4/12/86		Bootle	Hawthorne Road, Liverpool	2,000	L 1-2	J. Hothersall
11/12/86		Blackburn Park Road	Audley Hall	500	W 1-0	Garner
18/12/86		Witton	Redlam Brow		D 2-2	Parker 2
20/12/86	ch	Preston North End	Deepdale, Preston	1,000	D 3-3	Carlisle 2, +1
1/1/87		Bury	Gigg Lane, Bury	1,000	W 5-2	Garner, Parker 2, og, +1
8/1/87		Preston North End	Hole-i'th'-Wall	1,250	L 0-6	
15/1/87		Blackburn Park Road	Hole-i'th'-Wall		L 1-3	R. Hothersall
22/1/87		Bolton Wanderers	Pikes Lane, Bolton	350	L 0-6	
29/1/87		Darwen	Hole-i'th'-Wall	2,000	L 0-6	
5/2/87		Preston North End	Deepdale, Preston	3,000	L 2-7	J. Hothersall, Parker
12/2/87		Church	Hole-i'th'-Wall		L 0-2	
19/2/87		Macclesfield	Macclesfield Cricket Club, Victoria Road	2,000	L 2-3	Rushton 2
26/2/87		Stoke Swifts	Victoria Ground, Stoke	1,500	D 1-1	J. Hothersall
5/3/87		Witton	Redlam Brow		W 6-1	Carlisle 2, Jack Southworth, og, +2
12/3/87		Westhoughton	Wigan Road, Westhoughton		W 4-2	
26/3/87		Newton Heath	Hole-i'th'-Wall		W 3-0	Carlisle, +2
2/4/87		Witton	Hole-i'th'-Wall		W 4-2	
4/4/87		Bolton Wanderers	Hole-i'th'-Wall		L 1-2	Garner
9/4/87		Church	Pickup St, Spring Hill, Accrington	1,000	D 0-0	
11/4/87		Middlesbrough	Linthorpe Rd., Middlesbrough	5,000	L 1-2	Gill
16/4/87		Burnley	Turf Moor, Burnley	1,000	W 3-2	Jack Southworth, Carlisle, +1
23/4/87		Church	Hole-i'th'-Wall	1,000	W 2-1	R. Chadwick, Carlisle
25/4/87		Everton	Anfield, Liverpool	3,000	L 0-2	
30/4/87		Darwen	Barley Bank, Darwen		W 2-1	
2/5/87		Blackburn Park Road	Audley Hall		L 1-3	
14/5/87	ELCC SF	Accrington	Hole-i'th'-Wall		L 0-3	

94

1887-8

Date		Opponent	Venue	Att.	Result	Scorers
3/9/87		Heaton Park	Heaton Park, Manchester		W 6-0	Fielden 3, J. Hothersall, Carlisle, og
10/9/87		Chester	Faulkner Street, Chester		W 1-0	J. Hothersall
17/9/87		Bootle	Hawthorne Road, Liverpool	4,000	W 2-1	Carlisle, Costley
24/9/87		Blackburn Rovers	Leamington Street	5,000	L 2-3	Carlisle, Costley
1/10/87	LC	Darwen	Barley Bank, Darwn		L 2-5	Garner, +1
3/10/87		Halliwell	Hole-i'th'-Wall		L 1-3	Costley
8/10/87		Burnley	Turf Moor, Burnley		L 0-7	
15/10/87		Blackburn Park Rd	Audley Hall		W 4-2	Costley, Carlisle 3
22/10/87		Macclesfield	Macclesfield Cricket Club, Victoria Road		W 6-3	
29/10/87	ben	Blackpool South Shore	Cow Gap Lane, Blackpool		W 3-0	Fielden, Garner, Carlisle
5/11/87	FA	Blackburn Rovers	Leamington Street	5,000	L 1-5	J. Hothersall
12/11/87		Darwen	Hole-i'th'-Wall		D 2-2	Costley, Garner
14/11/87		Aston Villa	Hole-i'th'-Wall		L 1-2	Hunter
19/11/87		Blackburn Park Rd	Hole-i'th'-Wall	100	L 1-6	Cronshaw
26/11/87		Padiham	Wyre Street, Padiham		D 1-1	J. Hothersall
3/12/87		Accrington	Accrington Cricket Field, Thorneyholme Rd		L 1-6	Carlisle
17/12/87		Blackburn Rovers	Leamington Street		W 2-1	Chambers, +1
24/12/87		Darwen	Barley Bank, Darwn		L 0-4	
26/12/87		Cliftonville	Old Park Avenue, Belfast	4,000	W 2-1	Carlisle, +1
27/12/87		Fleetwood Rangers	Copse Ground, Station Road, Fleetwood		W 2-1	
31/12/87		London Caledonians	Leyton, Essex	500	L 1-3	Dewhurst
2/1/88		Bury	Gigg Lane, Bury	1,500	W 3-2	J. Hothersall, Costley, Cronshaw
14/1/88		Church	Pickup St, Spring Hill, Accrington		W 1-0	Garner
21/1/88		Leigh	Railway Road, Leigh	1,000	W 6-3	Smithson, Costley 2, J. Hothersall 2, Carlisle
28/1/88		Witton	Hole-i'th'-Wall	3,000	L 3-4	Garner, Costley 2
30/1/88		Aston Villa	Perry Bar, Birmingham		L 0-7	
4/2/88		Church	Hole-i'th'-Wall		W 4-2	Carlisle, Chadwick, J. Hothersall, Garner
11/2/88		Blackburn Rovers	Hole-i'th'-Wall		L 2-8	J. Hothersall, Fielden
14/2/88		Sunderland	Newcastle Road, Sunderland		W 3-1	
18/2/88		Blackburn Park Rd	Audley Hall		L 1-3	Dewhurst
25/2/88		Macclesfield	Hole-i'th'-Wall		W 3-0	J. Hothersall, Garner, +1
3/3/88		Newton Heath	North Road, Manchester		W 2-1	Dewhurst, +1
10/3/88		Darwen	Barley Bank, Darwn		L 0-6	
17/3/88		Church	Pickup St, Spring Hill, Accrington		D 2-2	Fielden 2
24/3/88		Gorton Villa	Abbey Hey, Gorton, Manchester		W 4-0	Garner 2, Fielden, Carlisle
31/3/88		Sunderland	Newcastle Road, Sunderland		L 1-4	
7/4/88		Blackburn Park Rd	Audley Hall		D 2-2	Costley, Frankland
14/4/88		Witton	Redlam Brow		L 1-4	og
28/4/88		Earlestown	Newton Common, Earlestown		W 4-3	J. Hothersall 2, Costley, Garner
5/5/88		Everton	Anfield, Liverpool	5,000	L 1-3	Dickson
19/5/88	ELCC SF	Blackburn Rovers	Hole-i'th'-Wall		L 2-5	Carlisle, J. Hothersall

1888-9

Date		Opponent	Venue	Attendance	Result	Scorers
1/9/88		Darwen	Hole-i'th'-Wall		D 1-1	J. Hothersall
3/9/88		Everton	Anfield, Liverpool	3,000	W 2-1	Heyes 2
8/9/88		Blackburn Park Road	Audley Hall	2,000	D 2-2	Dickson 2
15/9/88		Bury	Gigg Lane, Bury	1,500	W 5-2	Conway, Heyes 2, Carlisle, Strachan
22/9/88		Belfast Distillery	Broadway, Belfast	2,000	W 3-1	J. Hothersall 2, Carlisle
29/9/88	LC	Higher Walton	Hole-i'th'-Wall	300	L 1-2	Parker
6/10/88		Darwen	Barley Bank		L 1-6	Slater
-	FA	*Fleetwood Rangers*			w/o	
13/10/88		West Manchester	Old Trafford, Manchester		D 2-2	
20/10/88		Witton	Redlam Brow		D 2-2	J. Hothersall, Dickson
27/10/88	FA	Oswaldtwistle Rovers	Hole-i'th'-Wall		L 1-3	
3/11/88		Ulster	Ulster Cricket Club, Ballynafeigh, Belfast		W 3-0	Reid, Cooke, Riley
10/11/88	FC	Bootle	Hawthorne Road, Liverpool		L 0-4	
17/11/88		Southport Central	Sussex Road Sports Ground, Southport	1,000	L 1-5	J. Hothersall
24/11/88		Notts Forest	Gregory Ground, Lenton, Nottingham		W 3-2	Heyes, Dickson, + 1
1/12/88		Witton	Redlam Brow		L 2-4	
3/12/88		Blackburn Rovers	Leamington Street		L 2-4	
8/12/88		Royton	Thorp Road, Royton		L 1-4	Dodd
15/12/88	FC	Blackpool South Shore	Cow Gap Lane, Blackpool	1,500	L 0-3	
22/12/88		Blackburn Park Road	Hole-i'th'-Wall		W 2-1	
29/12/88	FC	Blackpool South Shore	Hole-i'th'-Wall	200	D 1-1	Heyes
5/1/89		Heywood Central	Phoenix Pleasure Grounds, Heywood		W 1-0	
19/1/89		Darwen	Barley Bank, Darwen		L 1-4	Prescott
11/2/89	ben	Blackburn Rovers	Leamington Street		L 1-6	
16/2/89		Hurst	Hurst Cross, Ashton-under-Lyne		L 2-3	Roberts, Kilner
23/2/89	FC	Bootle	Hawthorne Road, Liverpool		L 0-6	
2/3/89		Clitheroe	Waterloo Field, Clitheroe		L 0-4	
30/3/89		Irwell Springs	Broad Clough, Bacup		L 2-4	
6/4/89		Newton Heath Central	Newton Heath, Manchester		L 0-2	
12/4/89		Skelmersdale Recreation	Sandy Lane, Skelmersdale		L 1-2	
13/4/89		Farnworth Standard	Farnworth, Bolton		L 1-2	
27/4/89		Ramsbottom	"New ground", Ramsbottom, Lancs		L 4-5	
8/5/89		Blackburn Park Road	Audley Hall	500	D 2-2	
11/5/89		King's Own Regiment, Dublin	Hole-i'th'-Wall		W 1-0	
13/5/89		Everton	Anfield, Liverpool		L 1-6	Parker

Notes on the compilation of the above.

Some details of early football matches can prove chronically difficult to track down. Contemporary newspaper reports, if they exist at all, can be sketchy or contradictory, and the appearance of details such as crowd numbers or scorers are often dependent on the writer's whim or powers of observation. So sometimes, frustratingly, all you get is: "several thousand spectators", " a good sized crowd", "a goal from a scrimmage", or " the ball was rushed through".

Designated football reporters, at least in the earliest years, were few and far between. Accounts of games were often penned by a supporter who felt inspired enough by the result to jot something down and drop it off at the newspaper offices. The two provisos to these unsolicited contributions were that the writer's name and address had to be given, and that the more obviously biased accounts were rejected.

This extract from the football section (such as it was back then) of the *Blackburn Times* highlights the potential pitfalls for future researchers:

> We have occasional complaints as to reports where goals are disputed.
> We cannot make room for controversy on these matters, and must trust to our
> correspondents' good faith in supplying accurate details.
> Oct. 28th, 1878

So sometimes there are inaccuracies in, or discrepancies between, reports. Worse, sometimes the match isn't even mentioned in the local newspaper. This was either because there wasn't enough space in that particular issue, or because the game resulted in a defeat, thus dissipating the creative energies of the supporter who usually wrote the piece!

A case in point: it's well known that Warburton played his first game for Olympic in the Blackburn Association Challenge Cup semi-final in March 1880. But because of blanket newspaper coverage of the concurrent General Election, in that month football had to take a back seat, as it were, and further details of this vital game – even the opposition – have (so far) not come to light.

Another poser from the same season: according to the *Blackburn Times* Olympic defeated their Bolton namesakes 4-1 in the first round of the Lancashire Association Cup in September 1879. Yet in the official *History of the Lancashire Football Association* the Blackburn team do not appear in that season's first round draw. (Bolton Olympic were paired with Lynwood from Darwen.) Moreover, in a "Local News" snippet a year later in September 1880, we see the following: "The club ... have also joined the Lancashire Football Association". So what was the status of the previous year's "ghost" match with Bolton Olympic? Was it really a friendly, and had the writer got it wrong in presenting it as a Lancashire Cup match? Given the evidence, this is the conclusion I have come to.

Further information on Olympic's games is often available from sources other than Blackburn. Especially rich in detail are contemporary newspapers from Preston, Accrington, Sheffield, Liverpool, Nottingham, as well as the *Staffordshire Sentinel*, and Bolton's marvellous *Football Field*. A full list of such publications consulted is given in the Bibliography. Those people who gave generously of their time and knowledge, to help with the myriad awkward bits of research that helped to complete the above jigsaw, are mentioned in the Acknowledgements section.

In order to distinguish between two brothers playing at the same time, if no first name or initial is given when just one of them is playing, I think I'm following the convention of the time by assuming that the bare surname means the elder of the two. Thus "J. Hothersall" takes precedence over his younger brother "R. Hothersall" in the list of scorers. With the Southworths, there is less possibility of ambiguity, firstly because James or Jack/John is usually specified in the newspaper report, and secondly because Jack/John was the forward, and James the full back, so more than likely it was Jack/John who got his name on the scoresheet.

There are some discrepancies in the spelling of names (Costley/Crossley is the famous example). I have generally opted for what appears to be the most prevalent version, so "Carlisle", "Fielden", "Dickson", "Garner" and "Heyes" have got the vote. Again, I await possible corrections.

The early mist more or less disperses once the new decade of the 1880s gets into its stride. We see the emergence of specialist reporters, and whole newspaper columns devoted solely to football analysis and gossip. The football "extra", the match programme, and the specialist periodical and annual, catering to the increasingly literate populace, will shortly make an appearance. The soccer industry, soon to be a gargantuan money-spinner, is up and running.

I welcome additions, corrections, or comments, on any part of the book. It would be helpful if you could mention your own sources as and when necessary. My e-mail address is gphyth@btinternet.com

Location of football pitches in Blackburn in the 1880s

(See accompanying map)

Oozebooth (sometimes spelt Ouzebooth)

Olympic's first ever pitch. This is not to be confused with Oozehead Park, where the Rovers played their first ever games (see below). Oozebooth was an area of farmland that used to be situated near the summit of Shear Brow, between St James' Church and the old farmhouse, a couple of hundred yards to the east of, and across the path from, Hole-i'th'-Wall. It was also the original home terrain of Blackburn Cricket Club.

Oozehead Park

Near to St Silas' School, off Preston New Road. This was Rovers' first ever home pitch, on a terrain which was "rough", and which had "a pit in the centre being covered with planks and sods".

Little Harwood

Local teams were Blackburn North End, Little Harwood Echo (James T. Ward's first club, after Furthergate School), and occasionally Brookhouse Rangers. The pitch was on a recreation ground northeast of the town centre, close by the railway line to Clitheroe. Nowadays the terrain is part of the grounds of Daisyfield Primary School.

Knuzden

Out on the Accrington Road, east of town, this was the pitch of the Furthergate team.

Roe Lee

In the Pleckgate area of Blackburn, north of the Hole-i'th'-Wall ground, this was a temporary abode for the Olympic.

Cob Wall

The cricket field, near to Whalley New Road. Another temporary home for Olympic.

Ravenswing/Lammack

Home pitch of the Blackburn Law side, across Revidge Road from Corporation Park.

Grimshaw Park

On the site of the present St Mary's School, off Bennington Street, south of the town centre. Blackburn Pilgrims played here.

Audley Park

Home pitch of Blackburn Park Road, southeast of the centre of town, later known as Audley Hall. Park Road also played at Place Farm, near to the Workhouse (the present Queen's Park Hospital).

Cattle Market Field

A popular venue for a while, because of its central position, off Galligreaves Street. The short-lived Blackburn Association held its Cup final there, 1879 and 1880 – both times won by Olympic.

Alexandra Meadows

Home of the East Lancs. Cricket Club, and the natural choice for early Rovers games, as this was alongside the Blackburn Grammar School terrain, by Corporation Park.

Mill Hill (or Moorgate)

Black Star's ground, so where Tommy Gibson and Joe Beverley played many of their pre-Olympic games. In the southwest area of Blackburn, near the railway line.

Follywell Fields

Another home pitch of Brookhouse Rangers, which was Jimmy Costley's club until his move to Olympic in 1882. Jack Southworth's first ever junior club, Inkerman Rangers, played there. Situated behind the New Jerusalem Church off Anvil Street, roughly where the school on Swallow Drive is now.

Primrose Hill, Livesey

Out on the southwest edge of Blackburn, home to Livesey United, and Blackburn Perseverance, who also played at Cherry Tree Cricket Club, off Preston Old Road.

Redlam Brow

Southwest of Blackburn centre, just to the north of Preston Old Road, and Witton's home for most of the 1880's.

Gorse Bridge (or Whitebirk)

On the eastern side of town, near the Burnley Road and the canal. The Furthergate club and Blackburn Park Road sometimes played here. The pitch was behind the Gorse Bridge Mill. Further north, across the brook and between the iron works and the gas works, was the Greenbank playing area, home of Blackburn Zingari.

Ewood

This patch of the rural southern edge of the town was used for recreation well before the Rovers built the stadium there. Summer Fairs were held in the open space between the Bolton Road and the River Darwen. This was also the pitch of the Christ Church team.

The sports ground, a football pitch surrounded by a running track, dates from April 1882, when it was renamed Ewood Park. Before Rovers took over the lease in 1890, the ground was used for football, foot races, dog handicaps and trotting matches.

Leamington Street

Rovers' next ground after Alexandra Meadows. On the site of the present day Leamington Road Baptist Church. It cost £500 to construct, possessed a grandstand with a capacity of 600, and boasted six pay boxes arranged three on either side of a resplendent entrance archway that bore the club's name. Rovers stayed there from 1881 until 1890, when they decamped to their present stadium at Ewood Park.

Hole-i'th'-Wall

At the top of the dauntingly steep Shear Brow, behind the pub of the same name, this was originally the pitch of the Queen's Own side. When this team folded, being consumed by the Rovers, Olympic started to rent the terrain at the beginning of the 1879-80 season. The playing area is still there, visible from the back of the pub, and is now part of the grounds of St Mary's College. (For more details on the history of the ground, see Chapter 3.)

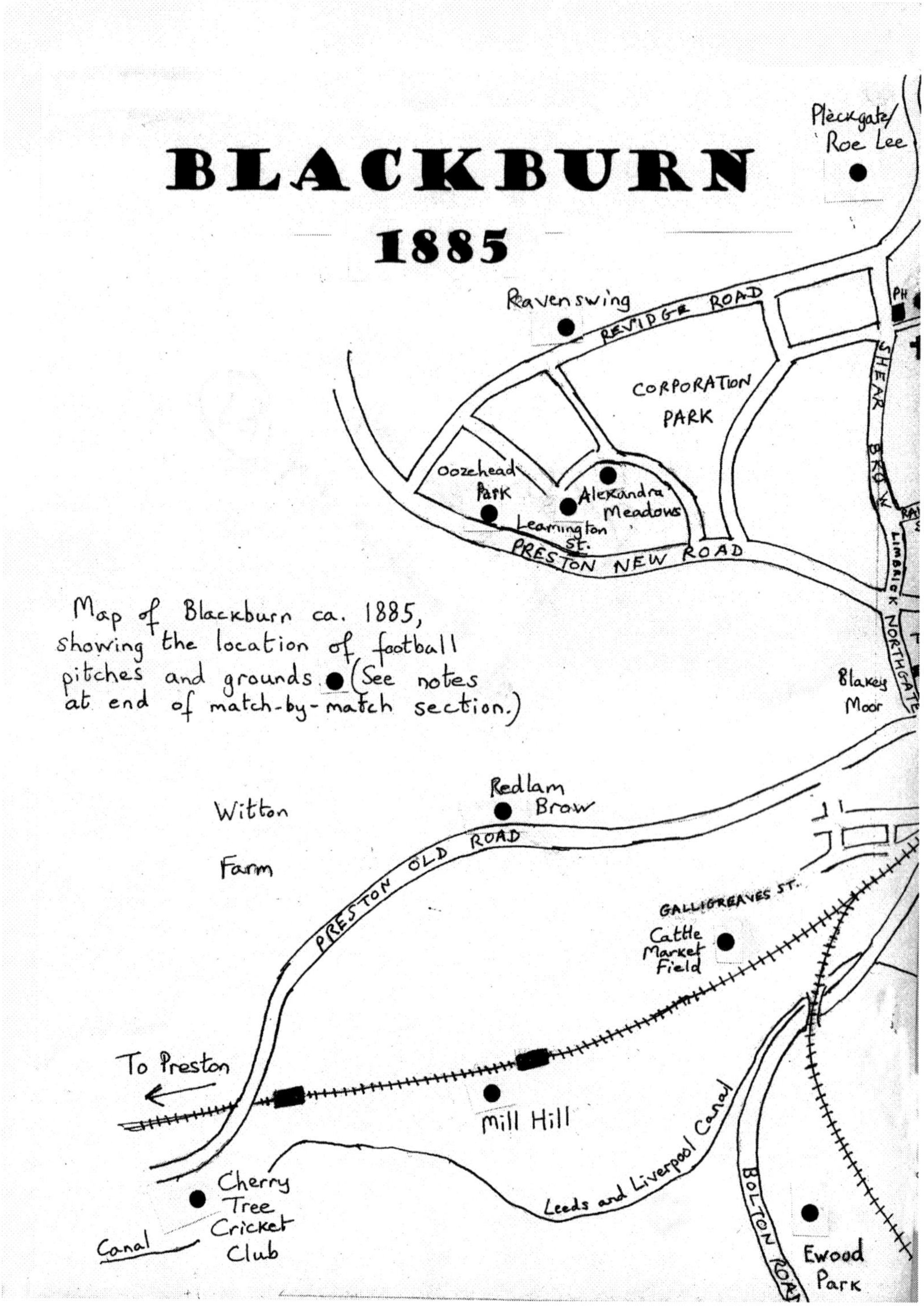
BLACKBURN
1885
Plèckgate/ Roe Lee
Ravenswing
REVIDGE ROAD
PH
CORPORATION PARK
SHEAR BROW
Oozehead Park
Alexandra Meadows
Leamington St.
PRESTON NEW ROAD
LIMBRICK
NORTHGATE
Map of Blackburn ca. 1885, showing the location of football pitches and grounds ● (See notes at end of match-by-match section.)
Blakey Moor
Redlam Brow
Witton Farm
PRESTON OLD ROAD
GALLIGREAVES ST.
Cattle Market Field
To Preston
Mill Hill
Leeds and Liverpool Canal
Cherry Tree Cricket Club
Canal
BOLTON ROAD
Ewood Park

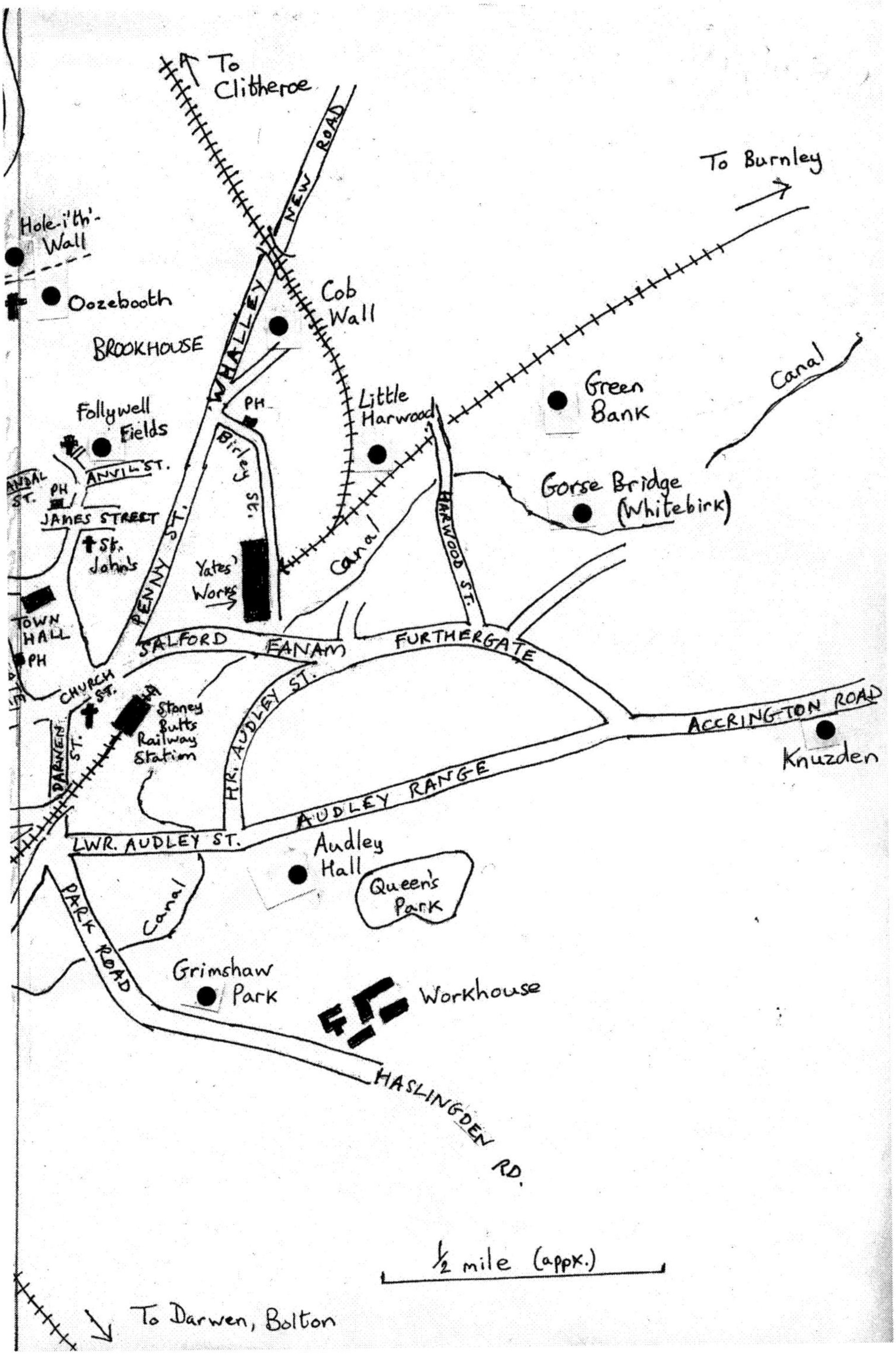

To Clitheroe
To Burnley
Hole-i'th'-Wall
Oozebooth
BROOKHOUSE
NEW ROAD
WHALLEY
Cob Wall
Canal
Green Bank
Little Harwood
PH
Follywell Fields
ANVIL ST.
PH
JAMES STREET
Birley St.
Gorse Bridge (Whitebirk)
HARWOOD ST.
St. John's
PENNY ST.
Yates' Works
Canal
TOWN HALL
PH
SALFORD
EANAM
FURTHERGATE
CHURCH ST.
Stoney Butts Railway Station
UPR. AUDLEY ST.
ACCRINGTON ROAD
Knuzden
DARWEN ST.
AUDLEY RANGE
LWR. AUDLEY ST.
Audley Hall
Queen's Park
PARK ROAD
Canal
Grimshaw Park
Workhouse
HASLINGDEN RD.
½ mile (appx.)
To Darwen, Bolton

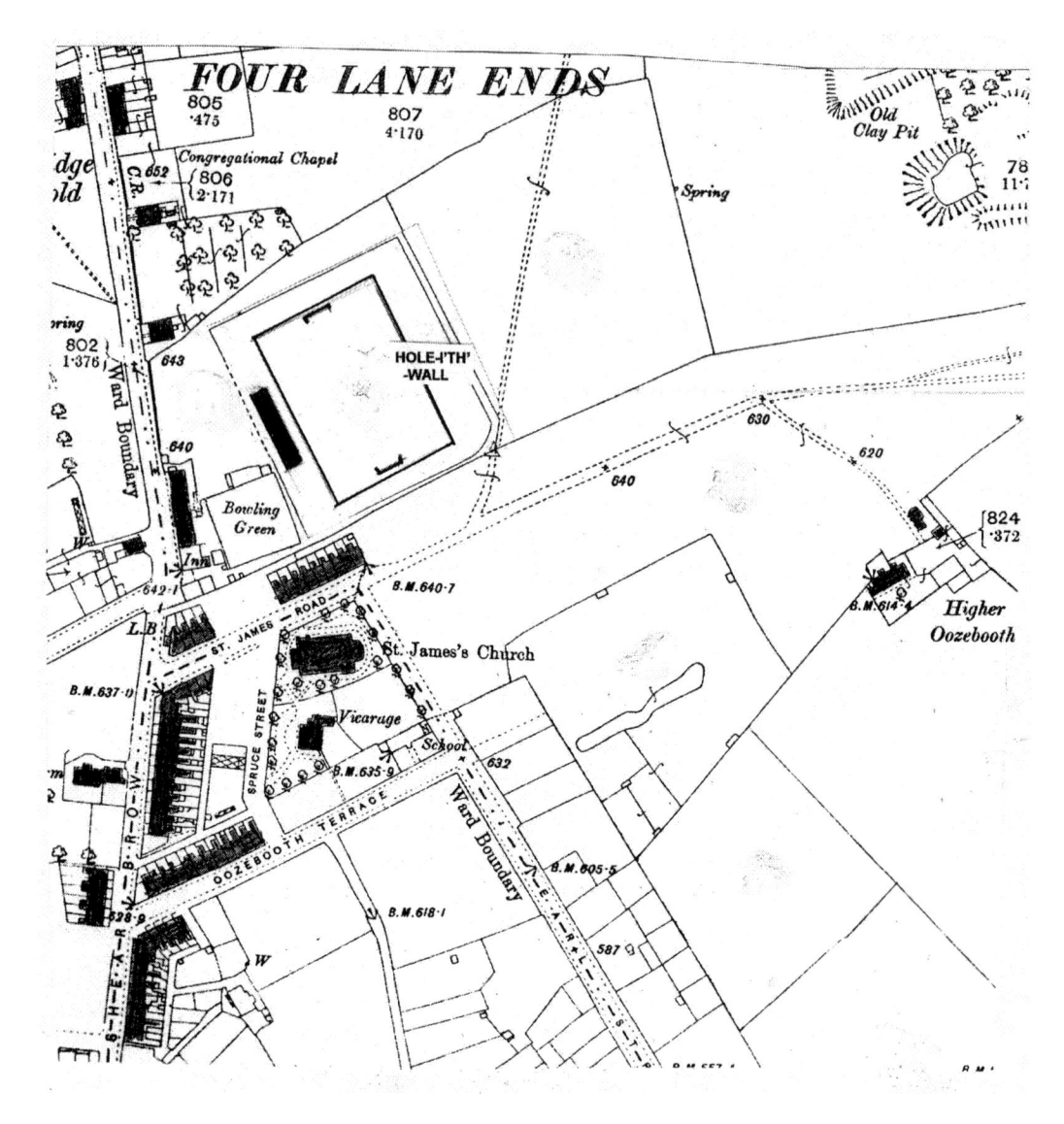

The area around Blackburn Olympic's home ground 1879-89, based on the 1893 OS map. The inn by the bowling green is the Hole-i'th'-Wall. The grandstand shown is the post-1884 structure, built "with its back facing the road". The main north-south road is Shear Brow. Olympic's first ever pitch was on open farmland between St James' Church and the Higher Oozebooth farmhouse. This terrain was also used by Blackburn Cricket Club.

APPENDIX II:

Sketches of the players, from contemporary sources

1. JACK HUNTER

Wherever Association Football is known and appreciated, among the moors of Lancashire and Yorkshire, on the heather of Scotland, or down amongst the Cockneys living within the sound of Bow Bells, the name of genial Jack Hunter, the former captain of the Blackburn Olympic, is a household word.

He, at any rate, is no stranger from over the Border, for he is Yorkshire born and bred, and one of the best of football exponents amongst us. Unlike some of our donners of the jersey, who have attained name and fame, he is no chitling of twenty, but has reached – for football players – the somewhat mature age of thirty-two, and has been for the long period of sixteen years one of the most devoted disciples of the "inflated leather".

Jack made his entry into this sublunary sphere at a little village named Crookes, near Sheffield, in 1852, amid surroundings decidedly bucolic, for his father was a gentleman's gardener at Norton, Derbyshire, where he removed shortly after the birth of our hero, and he himself was introduced to the life of the farm-yard, whistling merrily through a happy boyhood among the dairies and the milk pails, the cows and the poultry, like a sort of juvenile Patience of the gender masculine.

At Norton, the subject of our sketch commenced to take an interest in athletics, his love for football then of a very primitive kind, growing with his growth and strengthening with his strength. The death of his father's employer, and the break up of the establishment, necessitated a removal from Norton, and juvenile Johnny settled in Sheffield, commencing the trade first of butcher, and then after two or three years, that of silver cutler, at the establishment of Messrs. Walker and Hall.

At Sheffield he joined the famous Heeley club, playing back for a season or two, and then taking up his present post of centre half-back. For years he remained with Heeley, only leaving it some three seasons ago to join the Olympic at Blackburn.

His career with the Sheffielders is identified with the rise and progress of the club. Soon after joining them he was selected from the Yorkshire Colts to play in his first County match, which was against Glasgow, and played the same season against the Royal Engineers, and three times against London[1]. He next played twice against Slough, one match being at Windsor, and one at Sheffield. For six consecutive years he was one of the chosen to represent the County, and to take part in other important matches by the Football Blades, with one notorious exception, when for some unaccountable reason he was shelved. That same day, however, he was selected to play in his first international match – England against Scotland[2]. Since then he has played four times with England against Scotland, and three times against Wales, on one occasion receiving the high honour of captaining the English team.

Shortness of work at last compelled him to leave the county of his birth[3], and forsake the lily rose of York for the rich scarlet-hued flower of Lancaster. But not before his services had been highly appreciated and acknowledged, as a handsome gold Albert guard and massive silver Lever watch can testify, and which bears the inscription "Presented to Mr. John Hunter, by football friends, for his good play and captainship, April 1880." This, with a purse of fifty sovereigns, was a tribute, at any rate, to the value in which his services had been held.

On coming to Blackburn, as all the world and his wife know, he joined the Olympic, fighting manfully and bravely under the well-known pale blue and white banner, which has been victorious in many a stiffly-contested battle. The first season he joined them, the club won the East Lancashire Charity Cup, but owing to the residential qualifications he was not allowed by the powers that be to join in that triumph. The remainder of the club's subsequent history needs only a bare recital at our hands, for is it not known to every football votary, however youthful he may be? How, after a stiff tussle, the big trophy – the English Challenge Cup – was borne in triumph to

Blackburn by the victorious Olympians, who were the first team to bring it to the provinces; how Jack Hunter and his merry men received a welcome at the hands of thousands of their Blackburn admirers, will never be forgotten.

On the cinder path, also, Hunter has distinguished himself. He has won fifty-six prizes at athletic meetings at Sheffield Wednesday Sports, Sheffield Heeley, Doncaster and other gatherings, as well as winning two scratch hurdle races at the Sheffield Gymnasium Athletic Sports.

Hunter is now the well-known host of "The Mason's Arms", Blackburn, a noted house of call for lovers of football. The latest tips are here certain to be picked up, whilst his walls bristle with photographs of noted footballers and football clubs single and in groups. Fixture cards innumerable are interspersed, some, those issued by the Preston North End and Stoke clubs, to wit, being decidedly works of art. As may be expected the place of honour is assigned to the Olympians, who are photographed, as the clowns say, "altogether and one after another". Beneath this is a poetic effusion dedicated to the club by one Mr. Frank Archer, which runs as follows:

> Success to the Olympic club, Blackburn's rising team,
> United may its members stand, as they have always been.
> Carefully and skilfully, the tree they're creeping up,
> Credit they have gained since they won their splendid Cup.
> Each one we reward with praise, in favour may they rise,
> Sincerely they have struggled for and gained the massive prize.
> See their respected coaches, John Hunter in the field,
>
> To gain a point he's always there, you never find him yield.
> On guard you'll always see him, when the ball is flying high,
>
> One chance he never misses, when to score he makes a try.
> Let us give great praise to Tommy Gibson, too,
> You'll find at half-back, he and Astley, well know what to do.
> Midst goal we find T. Hacking, who has always striven hard,
> Praise we give to each full-back, S.A. Warburton and J. Ward.
> In every match T. Dewhurst and A. Matthews on right wing,
> Carefully have played together and honours tried to bring.
>
> Costley and J. Yates, fine play have always shown;
> Last we find G. Wilson, a credit we must own,
> United may they ever stand, in friendship prove sincere,
> By perseverance may they prove the cracks of Lancashire.
>
> *Football Field* (Nov 15th 1884)

[1] *Probably 1874. Sheffield traditionally played London three times in a season, once each under local rules, and once with a "mixed" rulebook. This stopped in 1877 when the whole country adopted the London FA rules.*

[2] *March 2nd 1878*

[3] *A diplomatic fudging; for the real reason, see Chapter 6!*

2. SQUIRE ALBERT WARBURTON

A fine name, you say! Truly so, and he's a fine man who owns it. So long as football rears its head proudly as the champion game of the North, so long will players and supporters alike regard with affection and esteem the gallant fellow who first led a Northern team to victory, and brought the English cup from the southern strongholds to adorn a Lancashire sideboard. This is the greatest achievement of a great career, and sporting England never forgets her heroes. But we must hark back to the early days before the metaphorical halo of fame surrounded, with its brilliant haze, the doughty footballer.

The epigrammatic sentiment that some men are born to greatness, some achieve greatness, and others have greatness thrust upon them is often quoted, and it can truly be said of

Warburton that when he entered the world on 26th January 1856, he was born to the greatness that he has since honestly acquired by conscientious work, discharged with an excellence, coupled with an unassuming modesty seldom combined to the same extent in the one individual.

Squire Albert opened his peepers to the light of day at Oldham, but he was not destined to kick up his heels for long there, as his parents removed to Bury, and subsequently, in 1861, to Blackburn, the boy being then five years of age. A brief period at St John's Schools, and then he was sent to learn the trade of a plumber.

We first find him in a conspicuous position on the football field in 1878, when he shared the defeat of Cob Wall in their cup-tie with Manchester Wanderers. Squire Albert – we like to repeat this name, it has such an unctuous roll to it – found his permanent position at full-back at the very commencement of his career. He did not remain long with Cob Wall, neither with St John's Young Men, with whom he played one or two matches. He was destined for higher flights, and on Easter Saturday 1878 he donned the Olympic light blue at Hole-i'th'-Wall, in a match with the Blackburn Rovers, when the latter succumbed by two to one.[1] On Easter Monday the Olympic met the Sheffield Zulus, and the savages caved in without scoring, the light blues again scoring two goals. As all the world knows, this was the inauguration of a triumphant history. The Olympic that season were well-nigh invincible, playing fifteen first team matches in succession without a reverse, the check coming when the Rovers in the return match took their revenge. The Olympic were naturally the winners of the Blackburn Association Cup. They met Livesey in the final tie and beat them, but the defeated team protested against Warburton on the grounds that he did not fulfil the time qualification, and the Committee ordered the draw to be replayed, with the same result.[2]

From that period until he severed his connection with the Olympic last season our hero appeared in every match, except when disabled, and was elected captain in the season 1882-3, succeeding Joe Beverley, who soon afterwards joined the Rovers. It would be wearisome to detail all the "doughty deeds of derring-do" achieved season after season by Warburton and his associates. It may be briefly mentioned that on the 21st August[3], 1882 the Olympic won the East Lancashire Charity Cup, and it was then that Warburton's election to the captaincy was assured.

We all remember the tremendous wave of enthusiastic excitement which swept over Lancashire as the season 1882-3 approached its termination ... (*the article here gives a description of the 1883 Cup Final and subsequent celebrations*) ... and how Warburton rode through the town carrying aloft the magnificent-looking trophy which represented so much to the world of sport.

Returning to lesser themes – by comparison – we find that Warburton is the only man who possesses a medal for every season in which the East Lancashire Cup has been competed for. The Olympic won it in 1882 and ran up in 1883, being knocked out by the Rovers, and this year Darwen won it.

Warburton has been engaged in the following county and international fixtures: March 4th 1881, International trial match at Bolton – Probables v. Improbables; March 18th, Lancashire v. Sheffield, when the Red Rose suffered defeat; December 3rd, Lancashire v. Birmingham, the County winning by five to four; September 30th 1882, North of England v. Sheffield, Warburton captaining the North, who turned up three men short, and were beaten; November 25th, Lancashire v. Bolton; December, Lancashire v. North of England ...

After winning the English Cup, dissension unhappily crept into the Olympic ranks. The green-eyed monster, as it is the pleasure of novelists to term jealousy, suggested to one or two aspiring youths that Warburton had been captain long enough. He declined to stand when nominated, and choice then lay between Hunter and Gibson. Another election was demanded, and this time Warburton was elected by a substantial majority. He, however, simply resigned immediately, and severed his connection with the club that probably owes more to him than any other for the position it now occupies. He only appeared on two occasions in the light blue after winning the Cup, and these were against Dumbarton and Aston Villa. After playing a game or two with Halliwell, and refusing overtures from the Rovers, Warburton threw in his lot with Darwen, being elected vice-captain, declining the higher honour which is held by J. Richmond.

It was not long before Warburton found himself pitted against his old associates. A drawn game with the Olympic in a friendly encounter was followed by another draw in the Charity Cup competition, but Darwen ultimately got the upper hand on the Olympic ground, and afterwards fought their way to victory for the trophy which the club now holds. The Olympic, however, beat Darwen in the Lancashire ties. That Warburton was a godsend for Darwen is proved by the fact that whereas a fortnight previously the Olympic beat them eight to love, with the aid of our hero they were able to keep the score in the next encounter to three to one.

Darwen are now in the third round of the English Cup competition, having beaten Fishwick Ramblers last Saturday, and today they victimise Southport in the Lancashire, and remembering their gallant fight with Queen's Park, there is opportunity no means remote for Warburton to repeat his former triumph.

He has not done much in other branches of sport, simply winning two second prizes at the Olympic Sports in 340 and 100 yards races.

Squire Albert became a Boniface in July last, when he took possession of the Dog and Partridge, James'-street, St John's, Blackburn, and surrounded himself with a host of football friends. He has been happily married ten years, and has a small family. He is a genial host and pleasant companion, and deserves all the good luck that can attend him. His appearance and sterling back play are too well known in Lancashire to need description, and we conclude by saying that as popular player, plumber and publican, we plump for Squire Albert Warburton.

Football Field (Nov 29th 1884)

[1] *The writer must mean 1880 here, as Olympic didn't play Rovers until February 1879, and the match with the Zulus was on Easter Monday 1880. Also, Warburton's debut for the Olympic was in the Blackburn Association semi, the week before the Rovers game mentioned here, which was won 1-0, and not 2-1.*

[2] *This seems like more confusion over dates. The Blackburn Association final in which Warburton participated was the 2-2 draw against Perseverance in April 1880. He did not appear in the replay though, so perhaps this is what the writer had in mind. See Chapter 3. The undefeated sequence referred to suggests 1878-9.*

[3] *Actually August 7th 1882*

Warburton's FA Cup Winner's Medal from the 1883 final.

3. THOMAS JAMES HACKING

A look round Lancashire custodians reveals several tried and true men, amongst whom Tom Hacking holds no second rank. He doesn't court popularity, but he is first in public favour, he plays seldom, but his admirers complain not if he puts in an appearance on important occasions. It will be a surprise to many that it is only due to pressure from his friends, and a desire to oblige, that Hacking plays football. He had no particular early training; he went between the Olympic posts for the first time in an emergency, totally ignorant of the simple rules of the game; and he performed so brilliantly that his destiny was sealed, and a goalkeeper he has remained ever since "willy nilly". Tom seems to have been truly "to the manner born".

Competing against the best clubs in England or Scotland, practising never, and often at long intervals, Hacking and the Olympic have probably the best goal record in the country for the matches of which the subject of this sketch has been engaged.

Hacking is a slightly-built, lithe athlete in appearance, black hair, dark complexion, and – but everybody knows him; what need for a description? He was born in June, 1857, and is therefore now between 27 and 28 years of age, stands 5 ft. 6½in. in height, and weighs considerably under 9 stones. Blackburn was his birthplace, and in Blackburn he has reeled off the strand of life already completed. When old enough he attended St John's School, the nursery of football, whence sprang Jimmy Brown, Beverley, Duckworth, Sowerbutts, and a host of staunch followers of the leather who have since donned the Rovers, Olympic, Park Road, and Witton colours. The Head Master, in the early days of these celebrities, had a great appreciation for the "sound body", hence the encouragement given to the young idea in the indulgence of outdoor sports; hence also the fruitful crop of stalwart young fellows who have made football in Blackburn, throughout Lancashire, aye, and over England, what it has been, and what it is at the present time. Some people are fond of attributing the popularity of the game to importations from over the border, forgetting that the original source was to be found in the nucleus of Lancashire lads who manfully struggled along at the period when "gates" were an "unknown quantity".

Hacking, when at school, was fond of cricket, jumping, and other branches of athletics in a general way, whilst he occasionally kicked a ball about under the rough and ready code of rules, or rather misrule, which formerly obtained. Jumping was his great forte, and even during his football career, "funny" men have dubbed him the "india-rubber doll", in recognition of his antics 'tween the sticks. But Hacking is no doll in a pantomime sense, though he bounced and bounced into public favour with very few rebounds. Tom has played football about four years, and the whole of that time with the Blackburn Olympic – or rather such portions of the time he could spare from business. Prior to his active connection with the club he had friends among its members and when one Friday night, Baldwin declined to play the next day, Tom was asked as a favour to act as substitute. The match was at Blackburn against Turton, and accordingly Hacking assisted the light blues to beat the villagers. At that period, we believe, Tom didn't even know what a corner kick was, but he did know how to use his hands, and this fact was speedily recognised.

The first match of importance in which he played was against the Edinburgh Hibernians on their Easter Lancashire tour, when the dispute with the Rovers occurred; in this the Olympic were victorious. In this season of 1880-81 Tom appeared in probably more matches than in any succeeding year. Since then he has chiefly confined himself to cup ties and big fixtures, and thus at a remarkably cheap expenditure of time and effort he finds himself in possession of four medals – the gold record for the first victors in the East Lancashire Charity Cup competition, 1881-82; the gold medal of the English Association commemorating the Olympic triumph in the struggle for the National trophy, 1882-3; the silver medal as runners-up in the Charity Cup competition the same year; and a silver medal for taking a similar position in the county competition last season.

The Lancashire committee have repeatedly chosen Hacking to fill the post of danger in county fixtures, and many have been the temptations and opportunities for him to obtain international honours, but the lack of "soaring ambition" has so far prevented this consummation. North, South, Out and About, and Ayont the Tweed players have had a taste of Hacking's prowess, and it would be difficult to mention any first class combination against whom he has not assisted the Olympic to do battle against, and generally to conquer.

Of course, the big year was 1882-3, the Olympic cup year, and it is worth recording in this connection that in the ties in this competition the Olympic scored thirty-six goals against six obtained by their opponents. These were Accrington three, Church none, Welsh Druids one, Old Carthusians none, Old Etonians one, and another which has slipped my memory for the moment.[1] This speaks volumes for Hacking's goal-keeping.

In 1882-3 he was chosen for the North v. South match at Birmingham, but the previous day a pitch from the train at Blackburn station knocked football out of him for a time. He was again unfortunate at the end of 1883, as when playing against Accrington in the final tie for the Charity Cup, he received a severe twist of the knee whilst executing one of his "indiarubber jumps", and this kept him down for nine months. His only appearance [for Olympic] last year was in the final for the County Cup against the Rovers.

There is no sign of decline of skill. Cool and agile as ever, Tom will hold his own against any set of forwards, and though he expresses a disinclination to appear in any matches beyond county cup ties, we hope to see him regularly under the crossbar.
Blackburn Standard (Jan 17th 1885), from *Football Field*

[1] *This was the one conceded in the 8-1 win over Lower Darwen.*

The Last Word: A Blackburnian with Toothache:

Thomas Hacking had played his last major game of football, but the fame outlived the deeds.

A dialect yarn of a Blackburn man with a raging toothache ("a big balloon i' thy cheek, besides four looms i' full swing at th' nerve") tells of the folk and commercial remedies the man tried before resorting to the one certain cure. A mustard plaster, a water-and-washing-soda mouthwash, brandy (breaking his teetotal pledge to Mrs. Lewis) and "Gregory peawdwer" all proved equally useless. Then:

"Id were last Monda' as aw met th'sensiblest chap as aw ever met i' my life, an' he sed these words to me:
"'Eh, Tum, tha'rt a letherheyd!'
"'Tell me summat as aw dorn't know,' I said.
"'Be off with tha to Tommy Hackin' and hav id eawt fost thing.'
"'Dusta mean Tommy Hackin' th' footbo'er?'
"'Ay,' he said; 'he con poo' teeth just as weel as he used to goal.'
"'Then he's a topper,' aw said; an' aw'll gooa to-day.'
"An' aw went, an' i' quarter ov an' heawr at after aw'd left his heawse, feelin' abeawt a ton leeter. When aw rung at his bell aw felt as miserable as a chap wod when he'd hed "now" said to him bi th' lass he'd proposed to; but when aw coom eawt aw felt summat like th' same chap wod iv th' lass hed said 'yigh' and kust him i' th' bergain. Sooa tha'll know wod to do next time as tha hes th' toothwerch – *an' see as tha does it!*"
Blackburn Standard (Apr 20th 1889)

4. THOMAS KENYON GIBSON

A Blackburn lad, bred and born, one of the genuine "18 carat, solid throughout" players, is "Tommy" Gibson, the subject of our present sketch. None deserve a higher place in the series of word pictures of "Popular Players" which has adorned our pages. Tom had played football "from his youth up", never swerving from the straight course, running with his head firmly set for the winning-post of excellence. And football has been play to Tom, just the salt of life, forming that best of recreations, change of occupation, from the continuous round of hard daily toil. He is an exemplification of that the old song maxim, "He who lives a good life is sure to live well." Like good wine he improves with age, and although he is in his 31st year he never played better than today. All honour to him, and good luck to the club that can retain such metal through the changing vicissitudes of football history.

Thomas Kenyon Gibson was born on the 24th November, 1853, in Ainsworth Street, Blackburn. Let us pass over his early youth, which was much the same as that of other boys – a little learning, a few troubles, and a great deal of play. We'll take up his football career in the season of 1876-7, when the James Street and Black Star Clubs amalgamated under the happy cognomen of Blackburn Olympic[1]. Jack Edmondson was captain of the new club, and Joe Beverley, along with Gibson, are now the only men in the Olympic ranks who played in the first game after the combination. Tom was then 23 years of age, no chicken, you'll say, but he proved himself a regular game young bird in those early days, when he was the favourite full back of the newly-born Olympic.

That same season the Livesey United, with the view to helping on their funds, instituted a cup competition, the ties for which were played off on their ground at Cherry Tree. The competing teams were Christ Church, St George's, St Mark's (now Witton), Olympic, Park Road, and Queen's Own. The Olympic carried it off, and this was the first trophy Gibson assisted in winning. The competition then dropped through, but in the season 1877-8 the Blackburn Football Association came into existence, and another cup of the value of about 35 guineas, was offered, the conditions being that the ultimate possessors should win it two years in succession, or three times in all. Again the Olympic came to the fore, obtaining the silver medals as the holders in the first year, and winning the cup outright at the second time of asking. This was rather rough on the promoters, who hardly anticipated such a summary disposal of their prize, and the competition was not renewed.

At this period Gibson had come to his present position at half-back. In 1878-9 the Olympic joined the Lancashire competition, but were, if we remember aright, thrown out in the first round[2], and the following season our hero was a member of the team beaten by Sheffield in the English ties, and then in the semi-final by the Rovers for the Lancashire Cup.

Steadily pursuing their upward climb, the Olympic gathered strength, and though in 1880-1 *(sic)* Darwen disposed of them in the National competition, they won the East Lancashire Charity Cup in 1882, beating the Rovers in the final.

The history of the memorable triumph of the Olympic in 1882-3, when they brought home the English Cup, amid unparalleled rejoicings, is an oft-told tale. Tom Gibson joined in that triumph, and worthily did his share in the fray. As we all know, last year Queen's Park proved too clever for the gallant band, and Rovers were good enough to take both County and National first honours.

Gibson has donned the Lancashire jersey almost times without number, always with credit to himself and advantage to the team. When London got such a slating at the hands of Lancashire, on the Leamington ground, Blackburn, in 1883, the match being for the benefit of the sufferers by the Altham Colliery explosion, this clever little Olympic half-back was captain. Three times has he engaged in the North v. South conflicts at Sheffield, and he has also appeared in the Probables v. Improbables trial match at Bolton.

The skippership of the Olympic has on many occasions been fittingly offered to and pressed upon Gibson, but, to use his own phrase, he's "no speaker", and it was *post-prandial* honours and duties that he fought shy of. On the field no one could be better qualified to lead a team to victory, if victory be possible, but oratorically Tommy prefers to take a back seat. In 1882, he was, however, persuaded to captain his team, but threw it up, and now shelters in the minor rank of vice captain.

Four years ago last September, Gibson took unto himself a wife and the comfortable home in Troy-street, Whalley-range, Blackburn is now peopled by the industrious parents and four bonny bairns. Thirteen years of hard and honest toil as an iron dresser at Messrs Yates's foundry go a long way to place him in a different category to many footballers we could name. Gibson's physique is by no means of a massive type, as he stands about five feet three or four inches in height, and weighs about nine stone thirteen. He is quiet, unassuming, and straightforward, not inclined to talk of his deeds, but rather leaving them to speak for themselves.

That this shining light has not been "hid under a bushel", is manifested by the fact that Gibson's friends are determined that eight years of valuable service in the football area shall not go unrewarded. We are glad to give extended publicity to the fact that a testimonial is in progress to which subscriptions are invited. The committee need have no fear as to the success of the movement "irrespective of club partisanship", for Gibson's friends rank on all sides. As an Olympian he is a redoubtable champion for his team, but as a player, pure and simple, he has ever

been ready through rough and smooth to advance the best interests of the game. This biographical sketch is not intended as an appeal for subscriptions, but no harm can be done by stating that the hon. secs. to the testimonial fund are Messrs. J. Edmundson *(sic)*, 48, Blackburn-street, and J. Foulds, 44, Charlotte-street, Blackburn.
Blackburn Standard (Dec 27th 1884), from *Football Field*

[1] *1876-7 is too early for the date of origin of Olympic, if the newspaper extract given at the beginning of Chapter 1 is to be believed. Also, the Blackburn Association was founded one year later than the date given here.*

[2] *Another error: Olympic didn't compete in the Lancashire Cup until two years later than this, and the FA Cup defeat against Sheffield was in 1880-1. The Lancs. Cup semi with Rovers was in 1881-2.*

5. JAMES WARD

We have this week to record the football doings of no Scotch player who has been imported from over the border, but those of a Lancashire boy born and bred – Jimmy Ward, the famous back of the Blackburn Olympic team. Blackburn is his native town, he having been born in Harwood-street, Furthergate, and in Harwood-street, Furthergate, he has lived ever since he was born twenty years ago on the 28th of this month. He was educated at the Furthergate School at the corner of Harwood-street, and there he now lives, the landlord of the Prince of Wales Inn, not a stone's throw from the house where he was ushered into this world of many troubles and few pleasures.

He is virtually a born footballer. As early as fourteen years of age he was a votary of the leather, joining the Little Harwood club as a forward on the left. Here he played for two years, and he was then drafted into the Blackburn Olympic second team, with whom he played once on the wing and once as full-back. Here his splendid display in the latter position brought him into prominence, and his light was not allowed to be kept under the second team bushel, being transferred into the first team as the left full back. His career with the Olympic, and his successes, many as they have been, are contemporaneous with the brilliant doings of the club with which he has been associated.

The big clubs which the Olympic has met have invariably had to encounter Ward at back, whose fine kicking, watchfulness and alertness have proved a tower of strength in the matches in which his club has been engaged.

Ward has played for his county many a time and oft. He championed Lancashire against Sheffield at Pike's-lane, when the county Palatine were defeated by the Blades by three to two, and again on the Bramall-lane ground in the return this season, when the red rose won by five to four. Ayrshire has also had to bite the dust to the tune of five to two by the victorious county of big chimneys and hard men.

Today Ward wins his international cap, playing with England against Wales at Blackburn. May victory rest upon the banner of St George!

In other walks of the athletic world Ward has not done much, but what he has, he has well done. He won a 100 yards sprint race at Harwood against Hammy Chippendale of £5 a side, beating his opponent by five yards. In jumping he has defeated the noted Aulty at Witton, whilst at the game known as "buck" playing[1] he has beaten Richard Smalley at Lammock, the match being for £25 a side.

In the matrimonial arena Ward is an early contestant, there is a hostess as well as a host at the Prince of Wales hotel, together with a very youthful successor to the athletic honours which his pater has won.
Football Field (Mar 14th 1885)

[1] *This would seem to be a less violent form of wrestling than the traditional Lancashire "all-in", with more in common with the Cornish style, in which the object was simply to upend and floor the opponent.*

6. JOE BEVERLEY

Joseph Beverley is a real Blackburnian. He was born in Buttery-street, and has resided in the town ever since that interesting event took place on the 12th November 1857. His father had been serving his country for 37 years, but at the time of Joe's birth he was pensioned off, and acting as winding master at Messrs. Hornby's Mills, Brookhouse. Joe received a fair education, attending St John's Schools until he was 15 years of age, when he went as clerk to a yarn agent in Blackburn. Quill driving, however, did not suit him, and he was apprenticed in iron turning. On completing his term he still worked at his trade, but at the present time he is not employed, chiefly owing to work being scarce.

    Joe commenced his football career in 1877 as one of the promoters of the Black Star F.C. He did not play, but was one of a deputation appointed to arrange for an amalgamation with the James-street club. This took place in February 1878, and the combination was named the Blackburn Olympic. After the preliminaries had been arranged the team for the following Saturday was selected, and not being able to make up the full complement, Joe volunteered his services in the event of the requisite number of men not turning up. The match was against his old school, St John's, and Beverley was put in goal. He prevented any score being made, and in the second half he was placed at centre forward, and kicked the only goal in the match, the Olympic winning by one to nil.[1] This was enough to give him a permanent place in the team, and he played as centre forward for the rest of the season, assisting to win a private cup put up for competition in Blackburn.

    The next season again saw him as centre forward, and this year they won the Blackburn cup. The following season he was elected captain, but the team still fought as a junior organisation, and again won the Blackburn cup, the trophy then becoming the property of the club. Beverley had now gone full back, that position being very difficult to fill, and in the next season – 1880-1 – the club came out amongst the cracks and entered the Lancashire Cup Competition, but they were disposed of in the first round. Joe's abilities were now recognised by the County Association, and along with Mr. Tom Scowcroft, of the Turton club, he played centre forward against North Wales at Accrington. Lancashire won by four goals to one, and in the same season he played as full back against Glasgow at Darwen, when the ground was covered with snow. The season 1881-2 again saw him captain of the Olympic, who ran up to the semi-final for the County Cup, when they were thrown out by the Rovers. However, later on they had their revenge by winning the East Lancashire Charity Cup in the first season it was competed for, defeating the Rovers by five goals to two. The only important match Beverley took part in this season outside his club's engagement was with the Improbables against the Probables at Pikes-lane.

    The following season saw him playing with the "enemy", the Rovers, as the companion of Fergy Suter. They were thrown out of the English Cup ties in the early stages by Darwen, but they won the Lancashire, their opponents in the final also being the "peaceful valley" representative. They afterwards also won the Charity Cup, Joe's old club, who had just carried off the English Cup, being their opponents. He thus obtained two gold medals, besides playing in the county matches against Sheffield and London, and in the trial match with North of England.

    The next season he continued his connection with the Rovers, and was one of the team who defeated Queen's Park in the final for the English Cup, for which he also received a gold medal. In this competition the Rovers scored 28 goals to two (Staveley and Queen's Park one each), which speaks volumes in favour of the defence of Beverley and Suter. He took part in one county match, viz., against Sheffield, and played with North *v.* South at Kennington Oval. His performance on this occasion was so good that he was chosen for the International match at Belfast. He also satisfied the powers that be by his exhibition against the representatives of the land of Erin, and took part in the matches against Scotland and Wales in the same season. The Rovers afterwards once more won the Lancashire Cup, and another gold medal was added to Beverley's stock.

    Last season he rejoined his old club, the Olympic, and they ran up to the final for the County trophy, being defeated by the Rovers at Preston by two goals to nil[2]. In the match Beverley obtained the only serious injury he has sustained during his long football career – a severe cut on the eye – which necessitated his retirement to have it stitched, but with that pluck which has always characterised his play he insisted on returning to the field of play.

The present season has seen him still in the Olympic ranks, but the club has been very unlucky in not obtaining an efficient centre, Beverley having generally had to take that position. He has also played in goal, notably against the Rovers when the Olympic won by four goals to three. Few players in Lancashire can boast of a more distinguished career than Beverley, and as a footballer there are few as genuine. Many a time has he led his team on to victory when defeat seemed inevitable, and from all appearances he seems likely to continue his successful career for a long time.

He stands 5ft. 8in., and turns the scales at 11 stone 12 pounds. Joe became a Benedict when very young, and is the proud possessor of a family of three bairns. He now resides at 72, Anvil-street, Blackburn, and it will be a long time ere the prowess of Joe Beverley is forgotten by Lancashire footballers.

Blackburn Standard (Jan 23rd 1886), from *Football Field*

[1] *This account of Olympic's first match doesn't square with the report in the Blackburn Standard 16th Feb. 1878. See Chapter 1.*

[2] *The score was actually 2-1 to the Rovers.*

7. JAMES COSTLEY

This week we once more introduce our readers to a member of the Blackburn Olympic club, Jimmy Costley. Though Blackburn to the backbone, Costley was not born there, but came into this world on the banks of the Mersey at Liverpool, where he resided until he was eleven years of age. That is now thirteen years ago, as he was born on the 18th January 1862.

After coming to Blackburn he attended the Park-road Congregational School, but left at an early age to work in a cotton mill. He stuck to spinning until about twelve months ago since which time he has been out of employment. Costley commenced his football career when but fourteen years old, and played outside left wing for the Brookhouse Rangers. It may be well to remark *en passant* that Costley resides at Brookhouse, and it was in this district that the Olympic was first formed.

He stuck to the Rangers for about five years, and in the summer of 1882 the Olympic Club organized a competition for junior clubs. The first prize was a clock and medals, which the Rangers won outright. The executive of the Hole-i'th'-Wall Club thought Costley showed signs of making a good player, and at length he was induced to leave his old club and join the Olympic second.

He first played with them in September 1882, and continued in the junior team till January 1883. At that time R. Wensby *(sic)* was Yates's partner on the left, and he was severely injured. Young Costley was therefore brought out of the second team and put alongside Yates. The pair soon made a name for themselves, and assisted the club to run through the English Cup ties, defeating the Old Carthusians in the semi-final, whilst at the Oval they met the Old Etonians, who had won the Cup from the Blackburn Rovers the previous year. This was the most exciting match Costley ever played in, and very few "professors" can equal his experience of starting with the second team at the beginning of the season, and finishing up by playing in the final tie for the English Cup. Our readers will remember that the allotted time expired without either side possessing the mastery, and an extra half hour was played. This showed the stamina of the Lancashire men, who had been specially trained. With about ten minutes to play our hero received the ball from Dewhurst, and kicked the crowning goal. Of course he got a gold medal, and the illustrated papers of the time had Costley kicking the goal which won the English Cup for the first time for a provincial club. In one of the illustrations Costley appears to have taken a tremendous kick, and is waiting patiently for the ball to go between two uprights about 28 feet high, whereas the all-important shot was made about four yards from the goal.

The following season, and, in fact, up to the present time, he has continued in his place as inside left. His abilities were duly recognised by the county authorities, who selected him for the match v. Ayrshire at Kilmarnock, and v. Sheffield at Bolton. He had his usual partner, Jack Yates, and on both occasions their play was of the highest order. They ran in the final for the Lancashire

Cup, which was played at Preston, and up to within a minute of the time – in fact it has since been understood that time had actually expired – the Olympians were leading. The teams again met a month later at Darwen, when the Rovers won by two goals to one, Costley obtaining a silver medal in lieu of a gold one he thought he was entitled to. In the same season the club was thrown out of the English Cup ties by Queen's Park.

The following year Costley was not selected for any county matches, chiefly owing to his club not nominating anyone, but only last Saturday he took part in the Gentlemen v. Players match at Preston[1], the committee of the Football Association thus showing that they appreciated the skill of the Olympian. On several occasions he has had offers to desert the Light Blues, but has withstood them all.

He is one of the little 'uns, and only stands 5ft. 6in., weighing 10st. 4lbs., but nevertheless he can "stand his own corner", and is not afraid of a little horse play, though he thinks it best to avoid it. He is a good dodger and a splendid shot at goal, and we think the Football Association, when choosing players for big matches, might do worse than select James Costley.
Blackburn Standard (Jan 30th 1886), from *Football Field*

[1] *Costley played twice in the Gentlemen vs. Players games, the first at Preston 5th Sep., 1885, and the second at the Oval on 20th Mar., 1886, in which he scored the winning goal. See text. He was never to receive an international cap.*

Author's note: Jimmy Costley may have played for Everton in their first ever Football League campaign in 1888-89, but matters are confused by the fact that there was another player with the same surname who turned out for Everton between 1886 and 1888. This was "E." or "T." Costley (so Edward/Ted?) according to the team lists for the Liverpool and District Cup Final on April 2nd 1887, which Everton won 5-0. An examination of specific dates and games is further proof that there were two Costleys playing at the time, one in Blackburn and another in Liverpool:

Sep. 4th 1886: Costley played for Blackburn Rovers vs. Halliwell (*Blackburn Times*)
Sep. 4th 1886: Costley scored 2 goals for Everton v. Astley Bridge (*Liverpool Courier*)

Professional players' initials are rarely given in those years, to distinguish them from amateurs. Throughout that autumn a Costley is playing some good games for Everton, whilst the Blackburn Costley is either struggling or injured. On November 13th, when the Rovers Costley is described as being "a shadow of his former self" (see Chapter 13) the Liverpool Costley is again playing a lively forward game for the Toffeemen.

And the following season:

Sep. 24th 1887: Costley scored for Blackburn Olympic vs. Rovers (*Blackburn Times*)
Sep. 24th 1887: Costley scored for Everton vs. Liverpool St John's (*Liverpool Courier*)

So which Costley played for Everton in 1888-89? Club archives give "J. T." Costley (6 Football League games, 3 goals), which could conceivably be either. However, records usually state that the player's previous club was Blackburn Rovers, which may be an error, meaning Olympic.

Extract from a letter written 1999 by Mrs. Muriel Cattow, Costley's granddaughter:

"Granddad worked at Hornby's Mill. He was a spinner in the cotton mill at Cob Wall, Blackburn and I used to take his lunch for him there. Mother used to say that wherever he went people would buy him a drink and he would come home drunk.

"Then one day he met Mrs. Lewis of Lee Hall mission and she got him to sign the pledge and he never drank again.

"He died at home. I was there when he came in, went upstairs to bed and died quickly. Blackburn Rovers escorted his coffin to the grave at Blackburn cemetery. He was a very gentle man, but still loved football. Rovers used to send him a season [ticket] until he died."

8. JACK SOUTHWORTH

Jack Southworth

Mr. John Southworth, of Park-terrace[1], has only been 22 years in the world, but he has been clever on the ball so long and has shown himself to be so capable a musician that he must have come into it with a kick and a flourish. He springs from an old Blackburn family, and lives with his father and mother, whose parents and their fathers before them for generations belonged to the town on the Blakewater.

When a lad of tender years he was caught up by the wave of enthusiasm which planted football in our midst, and gave to the world the first provincial clubs that brought the English Cup out of London. With both it has been Mr. Southworth's good fortune to be creditably identified. He commenced his football career when 12 years old, and formed a junior club which went by the name of Inkerman Rangers, which played its matches on Follywell Fields, behind the New Jerusalem Church. Of this team he was the captain during his connection with it. Later he played with the Brookhouse Rangers, and in the ranks both of that club and of the Brookhouse Perseverance he was often to be found. They were the nurseries of the Olympic club when it was rising into fame and they included such players as Costley, Parker, Whitehead and Joe Heyes. In course of time Southworth was promoted to a place in the Olympic second team in 1883-4.

His exceptional smartness on the ball was soon recognised by the committee, and he was made captain of the second string and first reserve man when there was a vacancy in the premier eleven. Twelve months later he had the chance of joining the Rovers, but his allegiance to the Light Blues was so strong that he could not entertain the suggestion. On a particular occasion when Accrington and Padiham met, the former with a man short, he was paid the compliment of being invited to fill the gap. It was an unfortunate engagement for him, as it turned out, for in the course of the game his knee gave way, and ended his career as a forward for several years.

Though his prospects were for the time blighted, he did not leave the field. He tried his hand at goal-keeping, and gave up his position on the inside left wing. Between the sticks he "came off" surprisingly well, and before the season ended he became the recognised goal-keeper for the first eleven, and played in the final tie of the Lancashire Cup when the Rovers beat the Olympians in Preston by 2 goals to 1. In the Charity Cup ties at the end of the season, he also took part, and was in at the victory of the Light Blues over Darwen, whom they defeated by one goal to none. They had, however, to subscribe to defeat when they encountered Accrington in the final.

The course of football like that of true love would seem never to run smooth. The Charity Cup ties were hardly out of the way when he found himself at Lancaster helping the Vale of Lune in a match against the Blackburn troop of the Duke of Lancaster's Own Yeomanry Cavalry. It proved another unlucky encounter, for this time the left knee gave way. With both shaky he could still keep goal, and in the season 1885-6 he signed with the Olympic as a professional.

In his leisure moments he had industriously studied music for some years, and in the summer months, from the age of 14, had been accustomed to accept engagements at Blackpool, Rhyl, and other popular resorts.

He had only played in two or three matches after becoming a "pro" when he got a berth at Chester in connection with the theatre there. In 1886 he was found goal-keeping for the Chester club, and there is no doubt that he made his mark as a custodian. Just before Christmas he returned to Blackburn, and, throwing in his lot with Olympic again, he came out as centre forward.

114

In the new position he was greatly admired, and observant men saw that with care he had a future before him. No one was more surprised or more gratified than Southworth himself that he found his knees strong again and his fleetness unimpaired. In the first match the Light Blues beat Witton by six goals to one.

At the end of the season overtures were made to him on behalf of the Rovers to play with them in the Charity Cup ties, but the time had not come when he felt disposed to sever his connection with the old club. It was not far distant, however, for in the very next season, 1887-8, he was found among the "Leamington lads", having signed as a "pro" in the position of centre forward. His first match with the Rovers was against the Olympians.

In the summer of last year he had an engagement to fulfil at Rhyl, but when once he returned to his native heath he did not miss a single Rovers' match. His dodging, his neat passing, his speed and his general accuracy in shooting won the hearts of the numerous frequenters of the Leamington ground, and the committee were so thoroughly satisfied and gratified with the form he displayed, that at the beginning of the present season they made him captain of the eleven.

Southworth is not merely a "battling" player, but he is to be depended upon. He was unable to play in the first match of the season against Sunderland, but after that there were only two occasions on which he was "minus". On each he had the most sufficient reason. In the one he was playing for his county at Edinburgh, and in the other he was one of the England eleven against Wales. If there was any lingering doubt as to his fitness for the post of Rovers' captain it was dispelled by his selection for the county and international fixtures.

Southworth has youth on his side. His record is more than satisfactory hitherto, but with fairly good luck his future will be more remarkable than his past has been.[2] He has consistently tried to deserve success of the highest order, and it will not be his fault if in the long run he does not command it. He is steady in habit, and with him heart and soul are in the game. He is built for speed, he plays an unselfish game, his judgment is excellent, and he can dodge and tackle as well as most folk. Whether on the wing, in goal, or as centre forward he has shown conspicuously good form, and there can be no doubt that he is not merely an all round player, but that as centre forward he has few if any equals and no superiors.
Blackburn Standard (Apr 20th, 1889)

[1] *Park Terrace is at the top of Shear Brow, a couple of minutes' walk from Hole-i'th'-Wall.*

[2] *Prophetic words! Southworth was to finish his career with 25 FA Cup goals, 2 Cup-winner's medals, 97 Football League goals (plus 36 with Everton), and 3 England caps.*

9. JAMES SOUTHWORTH

Mr. James Southworth is probably known by name by everybody in East Lancashire who takes any interest in athletics or football. He has gained fame in the football field as a full back for the Rovers[1], but the capacity in which he is represented above, and one in which he is perhaps better known, is as a 120 yards' sprinter. In athletic circles this year and last he has caused some commotion by the brilliant manner in which he has carried off many first prizes, and many persons can be found to back him heavily to win the championship next year.

So far this year he has not been seen with the Rovers' first team in the football field, but his services are at the disposal of the committee to play in any match in Blackburn.

Southworth's appearance before the world as an amateur sprinter is of a comparative recent date. The first occasion on which he competed in any athletic sports was at the Accrington Cricket Club Sports last year, where he succeeded in carrying off the first prize in the 120 yards' handicap. Since then his success as an athlete has been very marked, and in less than twelve months from that time he was looked upon by many as the future 120 yards' champion, so that from an obscure and unknown runner he gained in a short time a reputation almost second to none in the country. He continued to improve as time went on, and notwithstanding the fact that he was heavily handicapped at each consecutive race, he fully maintained his earlier successes. The next race in which he appeared after Accrington was at Lowerhouse where he won his heat, but owing to important business was compelled to leave before the final was decided. He was next seen at Bootle, and there again won the first prize in the 120 yards' handicap. At the Manchester Police Sports a week or two later the first prize again fell to him. The last time he ran last season was at Eccles in the Police sports and he there carried off the second prize.

At this time Southworth's leg gave way, and he decided to rest for a time. With care the limb regained its normal strength, and this year he again entered in the 120 yards' handicap and the 220 yards' handicap at the Accrington C.C. Sports. On this occasion his success was more marked than previously. Not only did he win the first prize in the first-named race, but he came in second in the 220 yards' race.

Some weeks later at Widnes he, for the first time, met Wilcock[2] in the 120 yards' scratch race. The race was a splendid one, and the subject of this sketch was beaten by about a foot. Southworth was, however, soon destined to wipe out this defeat, for a week or two later, at Witton, he defeated his formidable opponent in the 120 yards' race for the Feilden Cup.

Previous to that Southworth won the first prize at Lowerhouse. Since then he has won first prizes in 120 yard handicaps at Heywood, East Lancashire C.C. Sports, and Bury. In addition to the successes mentioned, he has won first prizes for football kicking at the East Lancashire C.C. Sports, Heywood, and Haslingden, and won the second prize in a 220 yards' hurdle race at Chorley. His brilliant performance at Witton in the subsequent race for the Feilden Cup, will be remembered by all who take an interest in athletics in Blackburn. Not only did he defeat Wilcock in the race for the cup, but carried off the first prize in a 120 yards' handicap.

James Southworth (left) pictured alongside his great sprint rival J.H. Wilcock. The trophy is the Feilden Cup, awarded to the winner of the 120 yards sprint.

"Do you think you can manage to carry off the championship next year?" our representative asked Mr. Southworth after gleaning the above facts.

"If I improve as much next year as I have done this I feel confident I can," was the reply.

Next year Mr. Southworth contemplates, along with a number of brother athletes, taking a short trip to America and there competing in a number of races. With careful training and ordinary luck he should next year carry off the championship if his friend of the other column[2] does not step in and spoil his little game.

Blackburn Weekly Standard (Oct 5th, 1889)

[1] *Both John and James Southworth played for Olympic until signing for Rovers in September 1887. See text.*

[2] *J. H. Wilcock: celebrated athlete and gymnast, born in Bradford, Southworth's great rival in the 120 yards sprints.*

APPENDIX III:

From *The Times*, April 2nd 1883:

> THE ASSOCIATION CHALLENGE CUP
> BLACKBURN OLYMPIC v. OLD ETONIANS
> Many interesting encounters have been furnished by the ties for this, the most important of the challenge cups, but probably none more so than the final match played at Kennington Oval between these clubs on Saturday. The weather was charming, and the attendance very large. The Etonians, who won the cup last year and in 1879, were successful in the toss, and at the outset defended the Harleyford-road goal. Hunter kicked off within a few minutes of half-past 3. The play at once became fast, the northerners being the first to act on the aggressive, and had it not been for Eton's back play they would speedily have scored. As it was, Gibson kicked the ball against the bar and it went behind. The Etonians now played up in a most determined style, and having run the ball down the ground Goodheart attempted to send the ball between the posts but failed. Even play followed, the forwards on either side making alternate attacks on the others' goal, but being well repulsed by the backs. Now came a most determined onslaught by the Lancashire team, and the downfall of the Etonian goal seemed inevitable. The ball was worked away, however, and a fine run down the ground ended in Goodheart sending the ball underneath the bar. The utmost enthusiasm greeted this achievement, and was continued when Eton very nearly repeated it. Nothing further of a distinct advantage was secured during the first portion of the game. The Etonians, however, soon after ends were changed, sustained a great loss, as Dunn in running the ball down the left side of the ground was cannoned against and thrown, he being unable to take further part in the match. Still the light blues had a slight advantage for a little while, but the northerners were not long before they assumed the aggressive and Matthews kicked a goal for them. Although both teams strove hard to gain some decisive score neither were able to do so during the customary hour and a half's play. The game was therefore prolonged for another half-hour. It seemed at one time probable that even the extension would not be sufficient to admit of the match being brought to a definite issue. During the first quarter of an hour nothing transpired, but subsequently Astley who had the ball well passed to him by Dewhurst gained the decisive point. Blackburn Olympic, the first northern club that has yet gained the cup, were thus successful by two goals to one. Mr. C. Crump was referee, and Mr. M. P. Betts and Mr. Pierce-Dix were the umpires.

Author's note:
The Thunderer gets it wrong:
  (a) It's spelt Goodhart
  (b) Dunn was injured *after* Matthews' equalising goal
  (c) Costley hit the winner, not Astley

APPENDIX IV:

Our Football Teams

Each Saturday, when days are cold
And warmer weather fleeting,
Our football teams turn out to give
Their "*visitors*" a beating.

At Leamington, to widespread fame,
They dread the "Blackburn Rover";
Or up above the Shire's Brow,
The "'Lympic" throws them over.

To these the "Wand'rer" struck his flag,
And "Eton" went a-weeping,
Whilst England gave her Challenge Cup
To Captain Hunter's keeping.

In crowded fields, the lusty cheer,
From throats nigh choked with cotton,
Proclaims the fact in far-off streets:
"A goal! A goal! Well gotten."

Then toe to toe; go on, brave "blues",
Through forest, town and heather;
And Blackburn still with cheerful voice
Shall hail the globe of leather.

Press on to goal and keep the cups
Ye both have won so bravely,
And point to all inquiring clubs,
"Old Wykehamists" and "Staveley".

Now in the final eight ye stand
To win or lose the trophy;
So here we'll part till "time" is called,
Then write another 'strophy.

Not fearing yet, I'll trust ye both
On any field before ye:
True samples of our Blackburn arms,
Our "*Arte et Labore*".

Charles Nightingale Stott (Jan/Feb 1884)
From *A Blackburn Miscellany* – see bibliography.

APPENDIX V:

EAST LANCASHIRE CHARITY CUP

Extract from *Things About Blackburn Rovers* (see bibliography)

It is a very old Cup. One Tuesday night in May, 1882, representatives of Blackburn Rovers, Olympic, Darwen and Accrington had a little confab at the White Bull Hotel, at Blackburn, and decided to get an "East Lancashire Charity Cup", which would be a magnificent trophy. The original idea, ambitious enough, was that the Cup should be 2ft. 10 in. in height, 150 ounces in weight, and 100 guineas in cost. Alterations and additions subsequently agreed upon added two inches to its stature, 50 ounces to its weight, and £50 to its cost.

The first draw was: Rovers v. Darwen, and Olympic v. Accrington, and arrangements were made for the getting in of subscriptions. Thanks to the keen interest of Mr. Thomas Whewell the brewer, Blackburn's contribution amounted to over £90. Darwen raised £23, and Accrington close upon £9. In the final Olympic beat Rovers 5-2 at Ewood Park. The total sum raised in gate money and subscriptions was over £240. Out of this, £146/12/- was paid for the Cup, £8/15/6 for its case, £22 for medals for the Olympic players, and £2/15/- for badges for the Rovers as runners-up. After the payment of sundry expenses a balance of £41 odd remained, and £40 was granted to the Blackburn and East Lancashire Infirmary.

On the body of the Cup is a scene of the game of football and on the reverse, a representation of the Infirmary. At the foot are four beautifully modelled figures of football players in different attitudes. Between them are four shields bearing the respective arms of Blackburn, Darwen, Accrington and Burnley, enamelled in the proper heraldic colours. Above the body, a string of Lancashire roses run round the Cup. The handles curve upwards from the body, and surmounted by models of a greyhound and lion to indicate fleetness and strength, the footballer's necessary (but not always present) requisites. Underneath the handles are the busts of Sir Robert Peel and the late Mr. Pilkington, who was virtually the founder of the Infirmary. On the neck of the Cup is the Lancashire coat-of-arms. The whole thing is surmounted by an exquisitely modelled group of Raphael's "Charity". The Cup is mounted on an ebony base, in which is cut the inscription "East Lancashire Football Charity Cup, 1882".

Author's note: the trophy later became the Lancs. FA Youth Cup, last awarded to Grange Youth from Wigan, in 1991. It now resides in the trophy room in the Lancashire FA headquarters at Leyland.

APPENDIX VI:

OLYMPIC PLAYERS WHO WERE SELECTED FOR ENGLAND

Name	Date	Opposition	Player's club
Jack Hunter	2/3/78	Scotland	Sheffield Heeley
	13/3/80	Scotland	
	15/3/80	Wales	
	26/2/81	Wales (capt.)	
	12/3/81	Scotland	
	18/2/82	Ireland	
	11/3/82	Scotland	
Joe Beverley	25/2/84	Ireland	Blackburn Rovers
	15/3/84	Scotland	
	17/3/84	Wales	
James Ward	14/3/85	Wales	Blackburn Olympic
John Yates	2/3/89	Ireland (3 goals)	Burnley
Jack Southworth	23/2/89	Wales (1 goal)	Blackburn Rovers
	7/3/91	Wales (1 goal)	
	2/4/92	Scotland (1 goal)	
Tommy Dewhurst	25/2/84	Ireland	Blackburn Olympic

(Dewhurst was originally chosen, then deselected for disciplinary reasons. See text.)

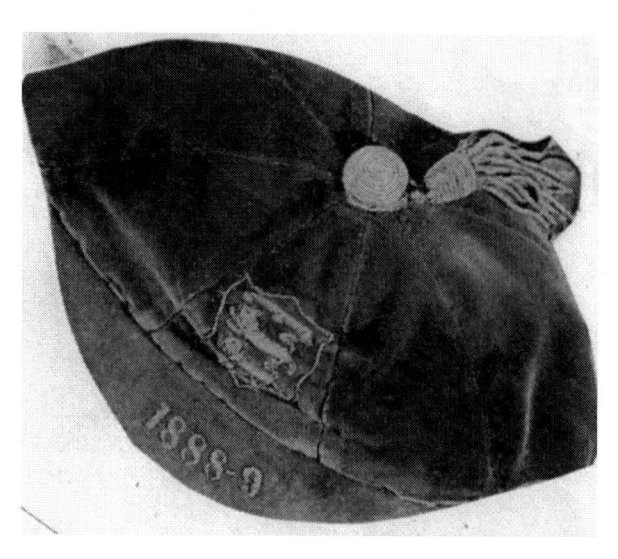

John Yates' England cap, auctioned at Sotheby's for a four-figure sum in May 2006.

BIBLIOGRAPHY

Lancashire FA committee meeting minutes 1878-1889
Football Annual 1882-86, ed. C. W. Alcock
Athletics and Football, Montague Shearman (London 1887)
History of Blackburn Rovers 1875-1925, Charles Francis (Blackburn 1925, Soccer Books 2005)
The History of the Lancashire Football Association 1878-1928, Sutcliffe and Hargreaves (Blackburn 1928)
Things About Blackburn Rovers, Harry Kay (Blackburn 1948)
Soccer: The World Game. A Popular History, Geoffrey Green (Pan 1956)
Association Football (4 vols.), Ed. Fabian and Green (Caxton 1960)
A History of Bolton Wanderers, Percy M. Young (Stanley Paul 1961)
Football in Sheffield, Percy M. Young (Sportsman's Book Club 1963)
A Century of English International Football, Farror and Lamming (Hale 1972)
A Century of Soccer 1875-1975, Harry Berry (Blackburn 1975)
The Giant Killers, Bryon Butler (Pelham 1982)
League Football and the Men Who Made It, Simon Inglis (Collins Willow 1988)
Everton: A Complete Record 1878-1988, Ross and Smailes (Breedon 1988)
Blackburn Rovers: A Complete Record 1875-1990, Mike Jackman (Breedon 1990)
Burnley: A Complete Record, Lee and Simpson (Breedon 1991)
A Team for All Seasons: A History of Northwich Victoria, K. R. Edwards (Cheshire County 1992)
The Official History of the Football Association, Bryon Butler (Queen Anne Press 1993)
Accrington FC – "Th'Owd Reds": The Formation, T. R. Slinger (TRS 1994)
Blackburn Rovers: The Official Encyclopedia, Mike Jackman (Breedon 1994)
The People's Game, James Walvin (Mainstream 1994)
Blackburn Rovers: An Illustrated History, Mike Jackman (Breedon 1995)
Rejected FC (Vols.2 and 3), Dave Twydell (Yore 1995)
The Official Illustrated History of the FA Cup, Bryon Butler (Headline 1996)
Olympic FC: The Forgotten Giant-Killers*, Graham Phythian (New Millennium 1998)
The Birth of Modern Football in Bolton and District: Turton Football Club, Peter Swain (Friends of Football 1998)
Halliwell Football Club: Its Development, Decline, Rebirth and Death, Peter Swain (Halliwell Local History Society 1999)
The FA Cup Complete Results, Tony Brown (Soccer Data 1999)
Darwen Football Club: Memories, Paul Breeze (Posh Up North 2001)
Saga of the Silkmen: The History of Macclesfield Town FC*, Graham Phythian (Carnegie 2001)
The Father of Modern Sport: The Life and Times of Charles W. Alcock, Keith Booth (Parrs Wood Press 2002)
The Lancashire Football Association: A Celebration of 125 Years, John Bullen (Lancs. FA 2003)
The Early FA Cup Finals and the Southern Amateurs, Keith Warsop (Soccer Data 2004)
The Forgotten Rivals: A History of Bootle Football Club 1880-1893, Tony Onslow (Countryvise 2005)
Play Up, Higher Walton!, Peter Holme (Landy 2006)
"*1883 Cup Final: Patricians v Plebeians*", Christopher Andrew *History Today* May 1983
"*Playing for Money: James J. Lang and Emergent Soccer Professionals in Sheffield*", Graham Curry (Taylor and Francis essay collection – website)
"*Early Sheffield Football*" Graham Curry *Soccer History* Winter 2004
Barrett's Directory of Blackburn and District 1884, 1891, 1897, 1901, 1903, 1906, 1909, 1915
Blackburn Worthies of Yesterday, George C. Miller (*Blackburn Times* 1959)
Blackburn and Darwen a Century Ago, Alan Duckworth (Landy 1989)
A Blackburn Miscellany, Ed. Bob Dobson (Landy 1993)
Blackburn's Old Inns, George C. Miller (Landy 1993)
Blackburn: A Pictorial History, Geoffrey Timmins (Phillimore 1993)

Blackpool: A Pictorial History, Ted Lightbown (Phillimore 1994)
BRFC: roversonline.com – website
Partick Thistle Early Years – website
William Billington: the Blackburn Poet – website
"Local Elite and the Working Class Response in the North-West 1870-95", Alice Russell *Northern History* 1987

*Available from the author

Newspapers consulted:

Accrington Times
Athletic News
Ayrshire Post
Bell's Life in London
Birmingham Gazette
Blackburn Standard
Blackburn Times
Blackpool Evening Gazette
Blackpool Herald
Bolton Evening Guardian
Bolton Evening Telegraph
Burnley Express and Advertiser
Darwen News
Dumbarton Herald
Edinburgh Times
Eton College Chronicle
Football Field
Glasgow Herald
Grimsby News
The Illustrated Sporting and Dramatic News
Kilmarnock Standard
Lancashire Evening Post
Leigh Chronicle
Lennox Herald
Liverpool Courier
Liverpool Daily Post
Liverpool Mercury
Manchester Guardian
North Eastern Daily Gazette
Northern Daily Telegraph
North Wales Guardian
Nottingham Evening Post
Pastime
Preston Guardian
Preston Herald
The Scotsman
Sheffield Independent
Sheffield Daily Telegraph
Southport Guardian
The Sporting Chronicle
The Sportsman
Staffordshire Sentinel
Sunderland Echo

The Times
Wrexham Advertiser

ACKNOWLEDGEMENTS

Thanks are due to the staff of the Local History or Community sections of the following Libraries:

> Blackburn
> Manchester Central
> Preston Harris
> Bolton
> Liverpool
> Sheffield
> Accrington
> Blackpool
> Burnley
> Darwen
> Nottingham
> Wrexham
> Fleetwood
> Birmingham Central
> Southport
> Bury
> Glasgow (The Mitchell Library)
> Dumbarton
> Kilmarnock (East Ayrshire)
> Middlesbrough Central
> Leigh
> Grimsby
> Sunderland

Also: British Library Newspaper Collection, Colindale, NW9

The following made invaluable contributions:
> Peter Holme, for permission to use archives and photographs from the National Football Museum, Preston, and for help in tracking down some of those elusive home venues;
> David Burgess of the Lancashire FA, for permission to take photographs of the County trophy and the East Lancs. Charity Cup, as well as access to Lancs. FA minutes;
> Mrs Catherine Lomax, for photographs of Warburton's medals;
> Nick Harling of Blackburn Museum, for permission to take photos, and for putting me right about the Oozebooth pitch;
> Albert Yates, for tireless support and liaison within Blackburn;
> Mark Shaw, landlord of the Hole-i'th'-Wall, for ale, liaison, and loan of the Robert Pate painting;
> Tony Onslow, for information on Bootle FC and early Everton FC;
> Ian Nannestad, for details on Grimsby Town;
> John Bibby, for loan of his copy of *Things About Rovers* (see bibliography);
> David France, for photocopies of Everton/Olympic match programme;
> Jan Gedzielewski, of St Mary's College, Blackburn, for permission to take photographs in the grounds;
> Matthew Tinker, for research into early Southport football;
> Robert Phythian, for computer services.

Picture Credits (page references)

Blackburn Local History Archives, 54
Blackburn Museum, 53
Blackburn Standard, 29. 36, 64, 67, 114, 116
Blackburn Times, 18, 35
Bolton Local History Archives, 68
FA Archives, 81
Football Field, 70, 71
David France (Everton memorabilia collection), 76
Illustrated Sporting and Dramatic News, 52
Lancashire FA, Leyland, 42, 86
Lancashire Telegraph, 120
Ted Lightbown, 47
Mrs. Catherine Lomax, 89, 106
National Football Museum, Preston, 4, 25, 49 (top)
Ordnance Survey, 62, 102
Robert Pate, 19 (bottom)
Sheffield Local History Archives, 23

The photograph of the Old Carthusians (p. 45) is published by kind permission of the Governing Body of Charterhouse.

Every reasonable effort has been made to trace owners of the copyright of visuals used herein. Details of any omissions or oversights should be communicated in writing to the author, c/o the publishers.

INDEX

Club abbreviations:
Acc – Accrington
BPR – Blackburn Park Road
BW – Bolton Wanderers
OC – Old Carthusians
OE – Old Etonians
Oly – Blackburn Olympic
Pers – Blackburn Perseverance
PNE – Preston North End
QPG – Queen's Park, Glasgow
Rov – Blackburn Rovers
Sheff – Sheffield Association
Wands – The Wanderers
Wed – Sheffield Wednesday

Precise locations (e.g., streets) are in Blackburn unless otherwise stated.
For further information on specific clubs, games and venues, see Appendix I.
Page numbers in **bold** type indicate illustrations.

A

Accrington Cricket Club Sports 115
Accrington FC 15, 27, 36, 39-40, 55, 56, 66, 68, 74, 75, 77
Accrington Times 27, 40
Adams, H. (Druids) 41
Ainsworth St. 108
Albion Mill, Ewood 80
Alcock, C. W. (FA official) 49, 61
    see also Football Annual
Alexandra Meadows 9, 23, 26, 98
Allan, David (QPG) 60
Alliance, The 77
Altham Colliery disaster 109
Amos, Andrew (OC) 43, 45
Anderson, William (QPG) 60
Anderson, William J. (OE) 48, 50
Anfield (Rd.), Liverpool 69, 77, 78
Anvil St. 99, 112
Archer, Frank (poet) 104
Arnott, Walter (QPG) 60
Arthur, "Herbie" (Rov) 57, 63, 66, 75, 76
Askew, Walter (Oly) 8, 9, 10, 16-17, 21, 24, 27, 28
Astley, Alfred (Oly) **4**, 8, 10, 16, 17, 27, 28, **81**
    death 80
    newsagent 38, 80
    treasurer 24
Astley, William (Oly) **4**, **81**, **124**
    East Lancashire Charity Cup game 36
    FA Cup games 39, 41, 46, 50, 57, 65
    first team debut 24
    forward 30
    full-back 28
    goalkeeper 65
    goals 31
    Lancashire Cup game 31
    last game for Olympic 78, 81*n*
    reserves 16
    retirement 80
Astley Bridge 31, 69, 113
Aston Villa FC 41, 55, 57, 60, 75, 79
Athletic News, The 73, 75
Athletics and Football 26
Audley Park 98
Aulty (long jumper) 38, 110

Avery, George (Rov) 10, 28, 36, 63
Ayrshire XI 110

B

Bainbridge, Herbert (OE) 48, 50, 51
Balaclava St. 54
Baldwin, W. (Oly) 16, 17, 21, 24, 25, 27, 107
Bamber, (Acc) 39
Barber, E. (Sheff) 24
Barber, H. (Sheff) 24
Barber, J. H. (Sheff) 24
Barley Bank, Darwen 11, 15, 30, **32**, 55, 58, 63
    see also Darwen
Barnsley 33
Barrett, Dr. (Oly) 75, 76
Barton, J. (Rov) 75
Beardshaw, W. (Sheff) 23, 24
Belfast 58, 77
Bell, (Oly) 69
Belthorn (coalmine) 65
Bennington St. 98
Beresford, (Rov) 75
Betts, Morgan (Wands) 49, 117
Beverley, Joe (Oly, Rov) **4**
    absences 21, 32
    birth 111
    captain of Olympic 20, 36
    death 80
    debut 8, 111
    East Lancs. Charity Cup games 36-7, 76
    FA Cup games 23-4, 30, 38, 39, 65, 66, 70
    family 112
    full-back 17, 31
    goalkeeper 8, 32
    goals 8, 9, 17, 24, 28, 30, 31, 70
    guest for Olympic 44
    "hidden in Blackpool" 69
    Lancashire Cup games 21-2, 31, 67
    last game for Olympic 78, 81*n*
    libero 22, 27
    one-armed throw-ins 8, 16, 17, 24, 38
    praise for 8
    representative honours 13, 111, 120
    return to Olympic (1884) 64
    Rovers player 11, 28, 56, 63, 72, 75
    wages dispute 71
Billington, William (poet) 6, 54, **54**, 63
Billy the Kid 20
Birley St. 53
Birtwistle, R. (Rov, Oly) 10, 57, 63
Blackamoor's Head, Inn, The 56
Black Star FC 7, 8, 99, 111
Blackburn Cricket Club 8, 102
Blackburn FA 7, 98
    trophy see Blackburn Olympic
Blackburn Law FC 7, 9, 98
Blackburn Olympic FC **4**, **52**, **81**, **124**
    2-3-5 system 26, 28, 30-1, 36, 46
    apple scrumping 65
    Blackburn FA Trophy **4**, 9, 10-11, 16-17, 79, 105, 109
    combination play 9, 16, 39, 46
    disputes on the pitch 20, 59
        see also disputed goals
    East Lancashire Charity Cup games 36-7, 55-6, 68, 74, 76
    England players 8, 33, 67, 120
    excursions 35, 37

125

FA Cup Final 1883 5, 8, 13, 48-52
FA Cup games 23-4, 30, 39-42, 45-6, 58-61, 66, 70, 74, 77
Football Combination, The 75, 77
grounds *see* Oozebooth, Hole-i'th'-Wall
high-scoring wins 15, 30, 58, 64
internal dissension 73
Lancashire Cup games 21-2, 31, 39, 58, 63-4, 65, 67-8, 77, 111
last games 78
Livesey United trophy **4**, 9, 109
origins 7-8
prize draws 71-2, 73, 74
reserves 10, 57
special training 14, 44, 47, 56
  banned from 66
team colours 8, 18, 36
wages dispute 71
see also Darwen, Blackburn Rovers, Preston North End
Blackburn Park Road FC 7, 16, 22, 55, 74, 78, 98, 99, 109
Blackburn Perseverance FC 16, 24, 99, 106*n*, 114
Blackburn Pilgrims FC 98
Blackburn Ragged School, The 72
Blackburn Railway Clerks, The 79
Blackburn Rovers FC
  FA Cup games 13, 17, 26, 48, 59, 61, 66, 72, 75
  Football League 75
  grounds 1875-1891
    see Alexandra Meadows, Leamington St., Ewood
  origins 7
  training at Morecambe 47
  vs. Olympic 10, 12, 17-18, 28, 31, 36-7, 57, 63-4, 66, 75, 76, 78
Blackburn School of Art, The 57
Blackburn Standard, The
  1878-81 7, 9, 16, 26, 27, **29**
  1882-3 8, 32, 34, 36, **36**, 37, 39, 52
  1884-9 54, 58, **64**, 65, **67**, 68, 73, **114**, **116**
  see also Appendix II
Blackburn St. 110
Blackburn Times, The
  1878-82 7, 10, 12, 13, 14, 15, 18, **18**, 21, 30, 32, **35**, 37
  1883-9 25, 36, 38, 41, 44, 48, 52, 53, 69, 77, 78, 79
Blackburn Zingari FC 99
Blackpool 44, 47, **47**, 55, 65, 68*n*, 69
  see also South Shore FC
Blackpool Evening Gazette 43
Blackpool Herald 65
Blackpool St. John's FC 39
Blakey Moor Market 7
Blenkhorne, Robert (Rov) 28
Blue Star FC 7
Boghead, Dumbarton 15, 57
Bolton Evening Guardian 15
Bolton Wanderers FC 15, 66, 67, **68**, 69, 71, 75
Boothman, Cllr. 7, 14, 21
Bootle FC 15, 22, 77, 78
Bottomgate 80
Bowen, E. (Druids) 41-2
Boyle's Clothing Store 35, 55
Bradbury, W. (Sheff) 23-4
Bradshaw, J. (Oly) 9, 16, 17
Bramall Lane, Sheffield 23, **23**, 29, 110
Bramham, William (Oly Secretary) **4**, 57, 65, **81**
  resignation 67
Brewer, Mr. (Sheff. Guardians) 33
Brickmakers' Arms, The, Burnley 79, **79**
Bridge Mill 21
Brindle, T. (Darwen) 16

British Football Association 66-7
Bromley-Davenport, W. (Oxf. Uni.) 58
Brookhouse 112
Brookhouse Rangers FC 16, 28, 38, 40, 112
Brown, (Acc) 39
Brown, A. J. (Oly) 16, 17, 24, 27, 28, 30, 31, 36
Brown, Jimmy (Rov)
  five-a-side team 29
  guests for Olympic 70
  Rovers games 28, 36-7, 63, 66
  sprinter 29
Bryce, (Acc) 39
Burnley FC 74, 75
Bury 105, 116
Butterworth, J. (Pers) 17
Buttery St. 8, 111

C

Cambridge University 26, 43, 48
Campbell, Charles (QPG) 60
Carlisle, (Oly) 73, 74, 75, 76, 78
Catterall, Mr. (caterer) 29
Cattle Market Field 10, 16, 17, 98
Cattow, Mrs. Muriel 80, 113
Cetewayo 20
Chadwick, E. (Rov) 75, 76
Chadwick, (Oly) 74, 78
Charlotte St. 110
Charterhouse *see* Old Carthusians
Cherry Tree Cricket Ground 9, 99
Chester FC 70, 114
Chesterfield 33
Chevalier, John (OE, Derby County) 48, 50, 65
Chew, (Acc) 39
Chippendale, Hammy (runner) 110
Chippendale, Thomas (poet) 54, 77
Christ Church FC 7, 10, 11, 109
Christie, Robert (QPG) 60
Church FC 22, 40-1, 70, 71, 74, 75
Church St. 8, 53, 67, 80
Clapham Rovers 43
Clayton-le-Moors 9
Clitheroe FC 15, 56
Cob Wall FC 11, 12, 15, 16, 98, 105
Cobbold, William (OC) 43, 45-6, 67
Coddington, William (MP) 55
College Road, Manchester 45
Colvin, E. G. (OC) **45**
Combination, The *see* Football Combination
Cook, J. (Oly) 9, 74
Cook, L. (Oly) 9
Corinthians, The 23, 48, 60, 67, 70-1
Corporation Park 7, 98
Costley, E. (*or* T.) Everton 76, 113
Costley, Jimmy (Oly) **52**, **81**, **124**
  birth 112
  Brookhouse Rangers player 16, 28, 38, 40, 114
  death 113
  debut for Olympic 40
  Everton player? 113
  FA Cup games 40, 41-2, 46, 50-1, 57, 59, 60, 65, 66, 70, 112
  "Gentlemen vs. Players" 71, 113
  goals 46, 51, **52**, 57, 58, 67, 113, 117*n*
  Lancashire Cup games 63-4
  last game for Olympic 78, 81*n*
  representative honours 58, 112-3

126

Rovers player 73
teetotal pledge 80, 113
Cotton Tree, The 35, 53, 56
Coupe, (Nelson) 70
Cow Gap Lane, Blackpool 44, 77
Cowlairs FC 30, 74
Crewe Alexandra FC 60, 75
Cricket and Football Times 12
Crook, (Oly) 40-1, 63
Crookes, Sheffield 33, 103
Crossley *see* Costley
Crump, Charles (ref.) 49, 66, 117
Cunliffe, (Oly) 13, 36

D

Dabulamanzi 33, 78
Darwen FC
   FA Cup games 13, 24
   vs. Old Etonians 13
   vs. Olympic 11, 15, 16, 30, 57, 58, 74, 78
   training at Blackpool 47
Darwen Ramblers 40, 57
Davis, J. (Druids) 41
Deepdale, Preston 53, 63
Denham, Mr. Nathan (bookseller) 72
Denton FC 74
Derby County FC 48, 65
Dewhurst, Mr. J. (cabinet maker) 72
Dewhurst, Tommy (Oly) **4, 81, 124**
   debut 31
   East Lancs. Charity Cup games 36-7, 56
   FA Cup games 39, 41, 46, 50-1, 57, 60, 66, 117
   goals 37, 41, 46, 55, 56, 58, 59, 70
   Halliwell player 73
   hidden down coalmine 65
   Lancashire Cup games 31, 63
   last game for Olympic 78, 81*n*
   old age 80
   representative honours 58, 59, 67, 120
   wages dispute 71
Dewsbury, Yorks. 57
Dickson (Oly) 75, 76
disputed goals 21-2, 66, 74
Distillery FC 77
Dodd (Oly, Heywood) 78
Dog and Partridge Inn, The 62, 70, 80, 106
Douglas, James (Rov) 28, 36, 63
Douglas, S. (Rov) 75
Drill Field, Northwich 30
Druids FC 20, 41-2
Duckworth, Johnny (Rov) 10, 28, 36
   Olympic player 8,9
Duckworth, Joseph (Oly) 58, 60, 63, 65
Duckworth, R. (Rov) 10
Duckworth, W. (Rov) 10
Duff (Partick Thistle) 74
Duke of Lancaster's Yeomanry XI 114
Dumbarton FC 15, 59
   "championship of Great Britain" 57
Dunn, Arthur (OE) 48, 50-1, 117

E

Eagley FC 15, 41, 64
Earl St. 38
East Lancashire Charity Cup **42**, 119

see also Blackburn Olympic, Darwen
Eastham, (Acc) 39
Eccles, Manchester 116
Eckroyd, (Oly) 75
Edinburgh 33
Edinburgh University FC 57
Edmondson, James (Oly) 9, 10
   treasurer 7
Enfield FC (Lancs.) 9, 10, 30, 31
England national XI 12, 33, 58, 67, 120
Eton College Chronicle 55
Etonian Ramblers FC 43
Euston Station, London 53
Evelyn, W. A. (OC) 43, 45
Everton FC 69, 74, 75, **76**, 77, 78, 80, 113
Ewood (Park) 11, 36, 99

F

FA Cup 11, 12, 18, **25**, 26, 28, **52**, 75
   see also Blackburn Olympic, Blackburn Rovers, Old Carthusians, Old Etonians
Farnworth Standard FC 78
Fecitt, Herbert (Rov) 66
Feilden Cup, The 116, **116**
Fielden, (Oly) 75, 76
Fish Lane 72
Fishwick Ramblers FC 106
Fleetwood Rangers FC 74, 77
Fletcher, (Oly) 74
floodlit football match, first ever 33
Foley, Charles (OE) 49, 50
Follywell Fields 99, 114
Football Annual, C. W. Alcock's 8, 33, 67
Football Combination, The 75, 77
Football Field 15, **70, 71**, 74, 78, 103-13
Football League, The 75, 77
Forrest, James (Rov) 63
Foulds, J. (Oly) 8, 9
Frankland, G. (Oly, Heywood) 78, 79
French, Thomas (OE) 49, 50
Furthergate FC 7, 9, 12, 98
Furthergate School 9, 110

G

Gaine, William E. L. (solicitor) 75
Galligreaves St. 10, 98
Garner, (Oly) 73, 74, 75, 79
Gentlemen vs. Players *see* Jimmy Costley
George Inn, The 21
Geronimo 20
Gibson, Tommy (Oly) **4, 81, 124**
   argument with Warburton 56, 58, 70
   attacking play 16, 17, 24
   birth 108
   Church player 56
   East Lancs. Charity Cup games 36
   FA Cup games 23-4, 39, 41, 46, 60, 66
   family 80, 109
   full-back 9
   half-back in 2-3-5 36, 76, 81
      see also Cup games
   Lancashire Cup games 31, 63, 67
   last game 78, 81*n*
   loyalty to Olympic 73, 74, 79
   lucky shirt 8
   missed train 22

praise for 29
representative honours 13, 22, 34, 58, 109
retirement 80
testimonial 110
three-quarter back 27
Gill, (Oly) 74
Gillespie, John (QPG) 60
Gillet, L. F. (OC) **45**
Glasgow Herald, The 30
Godalming, Surrey 43
Goodhart, Henry (OE) 48, 50, 51, 117
Gorse Bridge 99
Gow, J. J. (QPG) 60
Great Lever FC 31
Green, W. (Rov) 10
Greenwood, "Doc" (Rov) 10, 28, 36, 48
Gregson, Mr. (Lancs. FA) 70
Gregson, Richard (Rov) 75
Grimsby Town FC 64
Grimshaw Park 98

H

Hacking, G. (Pers) 17, 24
Hacking, John (Blackpool and Oldham Ath.) 24
Hacking, T. (Pers) 17, 24
Hacking, Thomas (Oly) **4**, **81**, **124**
  absences 32, 55, 69
  birth 107
  debut 25, 107
  dentistry 25, 69, 80, 108
  East Lancs. Charity Cup games 36-7, 55, 107
  FA Cup games 30, 39-40, 41-2, 50-1, 66
  great saves 29, 31, 40, 51
  identity 24-5
  injury prevents selection for North 25, 108
  Lancashire Cup games 31, 63
  last game for Olympic 78, 81*n*
  praise for 25, 29
  representative honours 40, 107
  scores a goal 65
Haigh, David (ref.) 42
Hall, J. G. (Crewe Alexandra) 75
Halliwell FC 63, 73, 113
Hancock St. 80
Hansell, Walter (OC) 43, 45, **45**
Hanson, W. (Oly) 10, 16, 17, 24
Hardman, E. T. (OC) 43, 45
Hargreaves, Fred (Rov) 10, 28, 36
Hargreaves, John (Rov) 36-7
Hargreaves, J. (Acc) 39
Hargreaves, W. (Oly) 30-1
Harrison, C. (Oly) 55
Harrower, W. (QPG) 60
Harwood St. 80, 110
Haslingden (Grane) 10, 116
Haslingden FC 9, 10
Haworth (Lower Chapel) 21
Haworth, J. (Rov, Oly) 10
Hawthorne Rd., Liverpool 77
Hayhurst, W. (shop) 14
Heeley *see* Sheffield Heeley
Hendon FC 41
Heyes, Joe (Rov, Oly) 75, 114
Heywood Athletic Sports 116
Heywood FC 78
Higher Oozebooth
  see Oozebooth

Higher Walton FC 77
Hindle, J. (Acc) 39
Hindle, Tom (ref) 74
Holden, J. (Oly) 73
Hole-i'th'-Wall **19**, 102
  athletic sports 1881 29
  football tournament 1882 38
  grandstand 29, 64, 102
    destroyed in gale 59
  history 15, 99
  improvements 18, 38
  pitch conditions 15, 31, 59
  pub 15, 22, **19**, **83**
  rugby game 57
  see also Blackburn Olympic
Hollins Grove 30, **32**
Holm, J. W. (QPG) 60
Holt, G. (Pers) 17
Hornby, Albert Neilsen ("Monkey") (Rov)
  guest for Olympic 41
  plays for Crewe Alexandra 60
Hornby, Sir Henry 14
Hornby's Mills 111, 113
Horrocks (Church) 41
Hothersall, Jack (Oly) 74, 76
Hothersall, Richard (Oly) 74, 79
Howorth, Roger (Rov, Oly) 36-7, 56, 57
Hughes, F. W. (Northwich Victoria) 59
Hunter, Jack (Heeley, Wed, Oly) **4**, **81**, **124**
  assistant trainer at Rovers 79
  athlete 33, 104
  benefit match 64
  boyhood 103
  captaincy 56, 118
  death 80
  debut for Olympic 32, 34
  England player 32, 33, 120
  FA Cup games 26, 39, 41-2. 45-6, 50-2, 60-1, 65, 66, 70, 74, 75, 103-4
  goalkeeper 78
  goals 42, 57, 70, 74
  injury 58
  Lancashire Cup games 63
  last game for Olympic 78, 81*n*
  New Brighton Tower FC coach 79
  praise for 33, 34
  pub landlord 35, 53, 62, 64, 79, 104
  retirement 79-80
  scout for amateur talent 74
  Sheffield player 26, 33-4, 103, 104*n*
  top hat tale 47
  Zulus player 33-4

I

Inkerman Rangers FC 114
Ireland national XI 78
Irwell Springs FC 78
Isle of St. Helena, The 80

J

James St. 7, 62, 70, 80, 106, 111
Jefferson, Thomas (Rov) 28
Jones, A. (Druids) 41
Jubilee St. 53

K

Kay, Harry 80
   see also Bibliography
Kennington Oval 13, 49, **49**, 63, 71
Kilmarnock Athletic FC 32, 55
Kilnhurst FC 35
King, R. S. (Oxf. Uni.) 58
King St. 80
King William St. 72
King's Own Regiment, Dublin 78
Kinnaird, Rt. Hon. Arthur **49, 52, 91**
   captain of OE 11, 13, 47
   FA Cup Final 1883 50-2
   headstand 48
   robust play 49
Knowl Meadow, Darwen 21
Knuzden 98

L

Lammock Athletic Sports 110
Lancashire Cup **86**
   see Blackburn Olympic, Rovers
Lancashire FA 13, 17, 22, 70
   Youth Cup 119
Lancashire League 79
Last, A. J. (OC) 43, 45
Leamington Rd. Baptist Church 99
Leamington St. 30, 55, 67, 71, 74, 75, 99
Leigh, (Oly) 69
Leigh FC 65
Lever, A. (Oly) 23-4
Lewis, Elizabeth 80, 113
Lewis, John (Rov) 10
Little, G. (Oly) 9, 69
Little Harwood FC 9, 98, 110
Liverpool Association 15, 18, 22
Liverpool St. John's FC 113
Livesey Utd. FC 9, 12
   trophy *see* Blackburn Olympic
Lloyd, J. (Druids) 41
Lofthouse, Joseph (Rov) 63
London Rd. Station, Manchester 45
Love, Jimmy (Darwen) 11, 16
Lower Chapel FC 21-2
Lower Darwen FC 40
Lowerhouse Athletic Sports 115, 116

M

Macaulay, Reginald (OE) 48, 50, 51
McCallum, A. (QPG) 60
McDonald, J. (QPG) 60
McDougall, J. K. (Scots. FA Pres.) 60
McGregor, William 75
McIntyre, Hugh (Rov) 28, 36-7, 63
   guests for Olympic 73-4
McLeod, W. (Cowlairs, Oly) 73-4
Mackereth, Andrew (Oly) 8, 9, 10, 16, 17
Manchester FC 60
Manchester Police Sports 116
Manchester Utd. FC *see* Newton Heath
Manchester Wanderers FC 105
Marchbank, L. (Pers, Oly) 17, 30
Marindin, Major Francis (FA President) 51, **52**
Marlow FC 41

Marsden, F. H. (Sheff) 24
Marshall, Thomas (Darwen) 11, 16, 34
Marshall, (Oly) 74
Mason's Arms, The 62, 64, 104
Matthews, Arthur (Oly) **4, 81, 124**
   debut for Olympic 21
   East Lancashire Cup games 36
   FA Cup games 39, 41-2, 50-1, 57, 58, 60, 117
   goals 21, 24, 27, 28, 31, 34, 40, 51, 57, 58, 59
   Lancashire Cup games 21, 31, 63, 67-8
   last game for Olympic 78, 81*n*
   picture-framer and gilder 24, 73
   praise for 29
   Presbyterian 24, 73
   representative honours 13
   reserve games 16
Matthews, W. A (Sheff) 24
Maxim, Sir Hiram Stevens 68*n*
Middlesbrough FC 71
Mill Hill 99
Mitella St., Burnley 79
Moorgate *see* Mill Hill
Mosforth, Willie (Wed) 80
Moss, William (Oly) 58, 60, 66
Mytton (Lancs.) 35, 37

N

Nailor (BW) 22
Nelson FC 70
New Brighton Tower FC 79
New Jerusalem Church 99, 114
News of the World Football Annual, The 5
Newton Heath FC 10, 57
Noble (Oly) 74
Norfolk, Duke of 23
Norris, Walter (OC) **45**
North Wales Guardian, The 20
Northgate 7, 14, 53, 62, 64
Northwich Victoria FC 30, 59
Norton, Derbys. 103
Nottingham Evening Post, The 60
Nottingham Forest FC 13, 17, 23, 26
Notts County FC 41, 58, 59, 61, 64, 67, 73
Novelli, P. C. (OE) 48

O

Old Bull Hotel, The 67
Old Carthusians FC 12, 34, 41, **45**
   1883 semi-final vs. Olympic 45-6
Old Etonians FC
   1883 FA Cup Final 49-52, **52**, 117
   vs. Darwen 1879 11, 13
   FA Cup record 17, 34, 41, 48
   vs. Rovers 13, 36, 48
   social rank 12
Old Westminsters FC 43, 59, 60
Old Wykehamists FC 58-9, 118
   "Willies" 58
Oldham 105
Olympia, Greece 8
Oozebooth 7, 8, 98, 102
Oozehead Park 98
Oswaldtwistle Rovers FC 64, 65, 77
Oswestry FC 60
Oval, The *see* Kennington Oval

129

Oxford University FC 17, 43, 58

P

Padiham FC 31
Padiham Church FC 39
Page, W. R. (OC) **45**
Paravicini, Percy de (OE) 48, 50
Parish Church, Blackburn 10
Park Road Congregational School 112
Park Terrace 114
Parker, W. ("Tich") (Oly) 73, 114
    FA Cup games 57, 60, 65, 74
    goals 57, 58, 59, 63
    Lancashire Cup games 63
    representative honours 58
    reserve for 1883 Cup Final 50
    scores last Olympic goal 78
Parry, Edward (OC) 43, **45**
Partick FC 30, 55
Partick Thistle FC 29, 74
Pastime (FA publication) 53
Paternoster Row (FA headquarters) 65
Peel, Sir Robert 119
Penny St. 53, 55
Pickup, J. W. (Pers) 17
Pierce-Dix, William (official) 33-4, 43, 45, 46, 49, 58, 117
Pike's Lane, Bolton **68**, 71, 110
Pilgrims FC 12, 43
Pilkington, Mr. (benefactor) 119
Pleckgate 15, 98
Powderhall, Edinburgh 57
Powell, A. (Druids) 41
Powell, J. (Druids) 41-2
Preston Herald, The 56
Preston New Rd. 7, 80, 98
Preston North End FC 18, 44, 56, 64, 66, 71, 72, 75, 79, 104
Preston Old Rd. 99
Primrose Hill 99
Prince of Wales Inn, The 71, 80, 110
Prinsep, J. F. M. (OC) **45**
Probables vs. Improbables
    (international trial match) 12-13, 105
professionalism 14, 55, 56, 69, 70, 72
Pyebank FC 34

Q

Queen's Own FC 7, 9, 10-11, 15, 99, 109
Queen's Park, Glasgow FC 29, 63, 66
    1884 FA Cup semi vs. Olympic 59-61

R

Railway Rd. 53, **53**
Ramsbottom, C. (Pers) 17
Randal St. 7
Ravenswing 98
Rawlinson, John (OE) 48, 50-1
Red Star FC 7
Redlam Brow 99
Renfrewshire Cup, The 29
Rhyl 115
Richards. Lewis (OC) 43, 45, **45**
Richmond, London 47, 55

Richmond, J. (Darwen) 105
Riley, Mr. (solicitor) 74
Rishton FC 22
Roberts, R. (Druids) 41
Roberts, S. (Druids) 41
Rodgers, W. (Sheff) 24
Roe Lee *see* Pleckgate
Rorke's Drift 33
Rostron, "Tot" (Darwen) 34
Rostron, Mr. (ref.) 22
Royal Engineers FC 33, 41, 43, 103
Ruabon, North Wales 20, 41
Rushton (Rov) 75

S

Saffron Walden 43
St. George's FC 10, 109
St. John's FC 7, 8, 105
St. John's School 107, 111
St. Mark's FC 7, 9, 16, 109
    see also Witton FC
St. Mary's College, Blackburn 15, **19**
St. Mary's FC 10
St. Mary's School 98
Salford Bridge 53, **53**
Scottish Athletic Journal, The 60
Scowcroft, Tom (Turton) 111
Sharples, (BW) 22
Sharples, Harold (Rov)
    guest for Olympic 31
Shear Brow 11, 15
    see also Hole-i'th'-Wall
Shearman, Montague (writer) 26
Sheffield Association 18, 20, 23-4, 33-4
Sheffield Daily Telegraph, The 20
Sheffield Exchange FC 29
Sheffield Gymnasium Athletic Sports, The 104
Sheffield Heeley FC 15, 33, 34, 103
Sheffield New Association 34
Sheffield Wednesday FC 13, 18, 26, 29, 33, 34, 41
    Sports 104
Sheffield Zulus 15, 33-4, 105, 106*n*
Slater, (Oly) 67, 69
Slough FC 103
Smalley, Richard (wrestler) 110
Smith, Dr. John (QPG) 60, 61
Smith, T. (Pers) 17
social divisions 12-13, 55, 71
Sorby, R. A. (Sheff) 23, 24
Sorby, T.H. (Sheff) 23, 24
Sotheby's 79, 120
South Shore FC 65, 72, 77
Southport FC 57
Southworth, James **116**
    Chester player 70
    Rovers player 75
    full-back 73, 74
    sprinter 70, 115-6
Southworth, John/Jack **114**
    Chester player 70, 114
    England caps 75, 115, 120
    goals 57, 75, 115
    goalkeeper 69-70, 114
    injury 69, 114
    musician 69, 114
    reserve (aged 16) 57
    Rovers player 75, 115

suspension 70, 71
Sowerbutts, Joseph (Rov) 63, 66
Sporting Chronicle, The 43, 46, 55
Sportsman, The 49
Standing, W. (Rov) 10
Staveley FC 22, 28-9, 118
Stoke FC 104
Stoney Butts Railway Station 22, 45, 46, 53, **53**, 62
Stott, Charles Nightingale (poet) 59, 118
Strachan, Thomas ("Tot") (Rov) 36, 56, 63
Strythe, (Leigh) 65
Sudell, Major William 56, 64, 67
Sunderland FC 66, 115
Suter, Jarvis (Partick Thistle) 74
Suter, Fergus (Partick, Darwen, Rov)
   Blackburn Rovers player 28, 36, 63, 66, 75, 76
   Darwen player 11, 16
   at Hunter's funeral 80
   same mill as Beverley 21
Swifts FC 12, 41

T

Taylor, T. (Oly) 16
team formations, development of 22, 26-8
Tel-el-Kebir 44
Third Lanark FC 70
Thompson, R. P. (OC) 43, 45, 46
Thornber, (Oly) 16
Thornliebank FC, Glasgow 29-30
Tod, A. H. (OC) **45**
Todmorden 49
Tontine St. 80
Town Hall St. 62
Townley, William (Rov) 75
Traynor, W. (Oly) 16
Trent Bridge, Nottingham 58, 60-1, 67
Troy St. 80, 109
Turf Moor, Burnley 79
Turner, (Rov) 66
Turton FC 15, 18, 22, 25, 26, 58, 107
Tyne Association 17

U

Ulster XI 77-8
Upton Park FC 59

V

Vale of Leven FC 59
Vale of Lune FC 114
Vanity Fair **49**
Vaughan, J. (Druids) 41
Victoria Station, Manchester 45
Victoria St. 53
Vintcent, Joseph (OC) 43, 45, **45**, 46

W

Wake, W. R. (Sheff) 24
Wakefield Trinity 57
Wales national XI 41, 67, 110
Walker, Robin (cabs) 18, 53, 67
Walker and Hall (cutler) 103

Walmsley, J. E. (Oly cttee.) 79
Walsall Swifts FC 57
Walsall Town FC 41
Walsh, H. (Pers) 17
Walton (Rov) 66
Wanderers FC, The 26
Warburton, E. (Pers) 17
Warburton, Squire Albert (Cob Wall, Oly, Darwen) **4, 52, 81, 124**
   argument with Gibson 56, 58, 70
   birth 105
   captaincy 38, 50, 51-2, 105
   Cob Wall player 16, 105
   cover goal 30, 31
   Darwen player 56, 58, 67, 105-6
   debut for Olympic 16-17
   Earl St. 38
   East Lancs. Charity Cup games 36, 105-6
   FA Cup games 24, 30, 39-40, 41-2, 46, 50-2
   goalkeeper 32, 71
   Halliwell player 105
   injuries 30, 40
   Lancashire Cup games 31
   medals **89, 106**
   praise for 29
   publican, plumber, poulterer 70, 80-1, 106
   representative honours 13, 29, 105
   response to heckler 53
   sprinter 29, 106
   three-quarter back 27
Ward, James (Oly, Rov) **4, 81, 124**
   athletic feats 38, 110
   birth 110
   Clitheroe player 56
   debut for Olympic 38
   eighteenth birthday 47
   England player 67, 110, 120
   FA Cup games 39-40, 41-2, 46, 50-1, 57, 60
   family 110
   goals 69
   last game 78, 81*n*
   Lancashire Cup games 63
   Little Harwood player 16
   pub licensee 71, 80, 110
   representative honours 58
      see also England player
   Rovers player 72, 73
   schooldays 9, 110
   turns up without kit 71
Warsop, Keith 14*n*
Warwick St. 73
Watt, William (QPG) 60, 61
Wednesbury Town FC 57
Wellington Inn, The 80
Wensley, R. (Oly) 30, 36
West Bromwich Albion FC 72
Westwell, Robert (Oly) 8, 9, 10, 16, 17, 21, 22, 24, 27, 28
Whalley New Rd. 80
Whalley Range, Manchester 45
Whalley-range, Blackburn 109
Wharncliffe Charity Cup 33, 34
Whewell, Thomas (brewer) 119
White Bull Hotel, The **53**
White Star FC 7
Whitebirk *see* Gorse Bridge
Whitehead, W. (Oly, Witton) 57, 65, 66, 69, 114
Whiteside, (Oly) 20, 78
Whittaker, W. J. (Acc) 39, 40
Widnes Athletic Sports 116

Wilcock, J. H. (sprinter) 116, **116**
Wilkinson, (Acc) 39
Williams, W. (Druids) 39
"Willies" *see* Old Wykehamists
Wilson, A. (Pers) 17
Wilson, George (Oly, PNE) 21, **81**, **124**
   debut for Olympic 38
   FA Cup games 39-40, 41-2, 46, 50-1
   goals 38, 39, 40, 41, 42, 46, 56
   ineligible for Lancs. Cup tie 39
   Preston North End player 56, 64
   pub landlord 56
   Sheffield New Association player 14, 35
Winchester School *see* Old Wykehamists
Witton FC 7, 22, 30, 32, 74, 75
Witton Sports 38, 110
Wolverhampton Wanderers FC 79
Woolfall, A. ("Woody") (Rov, Oly) 28, 56, 60, 63
Wrexham FC 18, 22, 26, 30
Wynnstay Park, Ruabon 20
Wynyard, E. G. (OC) **45**

Y

Yates, Fred (Oly committee member) 64, 66
Yates, James (Acc) 24, 39
Yates, John (Oly, Acc, Burnley) **4**, **81**, **124**
   Accrington player 65, 79
   Burnley player 71, 79
   death 79
   early games for Olympic 21, 24
   East Lancs. Charity Cup games 36
   England cap 71, 79, **120**
   FA Cup games 24, 39-40, 41-2, 46, 50, 57, 60-1
   goals 24, 27, 28, 31, 34, 37, 40, 42, 46, 57, 58, 70
   Lancashire Cup games 21, 31, 63
   last game for Olympic 78, 81*n*
   praise for 29
   pub licensee 79
   referees a game 47
   representative honours 58
      see also England cap
   wages dispute 71
Yates, Sydney (club patron and president, foundry owner) 29, 35, 37, 38
   contribution to FA Cup expenses 14, 44, 55
   death 74
   death of wife 55
   illness 53, 64
   resignation 64
   return 73
see also Mytton
Yorkshire Colts 103

Z

Zulus, The
   see Sheffield Zulus

THE AUTHOR

Graham Phythian has written books on many topics, including local history and football. He was born, and is resident, in Manchester. He was a student at Exeter University, where between writing a thesis on Zola (Emile, not Gianfranco) and sampling the scrumpy he represented his College at football. His other interests include chess, theatre, cinema, country walking, and real ale.